Heart and Brain

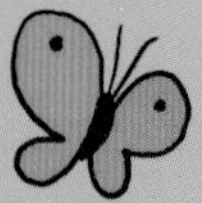

GUT INSTINCTS

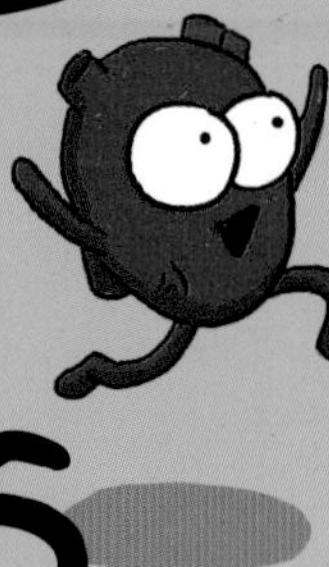

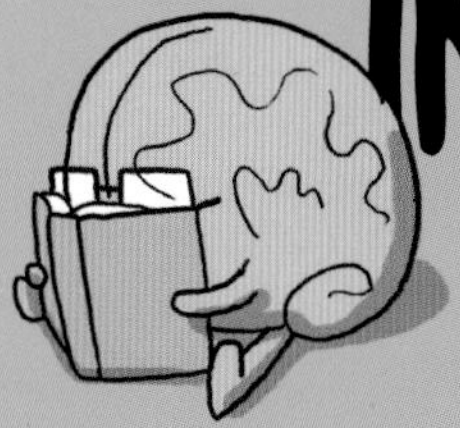

Heart and Brain: Gut Instincts

Andrews McMeel Publishing
a division of Andrews McMeel Universal
1130 Walnut Street, Kansas City, Missouri 64106

www.andrewsmcmeel.com

16 17 18 19 20 TEN 10 9 8 7 6 5 4 3 2 1
ISBN: 978-1-4494-7978-7
Library of Congress Control Number: 2016941521

Editor: Julie Bunge
Art Director, Designer: Diane Marsh
Production Editor: Erika Kuster
Production Manager: Chuck Harper

ATTENTION: SCHOOLS AND BUSINESSES
Andrews McMeel books are available at quantity discounts with bulk purchase
for educational, business, or sales promotional use. For information, please
e-mail the Andrews McMeel Publishing Special Sales Department:
specialsales@amuniversal.com.

Cast of Characters

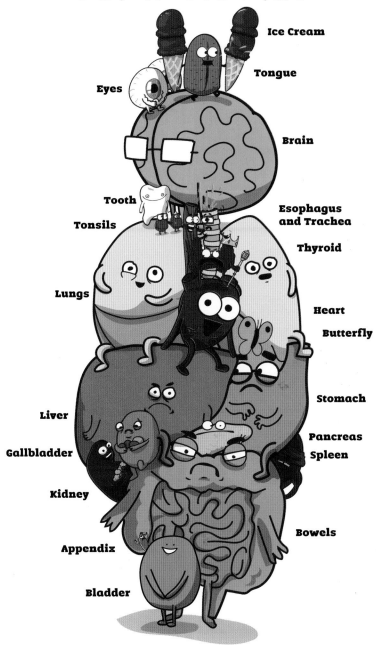

Ice Cream

Tongue

Eyes

Brain

Tooth

Esophagus and Trachea

Tonsils

Thyroid

Lungs

Heart

Butterfly

Liver

Stomach

Gallbladder

Pancreas

Spleen

Kidney

Bowels

Appendix

Bladder

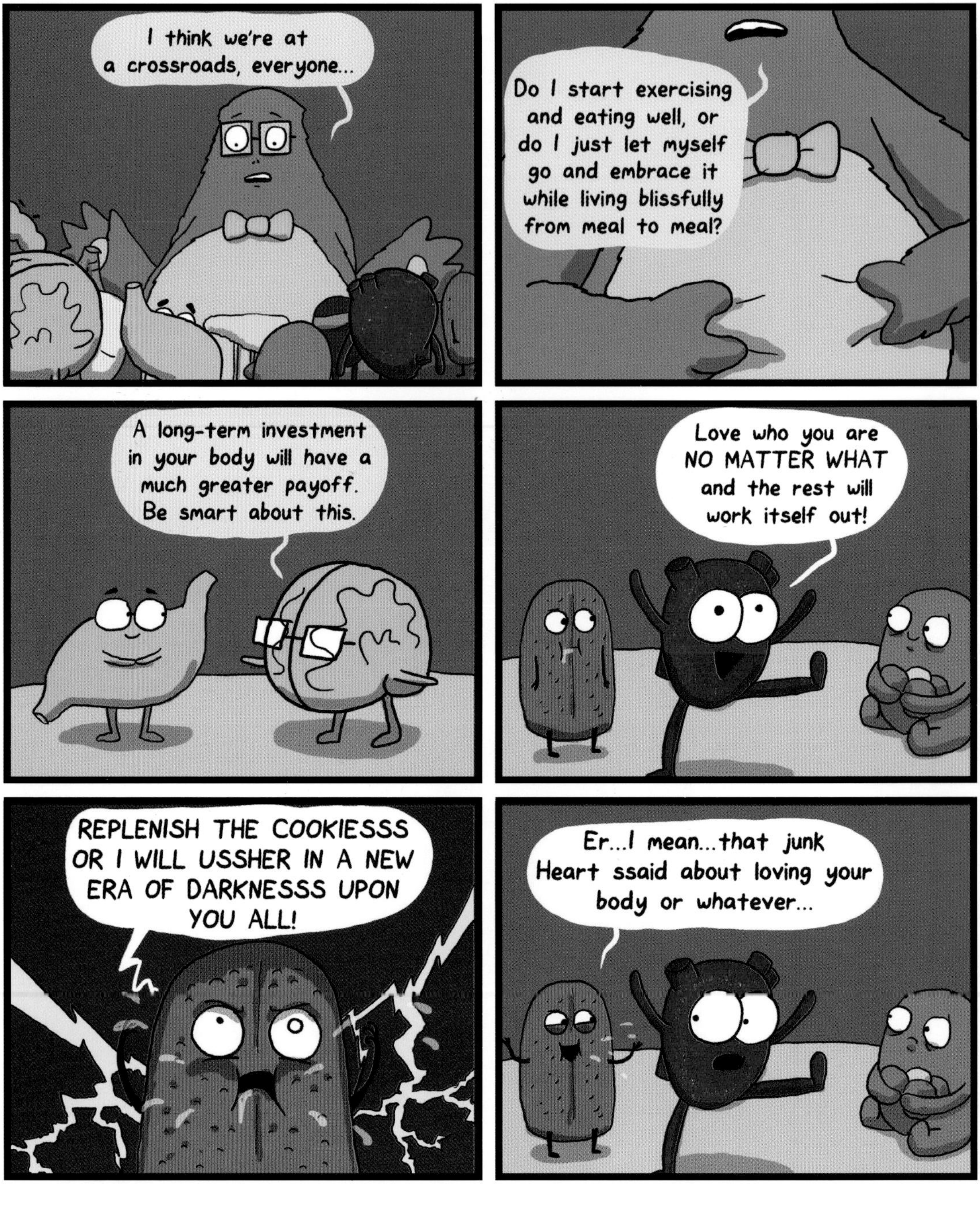
I think we're at a crossroads, everyone...
Do I start exercising and eating well, or do I just let myself go and embrace it while living blissfully from meal to meal?
A long-term investment in your body will have a much greater payoff. Be smart about this.
Love who you are NO MATTER WHAT and the rest will work itself out!
REPLENISH THE COOKIESSS OR I WILL USSHER IN A NEW ERA OF DARKNESSS UPON YOU ALL!
Er...I mean...that junk Heart ssaid about loving your body or whatever...

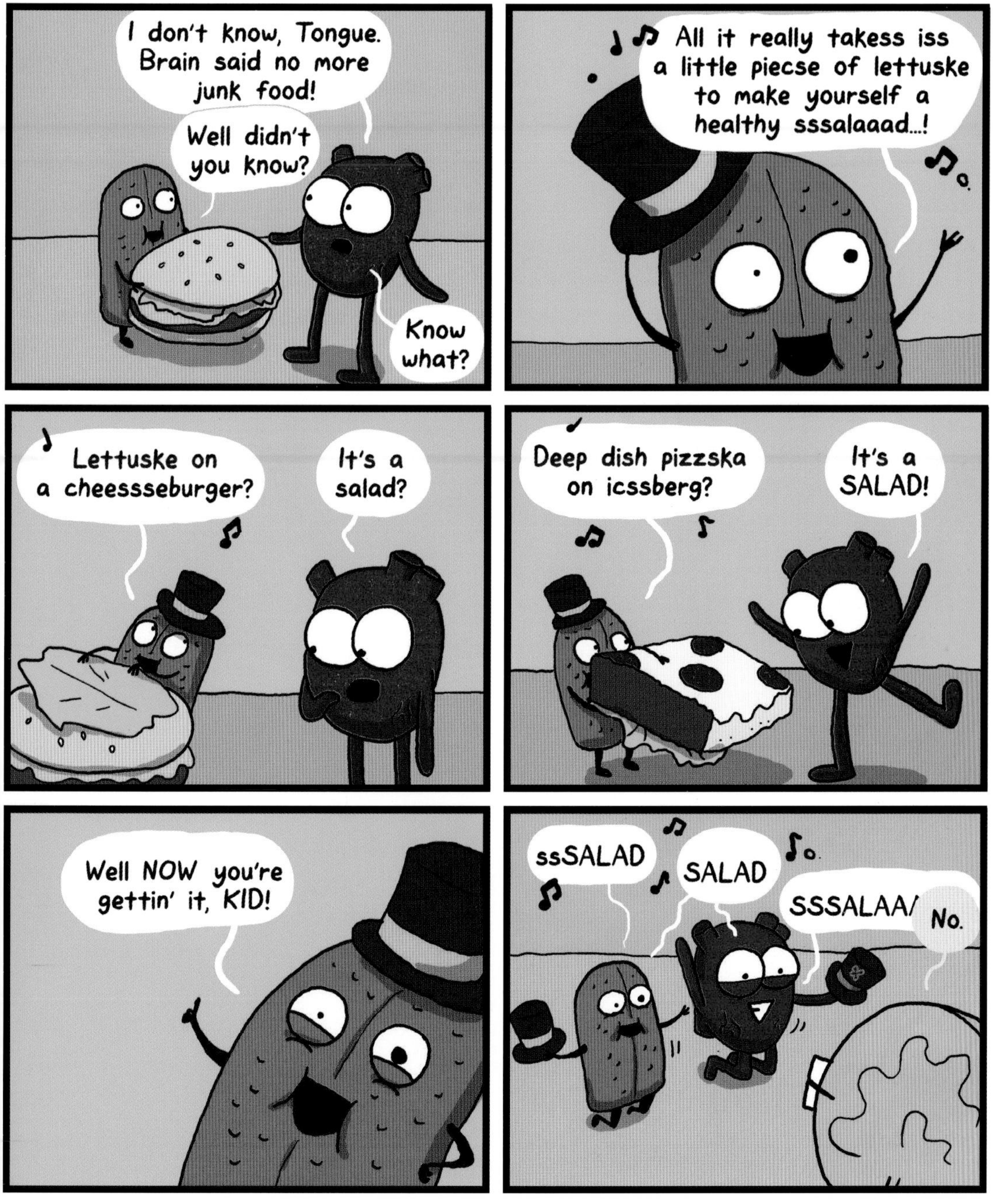
I don't know, Tongue. Brain said no more junk food!
Well didn't you know?
Know what?
All it really takess iss a little piecse of lettuske to make yourself a healthy sssalaaad...!
Lettuske on a cheessseburger?
It's a salad?
Deep dish pizzska on icssberg?
It's a SALAD!
Well NOW you're gettin' it, KID!
ssSALAD
SALAD
SSSALAA
No.

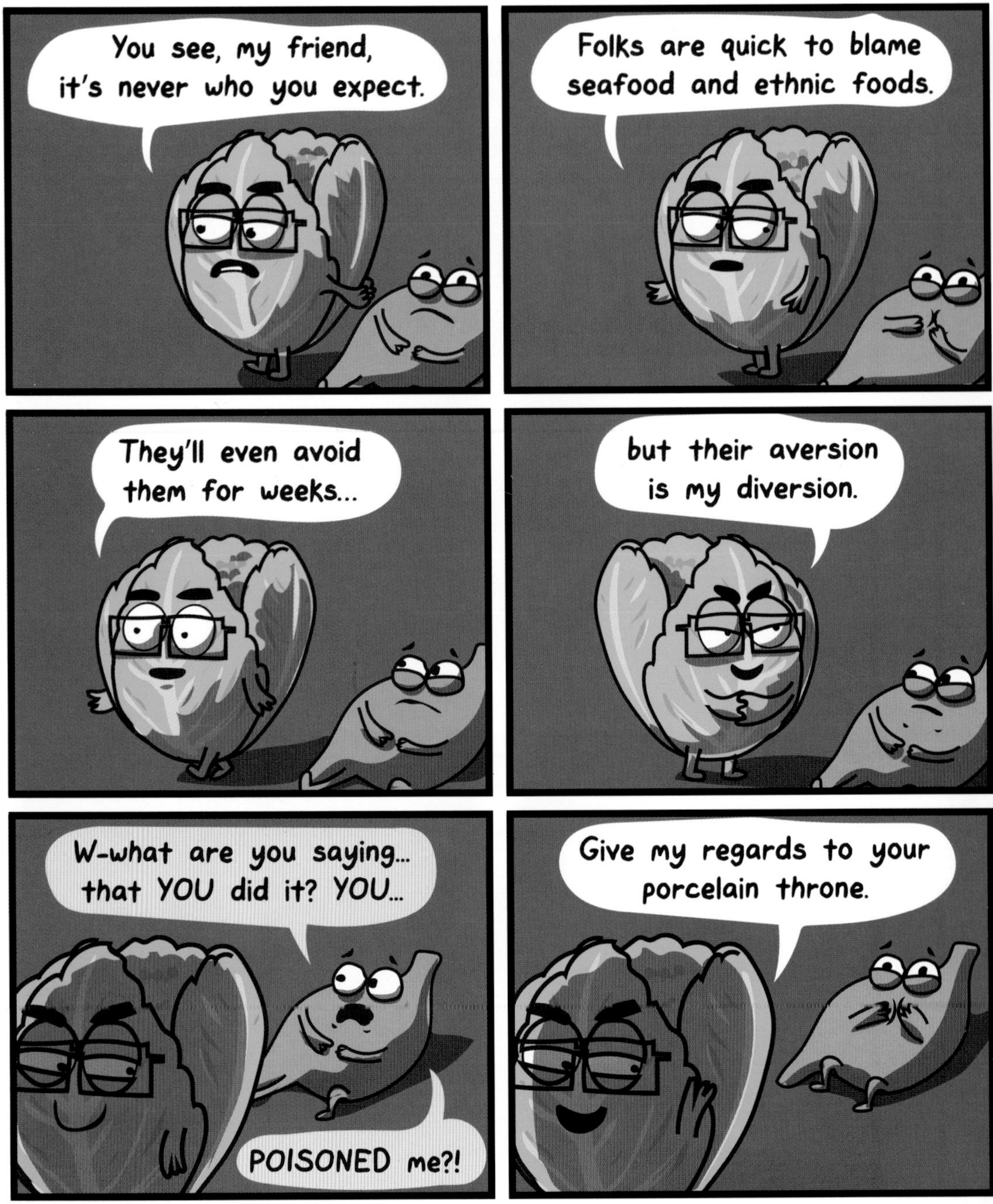
You see, my friend, it's never who you expect.
Folks are quick to blame seafood and ethnic foods.
They'll even avoid them for weeks...
but their aversion is my diversion.
W-what are you saying... that YOU did it? YOU...
POISONED me?!
Give my regards to your porcelain throne.

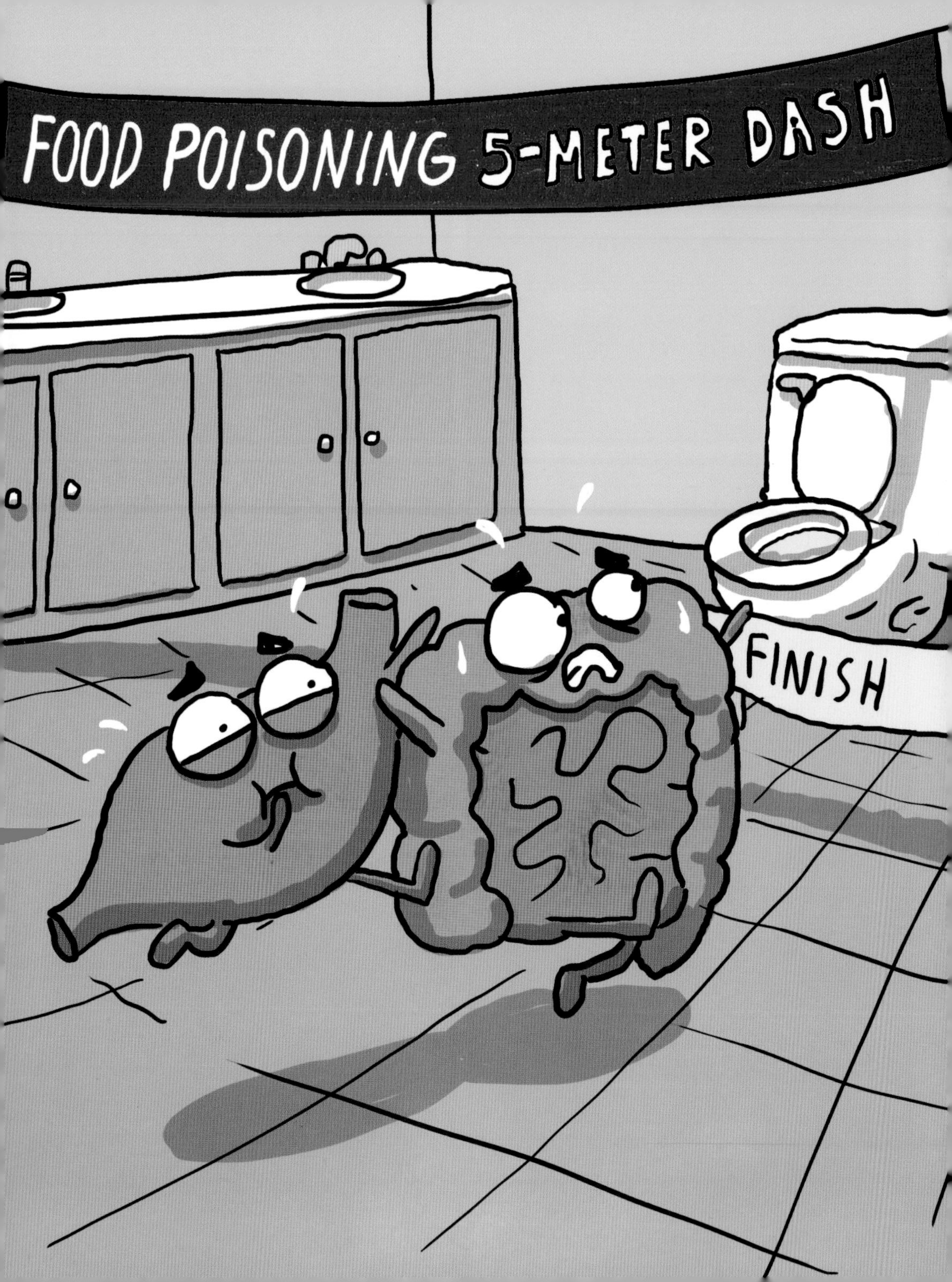
FOOD POISONING 5-METER DASH
FINISH

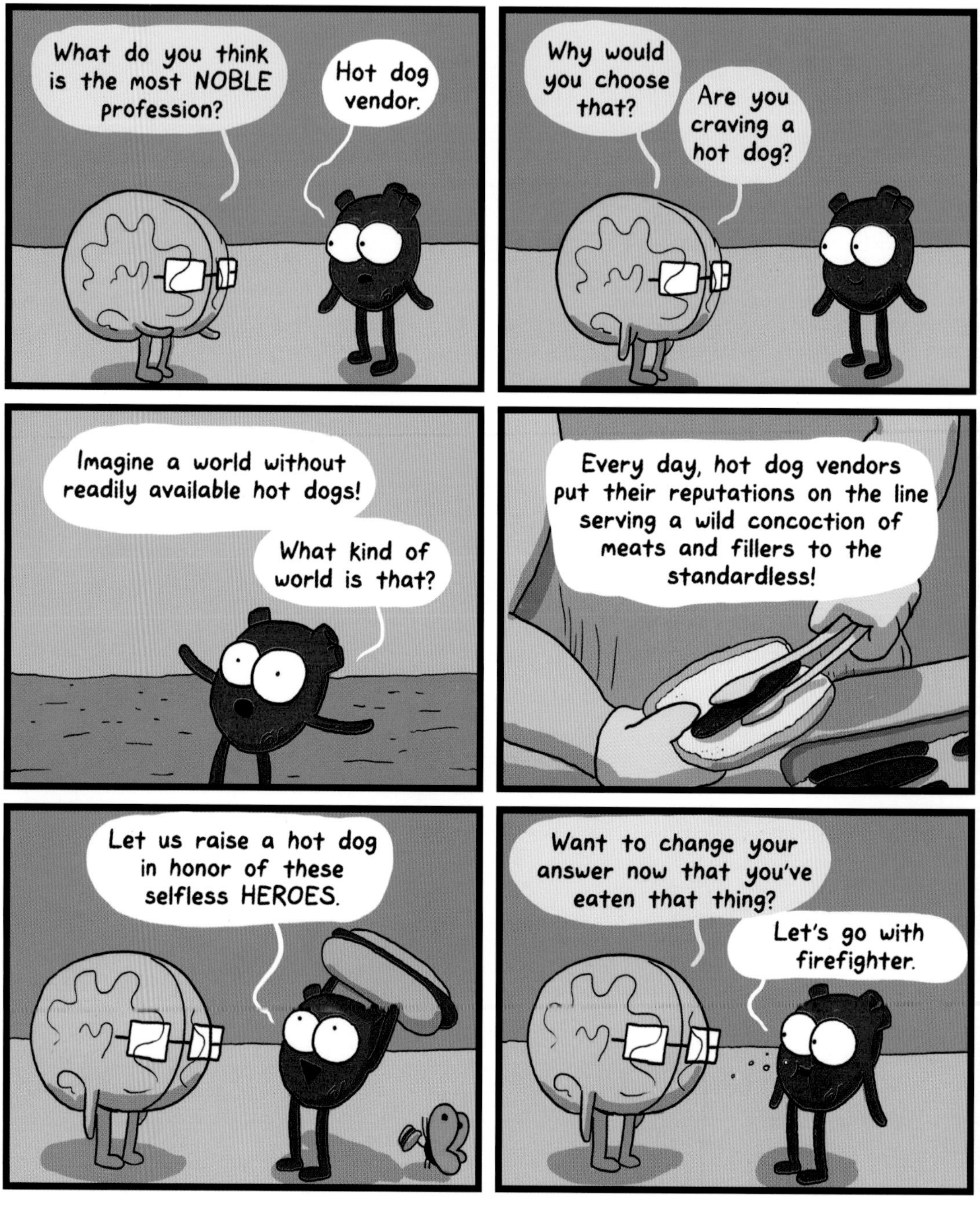
What do you think is the most NOBLE profession?
Hot dog vendor.
Why would you choose that?
Are you craving a hot dog?
Imagine a world without readily available hot dogs!
What kind of world is that?
Every day, hot dog vendors put their reputations on the line serving a wild concoction of meats and fillers to the standardless!
Let us raise a hot dog in honor of these selfless HEROES.
Want to change your answer now that you've eaten that thing?
Let's go with firefighter.

I am SO full!
Don't forget deSSSERT!
Dessert? Are you joking? I'm at capacity. Forget it.
What do YOU think, Ssweet Tooth?
Hewo!
Aw!
There's ALWAYS room for dessert!
There's ALWAYS room for dessert!
You know what? I think I actually CAN make room for dessert!
Imagine that!

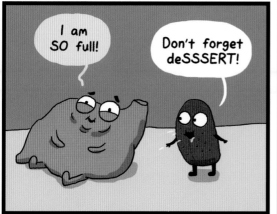

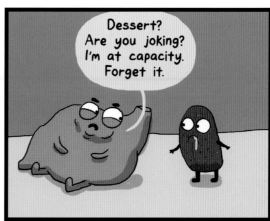

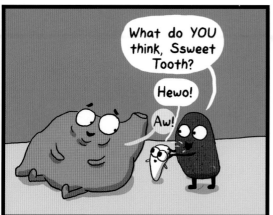

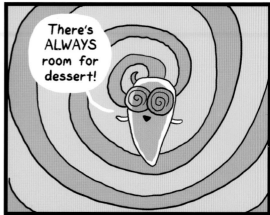

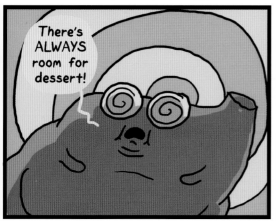

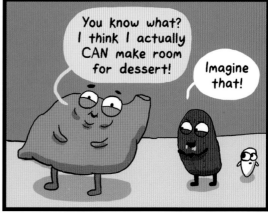

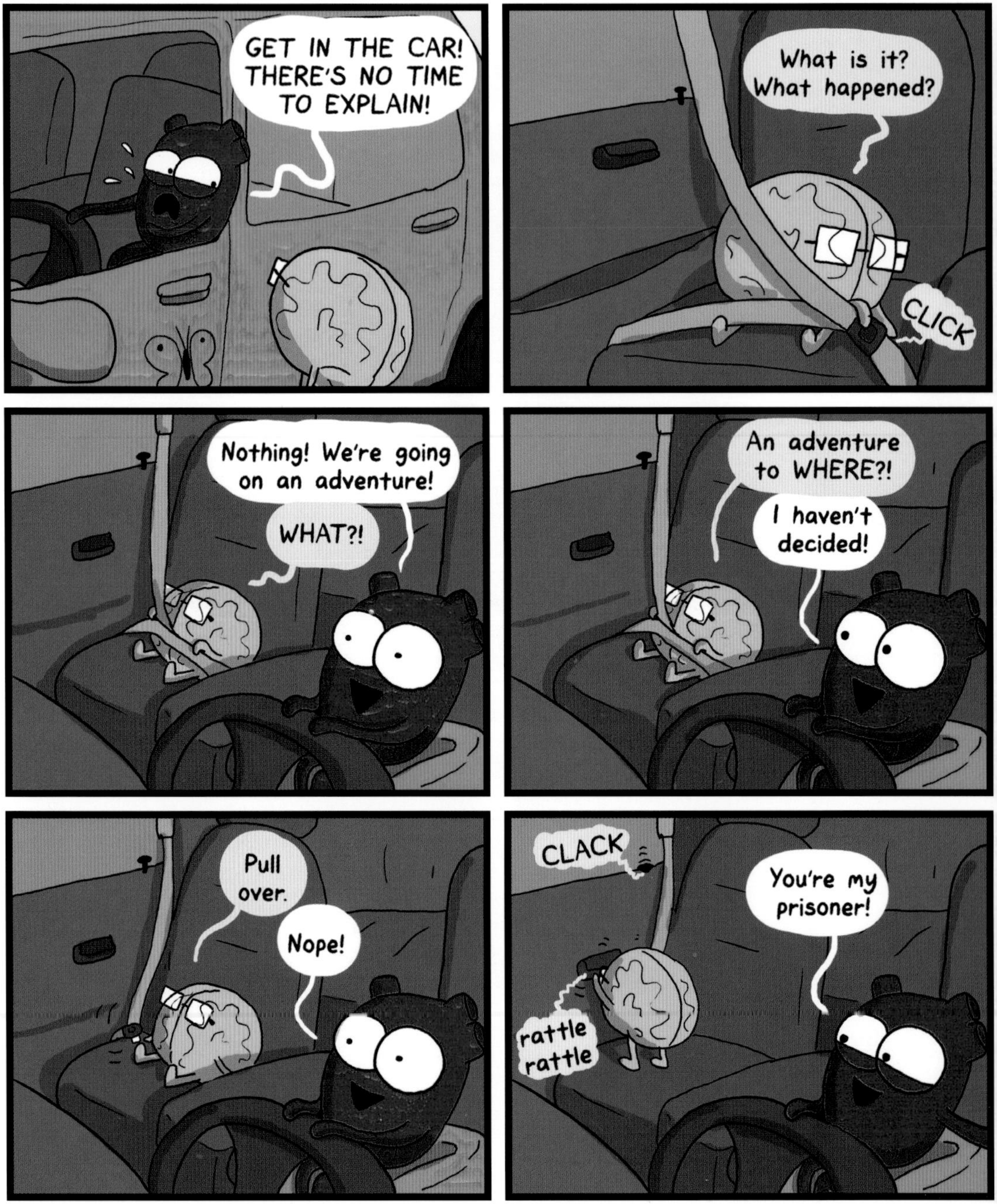
GET IN THE CAR! THERE'S NO TIME TO EXPLAIN!
What is it? What happened?
CLICK
Nothing! We're going on an adventure!
WHAT?!
An adventure to WHERE?!
I haven't decided!
Pull over.
Nope!
CLACK
You're my prisoner!
rattle rattle

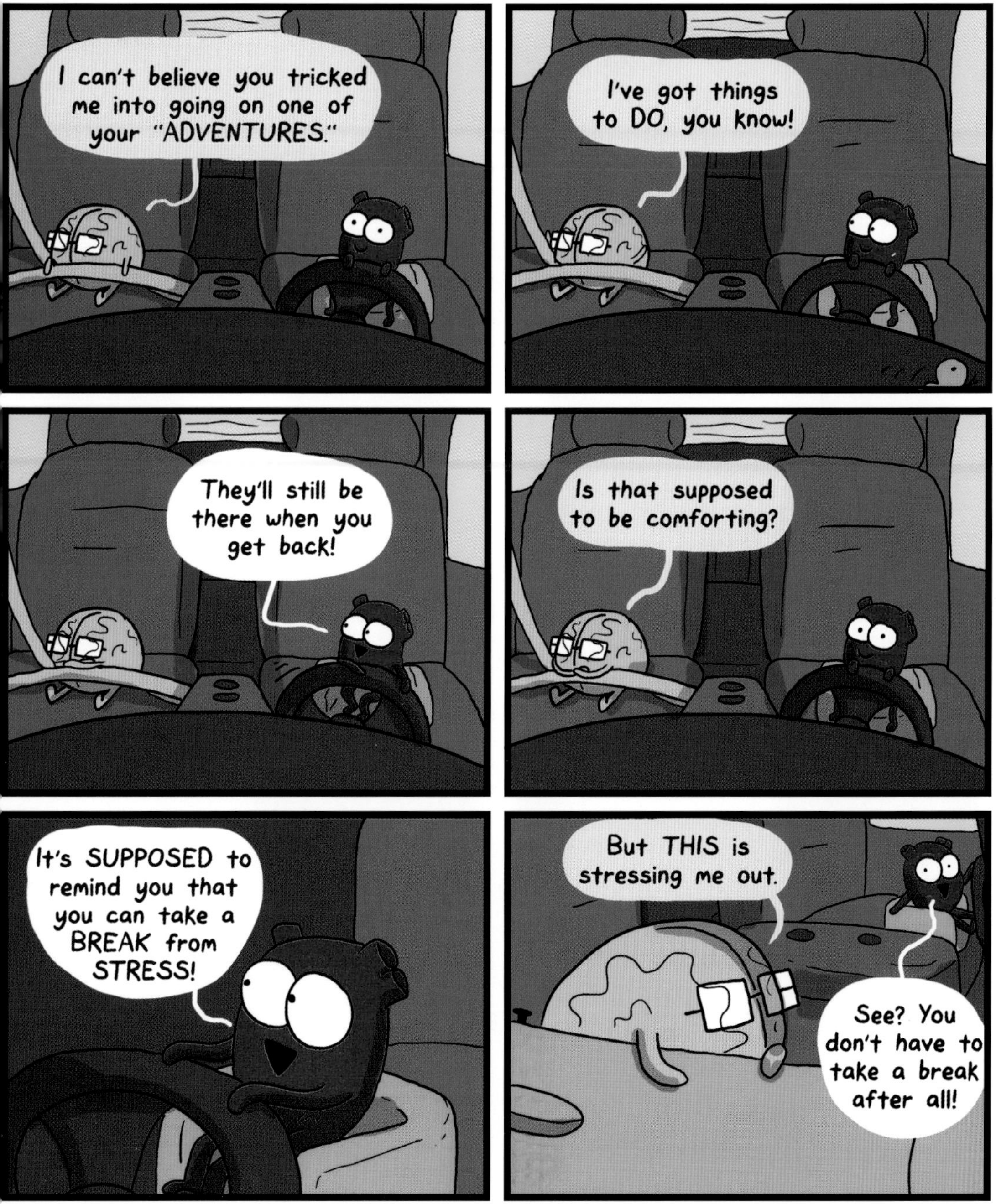
I can't believe you tricked me into going on one of your "ADVENTURES."
I've got things to DO, you know!
They'll still be there when you get back!
Is that supposed to be comforting?
It's SUPPOSED to remind you that you can take a BREAK from STRESS!
But THIS is stressing me out.
See? You don't have to take a break after all!

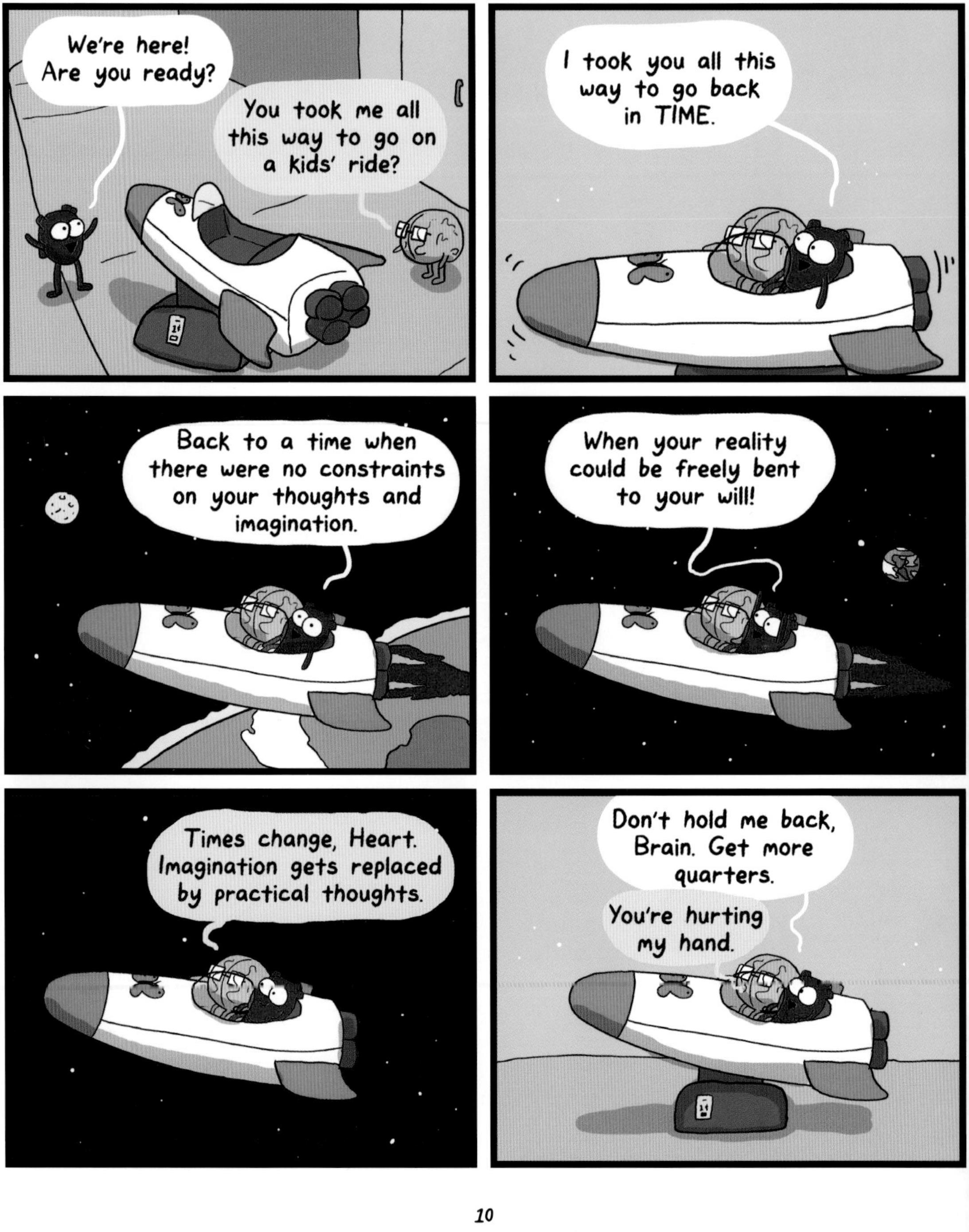
We're here! Are you ready?
You took me all this way to go on a kids' ride?
I took you all this way to go back in TIME.
Back to a time when there were no constraints on your thoughts and imagination.
When your reality could be freely bent to your will!
Times change, Heart. Imagination gets replaced by practical thoughts.
Don't hold me back, Brain. Get more quarters.
You're hurting my hand.

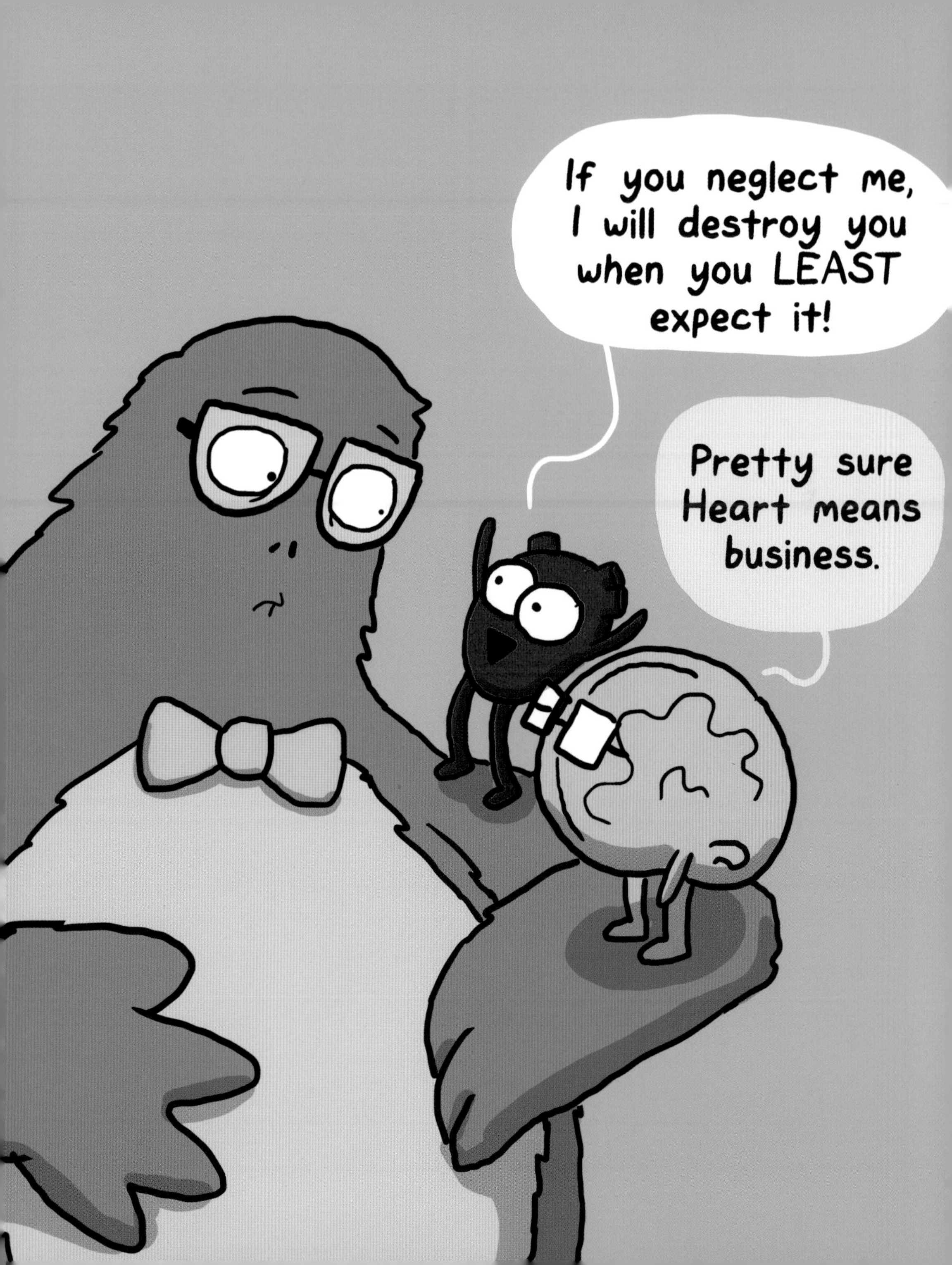
If you neglect me, I will destroy you when you LEAST expect it!
Pretty sure Heart means business.

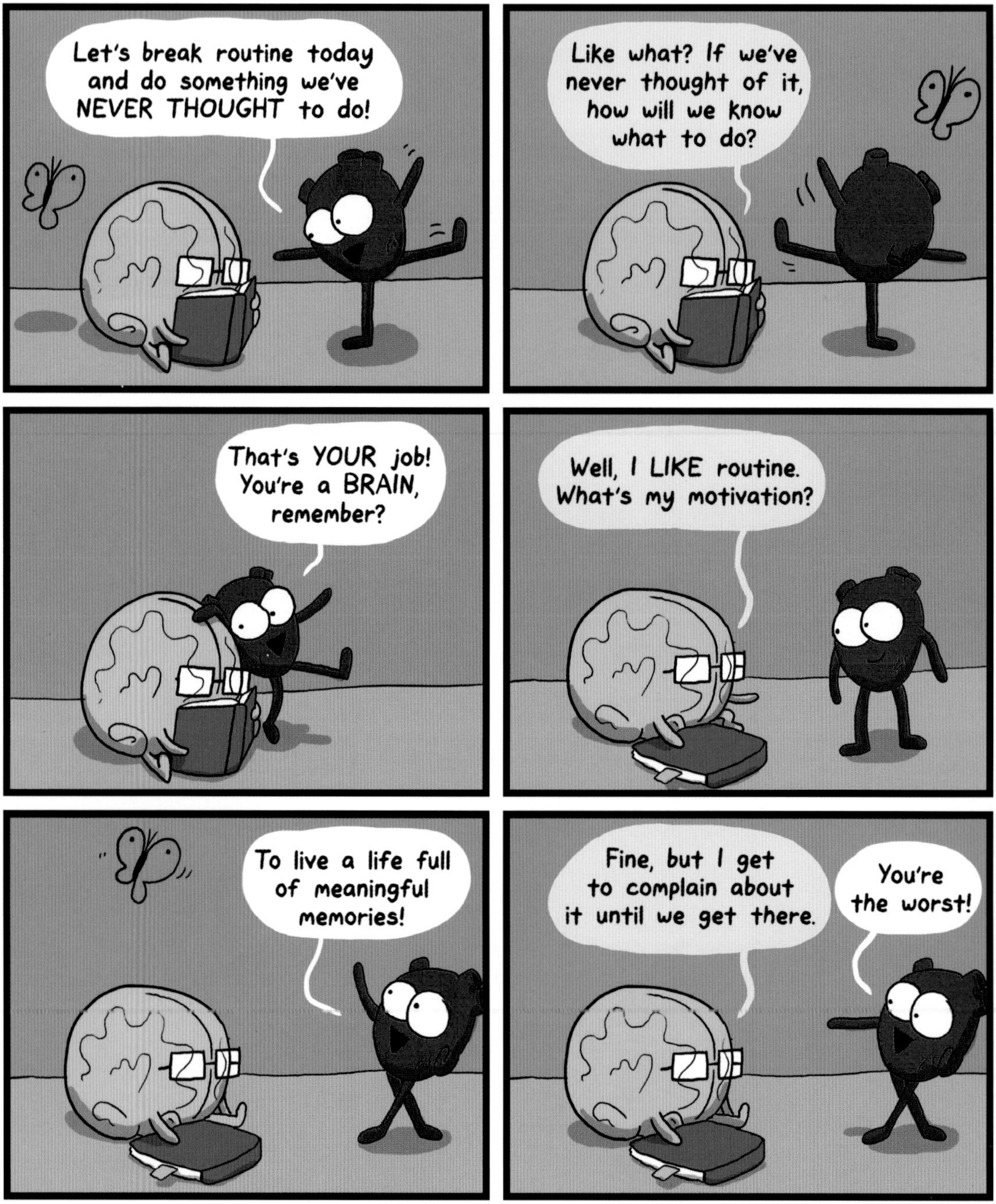
Let's break routine today and do something we've NEVER THOUGHT to do!
Like what? If we've never thought of it, how will we know what to do?
That's YOUR job! You're a BRAIN, remember?
Well, I LIKE routine. What's my motivation?
To live a life full of meaningful memories!
Fine, but I get to complain about it until we get there.
You're the worst!

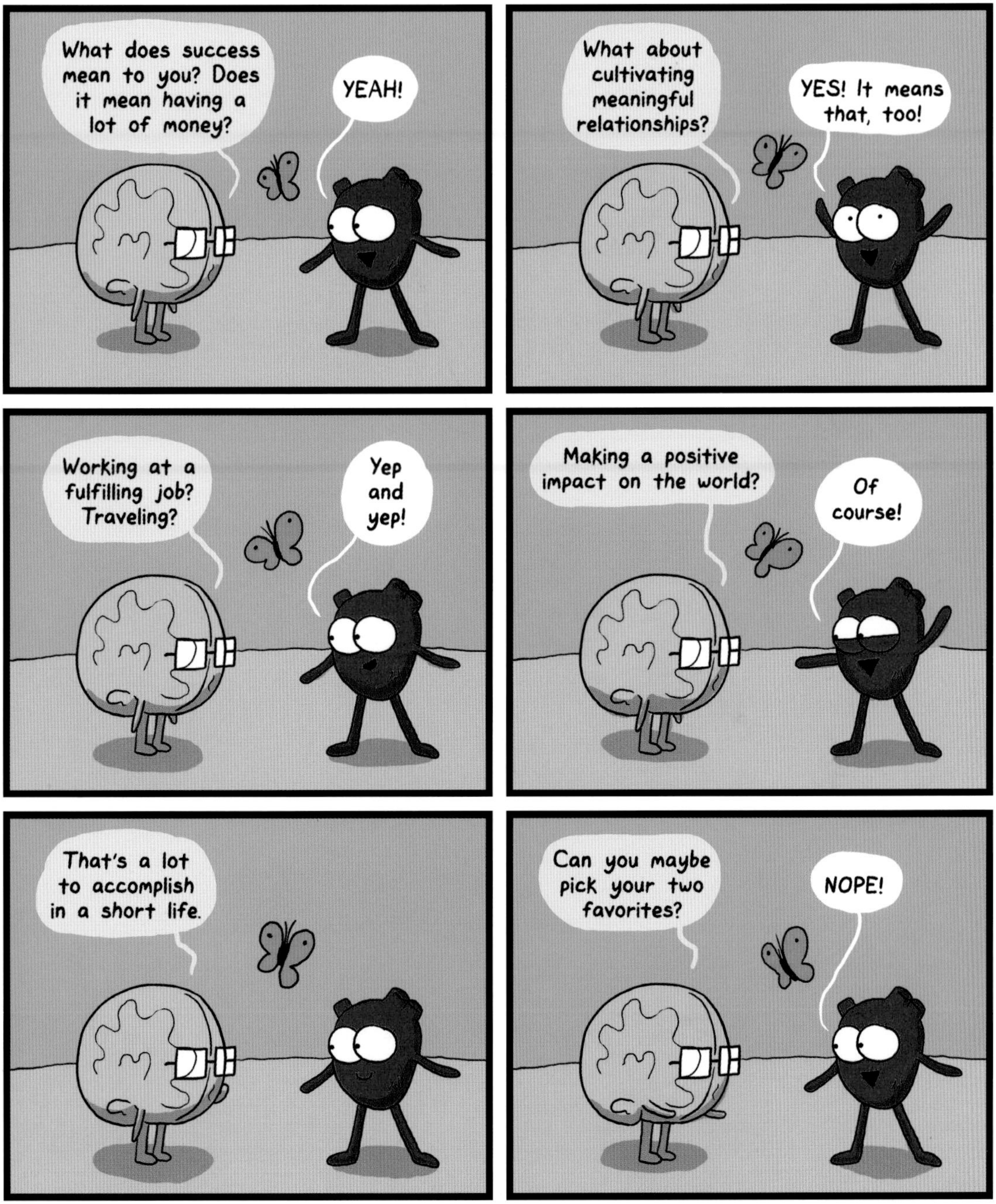
What does success mean to you? Does it mean having a lot of money?
YEAH!
What about cultivating meaningful relationships?
YES! It means that, too!
Working at a fulfilling job? Traveling?
Yep and yep!
Making a positive impact on the world?
Of course!
That's a lot to accomplish in a short life.
Can you maybe pick your two favorites?
NOPE!

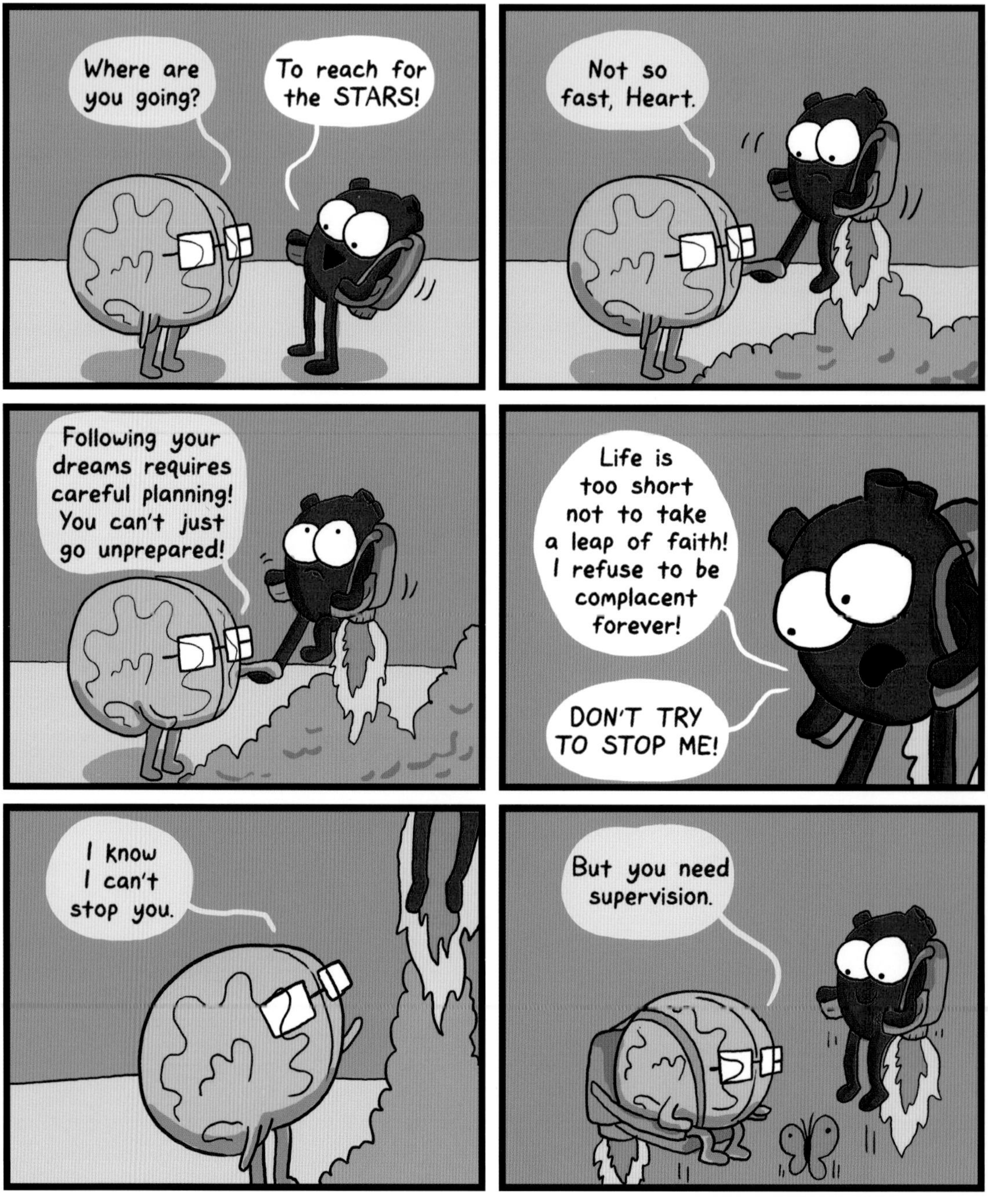
Where are you going?
To reach for the STARS!
Not so fast, Heart.
Following your dreams requires careful planning! You can't just go unprepared!
Life is too short not to take a leap of faith! I refuse to be complacent forever!
DON'T TRY TO STOP ME!
I know I can't stop you.
But you need supervision.

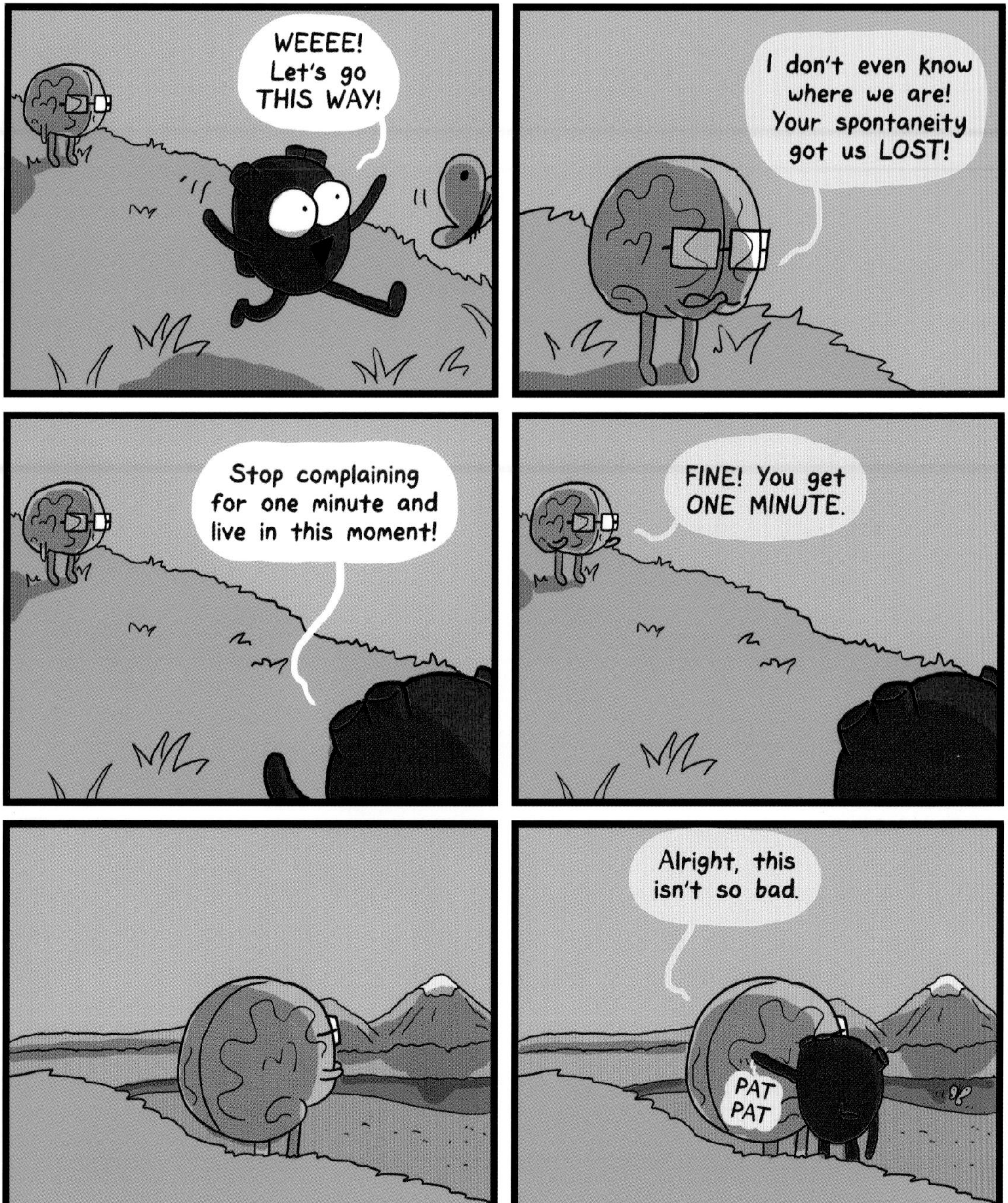
WEEEE! Let's go THIS WAY!
I don't even know where we are! Your spontaneity got us LOST!
Stop complaining for one minute and live in this moment!
FINE! You get ONE MINUTE.
Alright, this isn't so bad.
PAT PAT

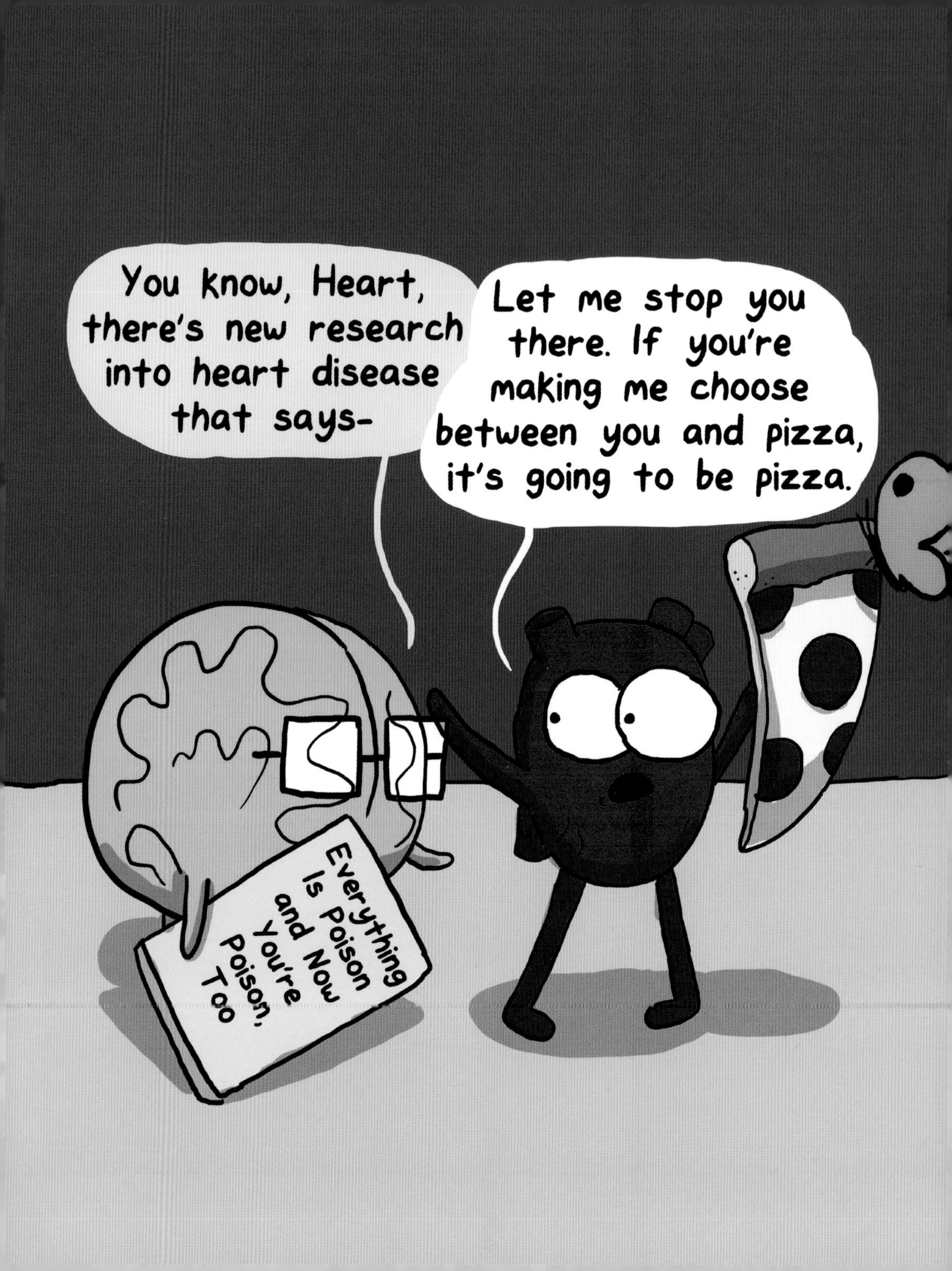
You know, Heart, there's new research into heart disease that says-
Let me stop you there. If you're making me choose between you and pizza, it's going to be pizza.
Everything Is Poison and Now You're Poison, Too

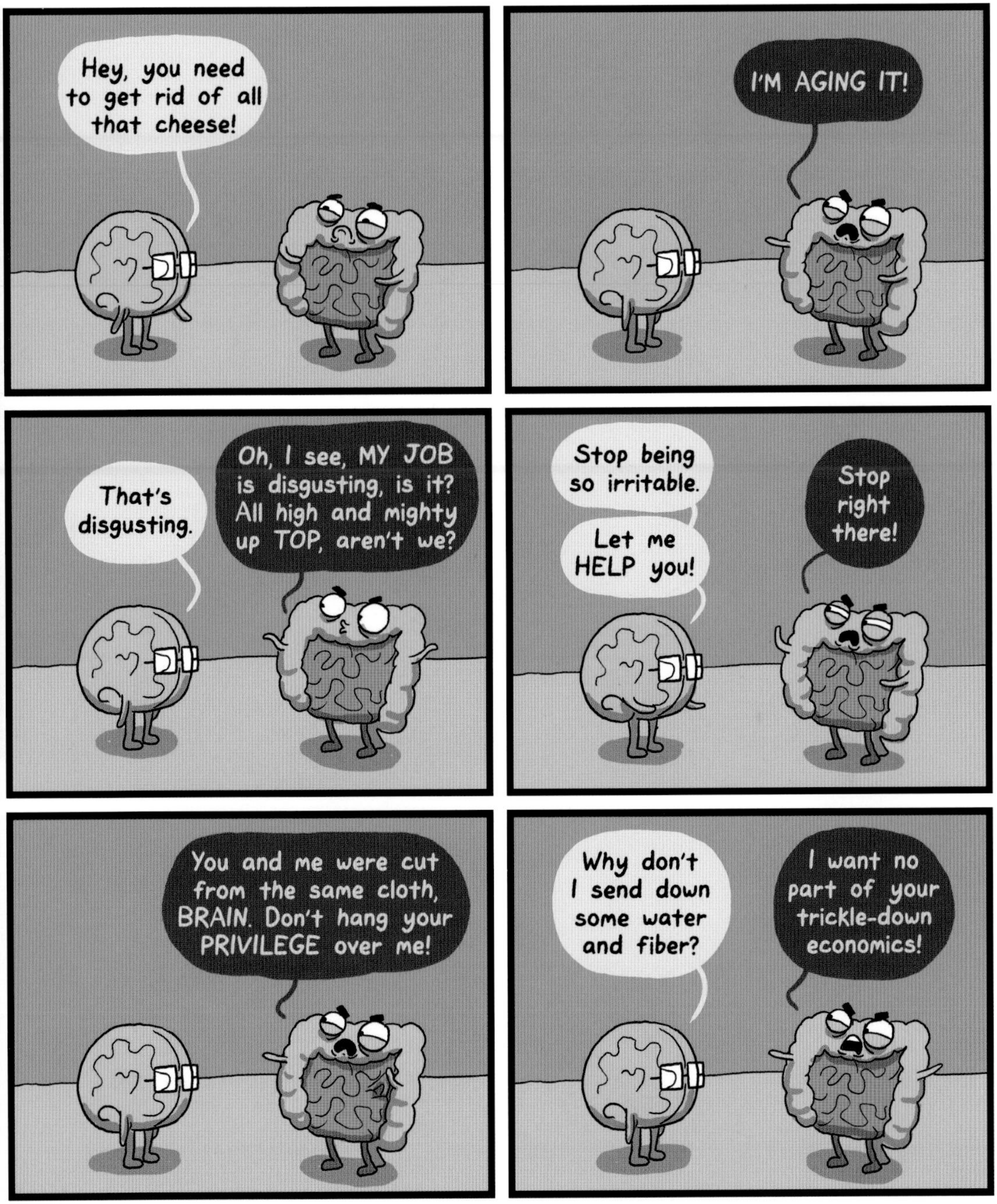
Hey, you need to get rid of all that cheese!
I'M AGING IT!
That's disgusting.
Oh, I see, MY JOB is disgusting, is it? All high and mighty up TOP, aren't we?
Stop being so irritable.
Let me HELP you!
Stop right there!
You and me were cut from the same cloth, BRAIN. Don't hang your PRIVILEGE over me!
Why don't I send down some water and fiber?
I want no part of your trickle-down economics!

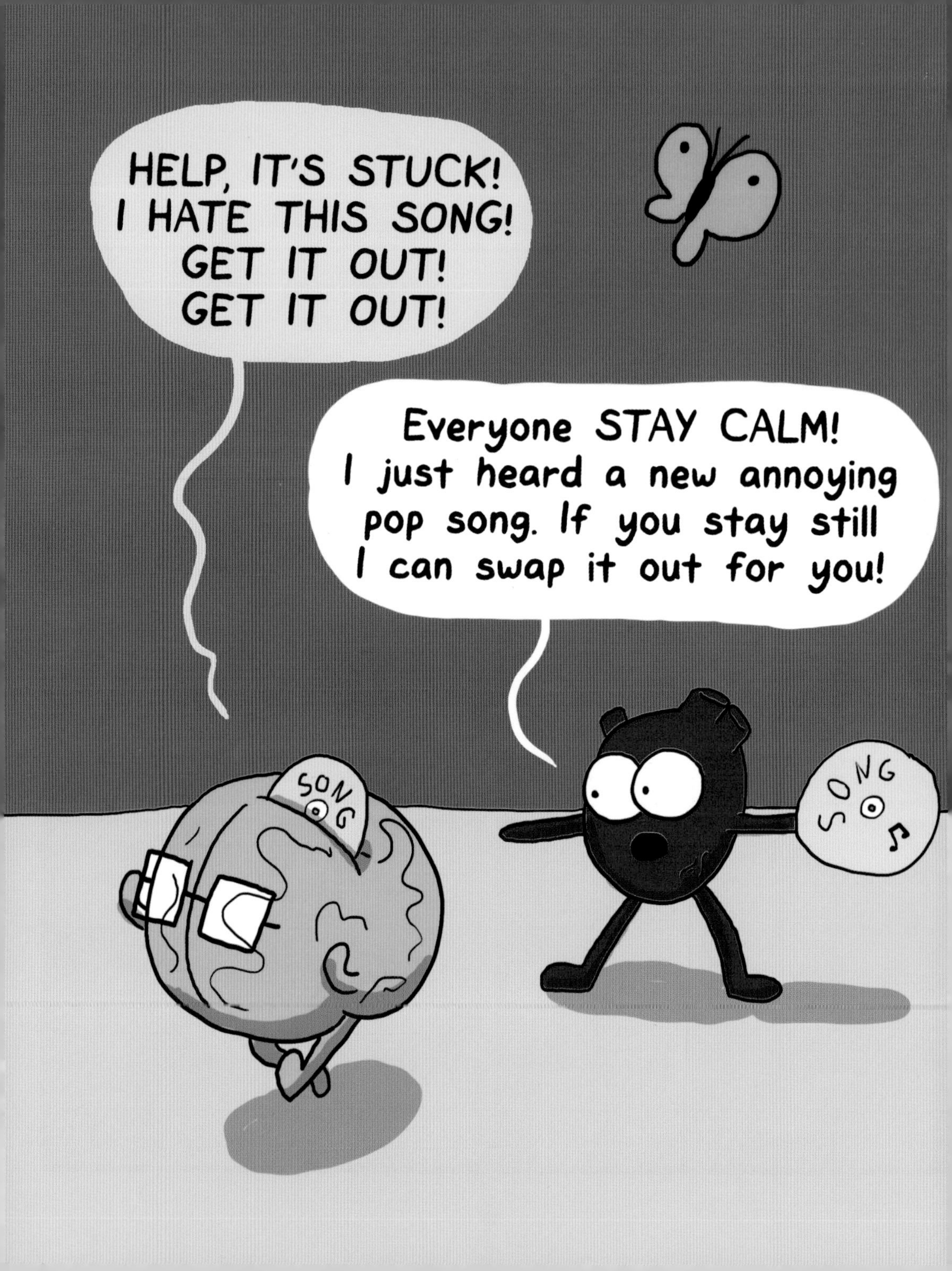
HELP, IT'S STUCK! I HATE THIS SONG! GET IT OUT! GET IT OUT!
Everyone STAY CALM! I just heard a new annoying pop song. If you stay still I can swap it out for you!
SONG
SONG

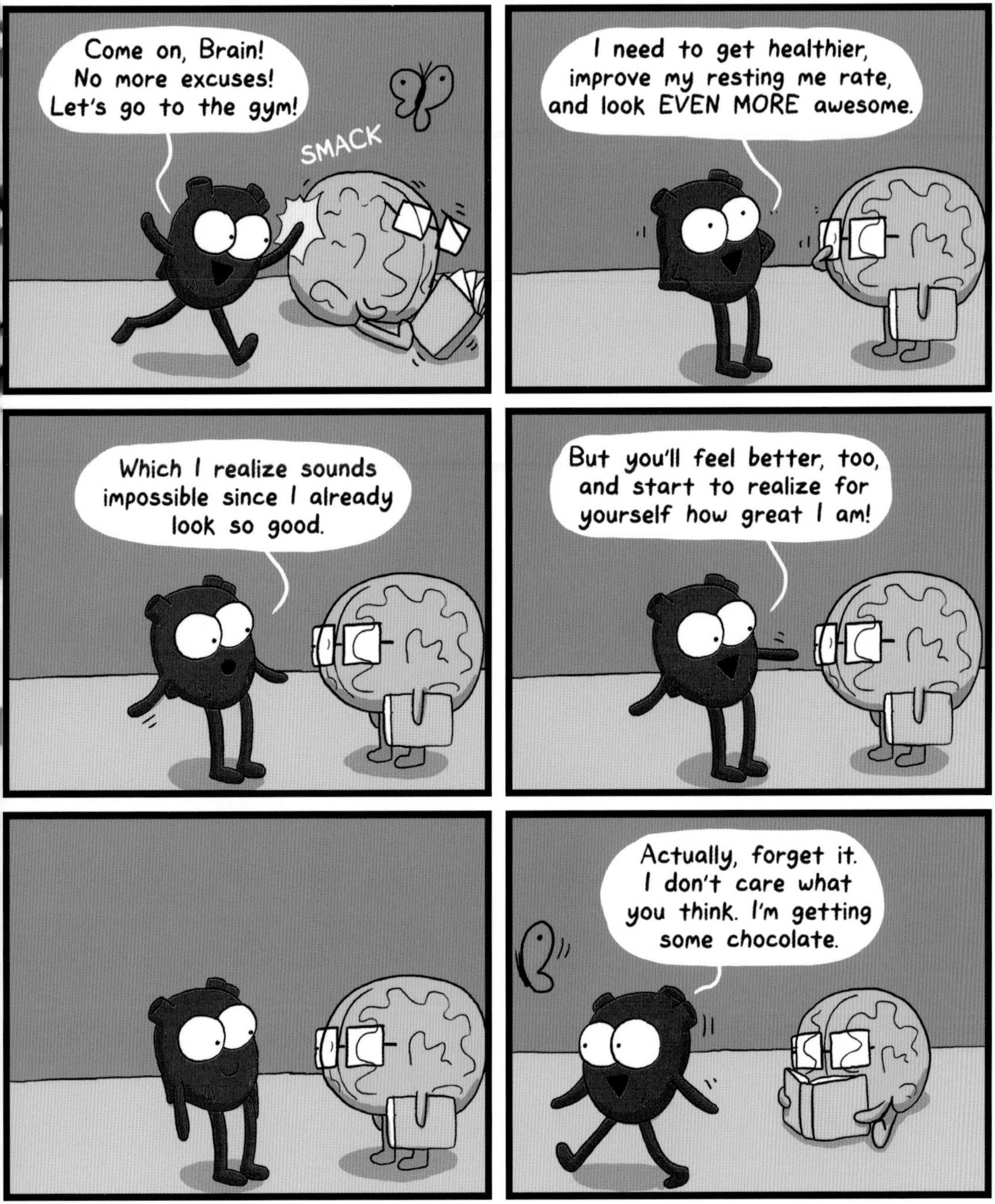
Come on, Brain! No more excuses! Let's go to the gym!
SMACK
I need to get healthier, improve my resting me rate, and look EVEN MORE awesome.
Which I realize sounds impossible since I already look so good.
But you'll feel better, too, and start to realize for yourself how great I am!
Actually, forget it. I don't care what you think. I'm getting some chocolate.

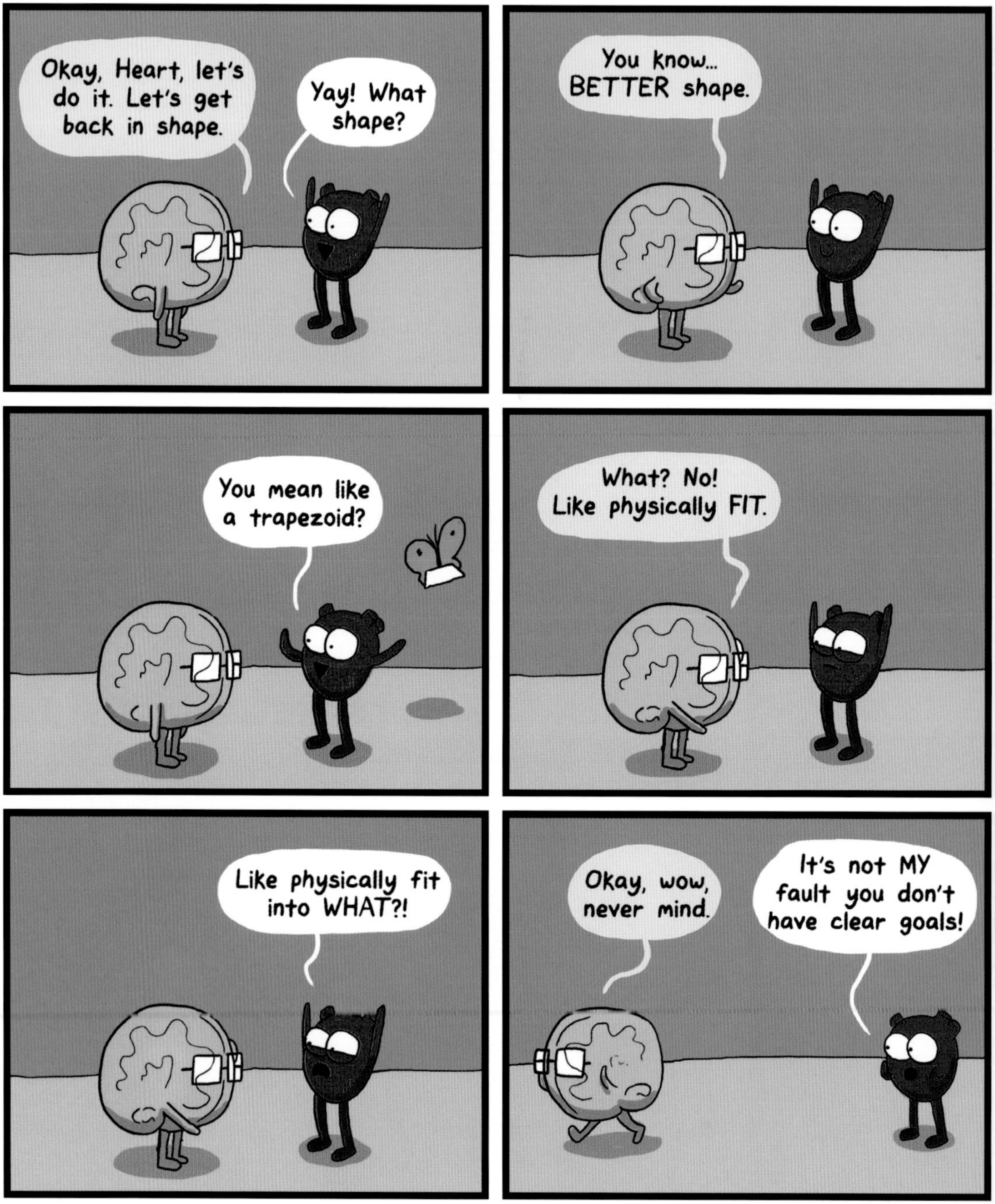
Okay, Heart, let's do it. Let's get back in shape.
Yay! What shape?
You know... BETTER shape.
You mean like a trapezoid?
What? No! Like physically FIT.
Like physically fit into WHAT?!
Okay, wow, never mind.
It's not MY fault you don't have clear goals!

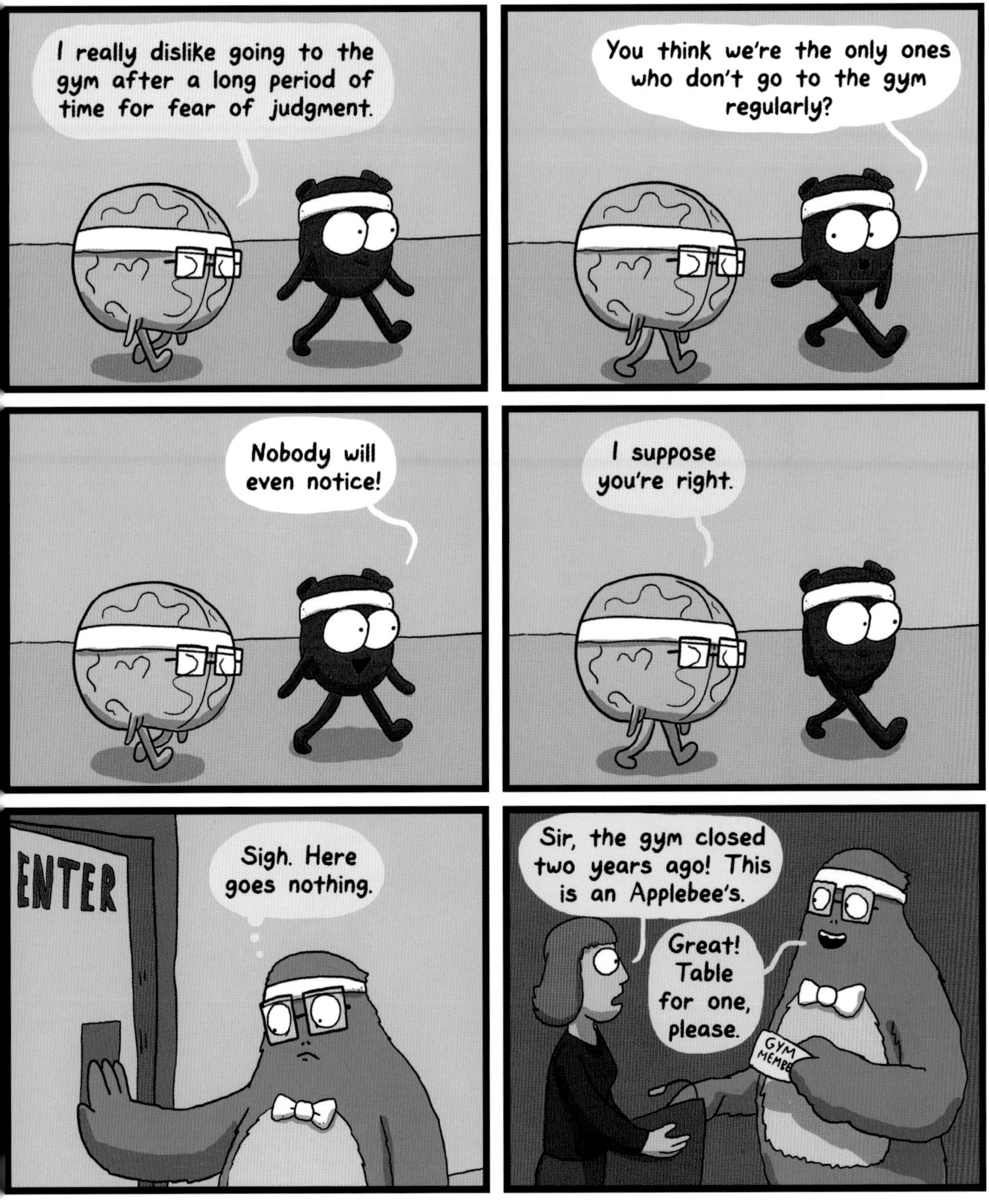
I really dislike going to the gym after a long period of time for fear of judgment.
You think we're the only ones who don't go to the gym regularly?
Nobody will even notice!
I suppose you're right.
ENTER
Sigh. Here goes nothing.
Sir, the gym closed two years ago! This is an Applebee's.
Great! Table for one, please.

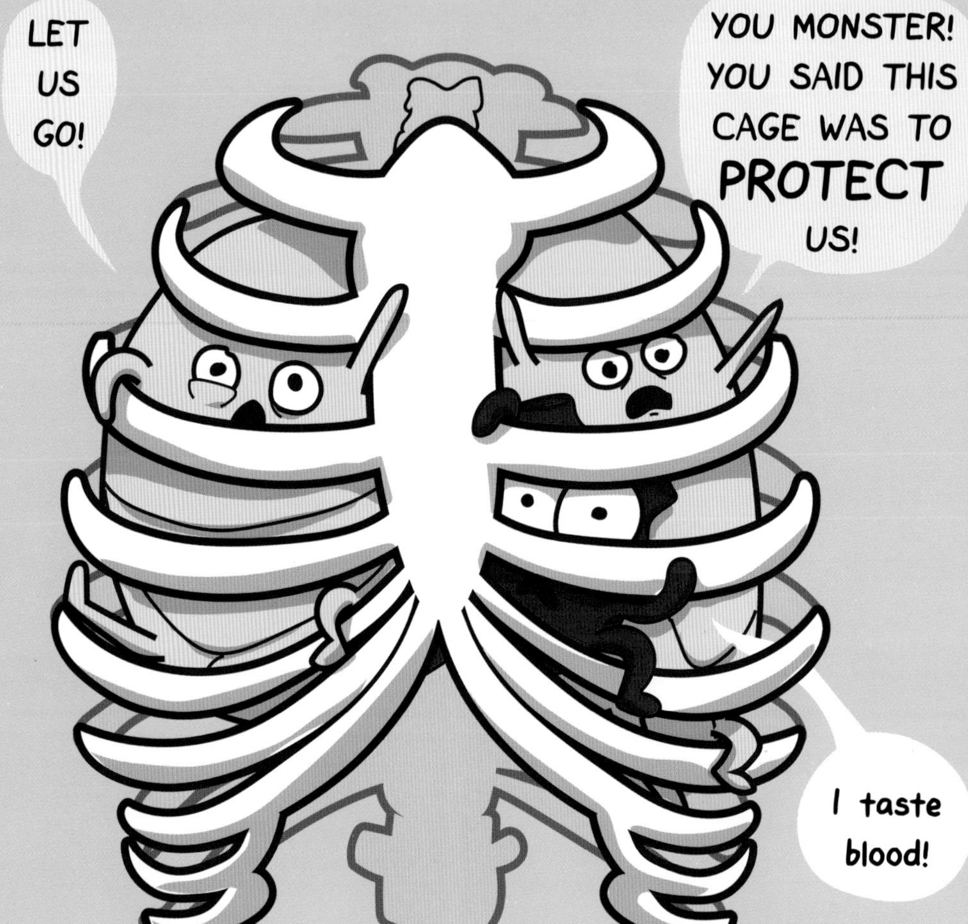
LET US GO!
YOU MONSTER! YOU SAID THIS CAGE WAS TO PROTECT US!
I taste blood!

What happens during a run.

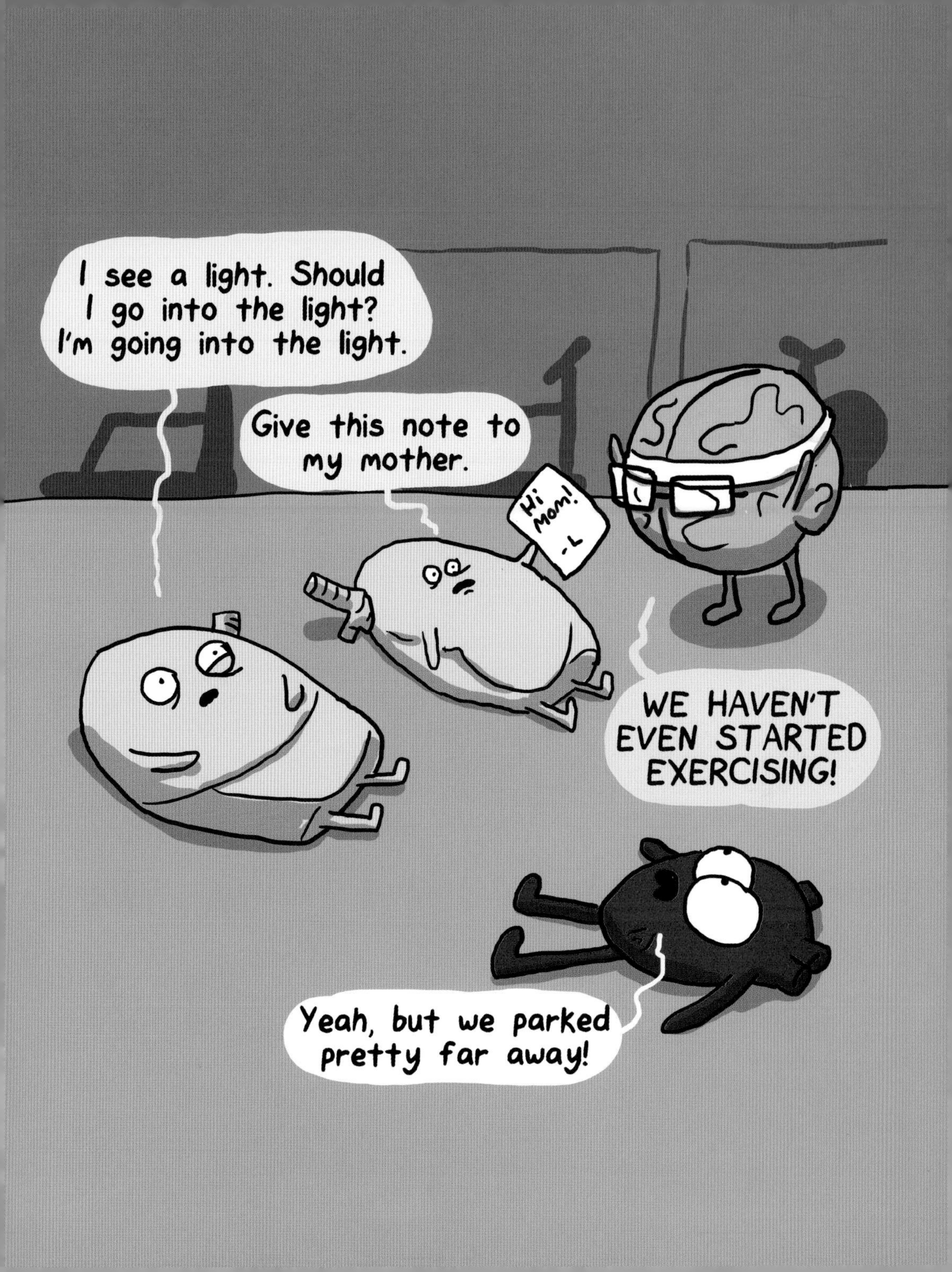
I see a light. Should I go into the light? I'm going into the light.
Give this note to my mother.
Hi Mom! -L
WE HAVEN'T EVEN STARTED EXERCISING!
Yeah, but we parked pretty far away!

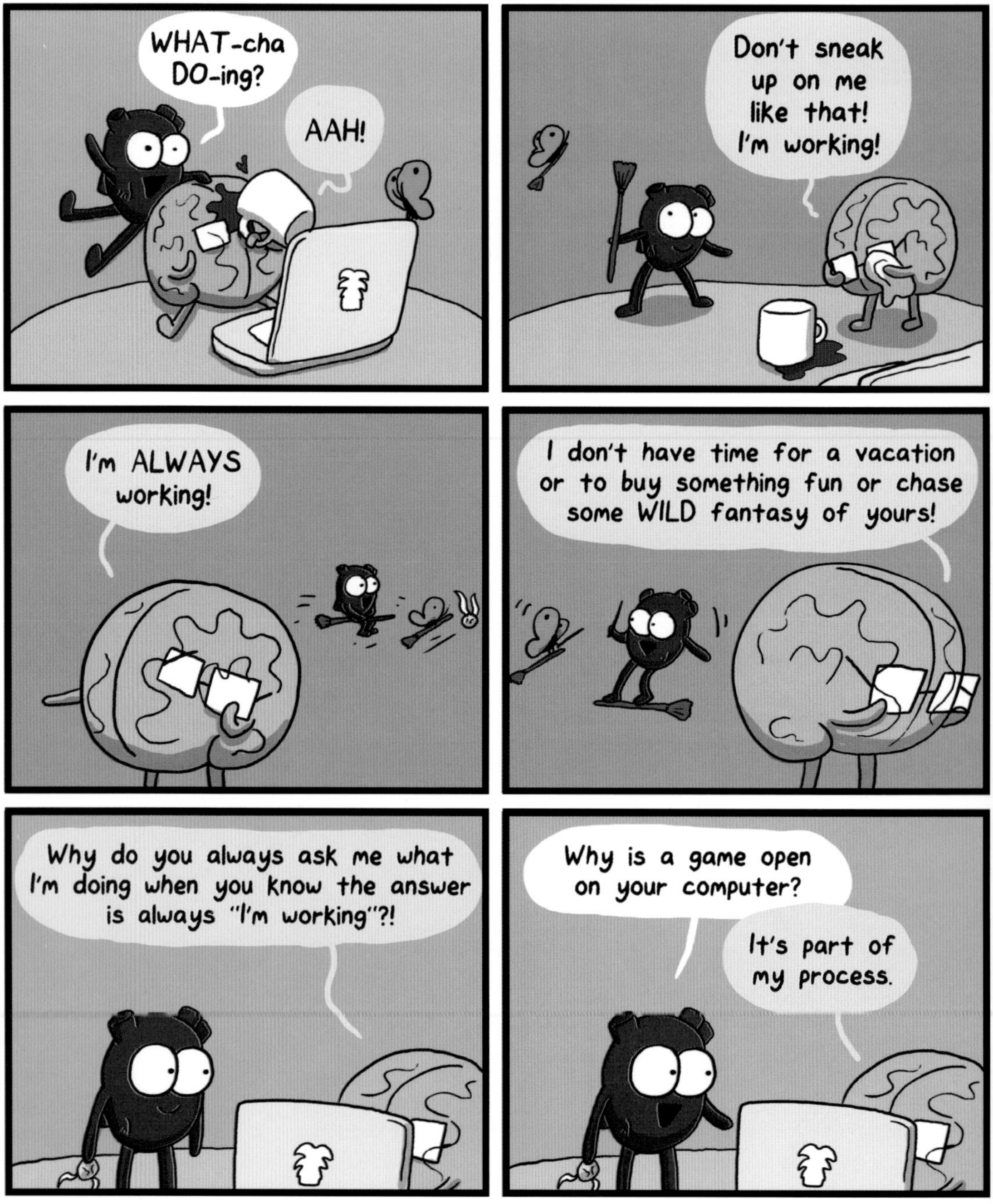
WHAT-cha DO-ing?
AAH!
Don't sneak up on me like that! I'm working!
I'm ALWAYS working!
I don't have time for a vacation or to buy something fun or chase some WILD fantasy of yours!
Why do you always ask me what I'm doing when you know the answer is always "I'm working"?!
Why is a game open on your computer?
It's part of my process.

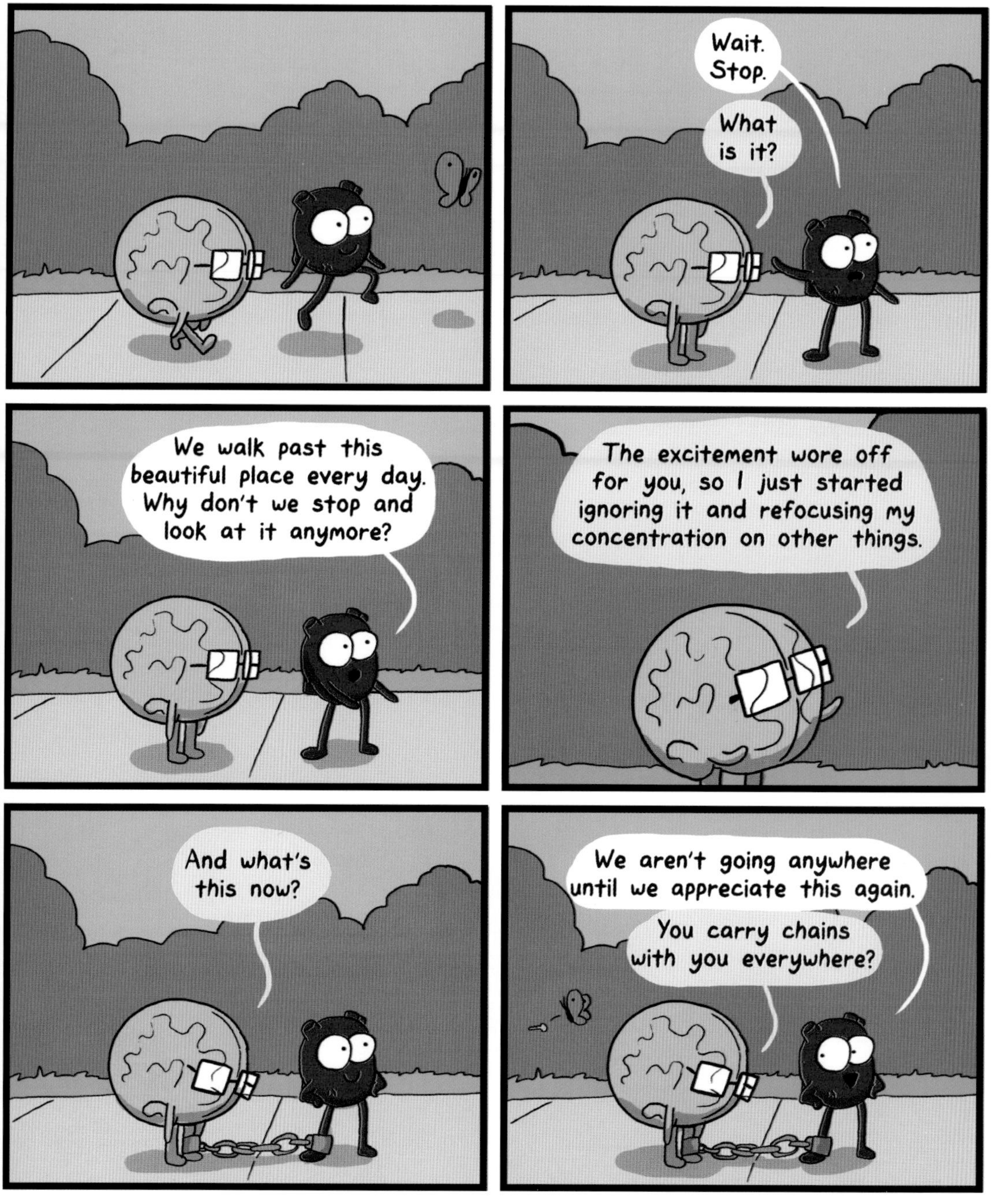
Wait. Stop.
What is it?
We walk past this beautiful place every day. Why don't we stop and look at it anymore?
The excitement wore off for you, so I just started ignoring it and refocusing my concentration on other things.
And what's this now?
We aren't going anywhere until we appreciate this again.
You carry chains with you everywhere?

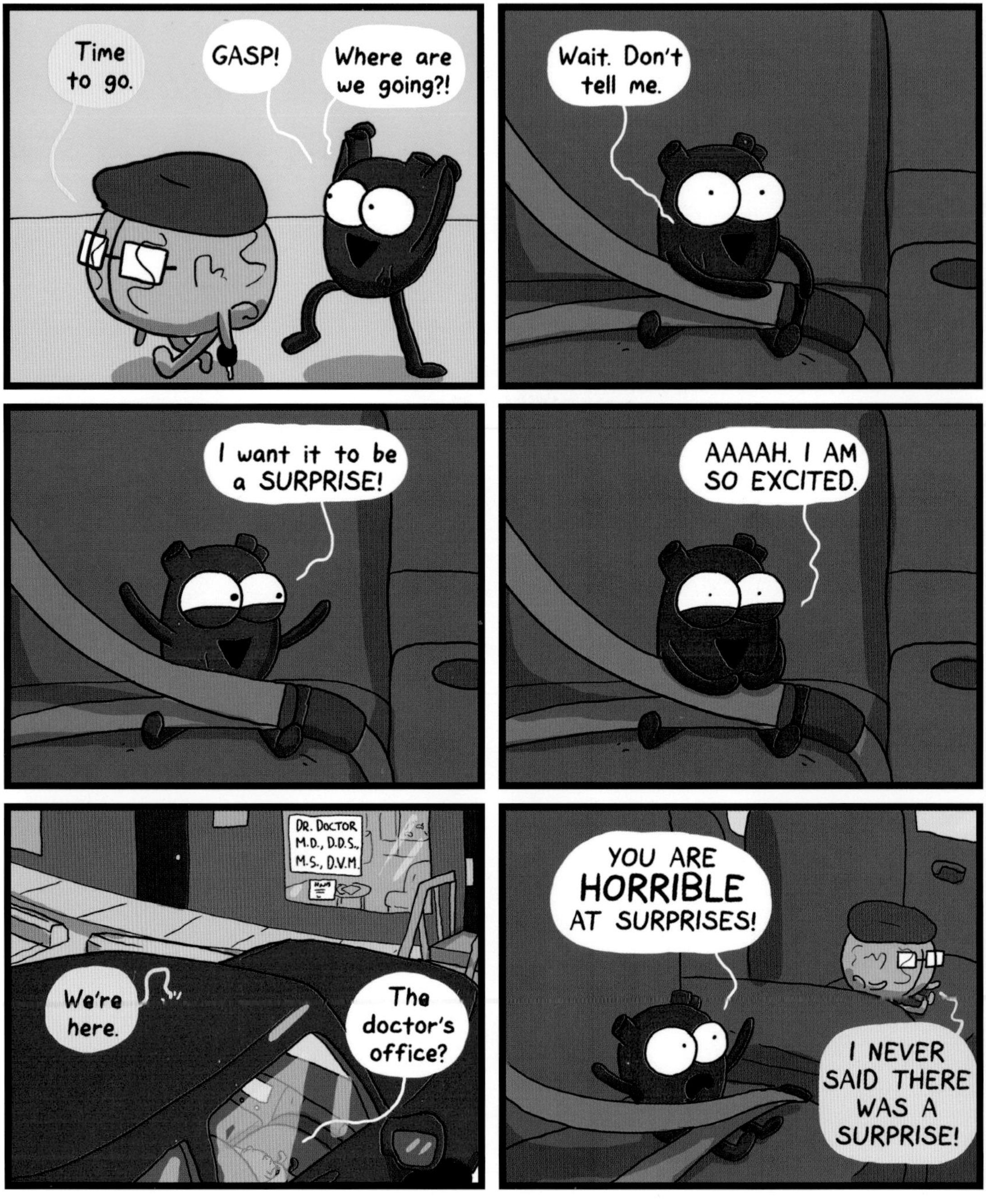
Time to go.
GASP!
Where are we going?!
Wait. Don't tell me.
I want it to be a SURPRISE!
AAAAH. I AM SO EXCITED.
DR. DOCTOR M.D., D.D.S., M.S., D.V.M.
We're here.
The doctor's office?
YOU ARE HORRIBLE AT SURPRISES!
I NEVER SAID THERE WAS A SURPRISE!

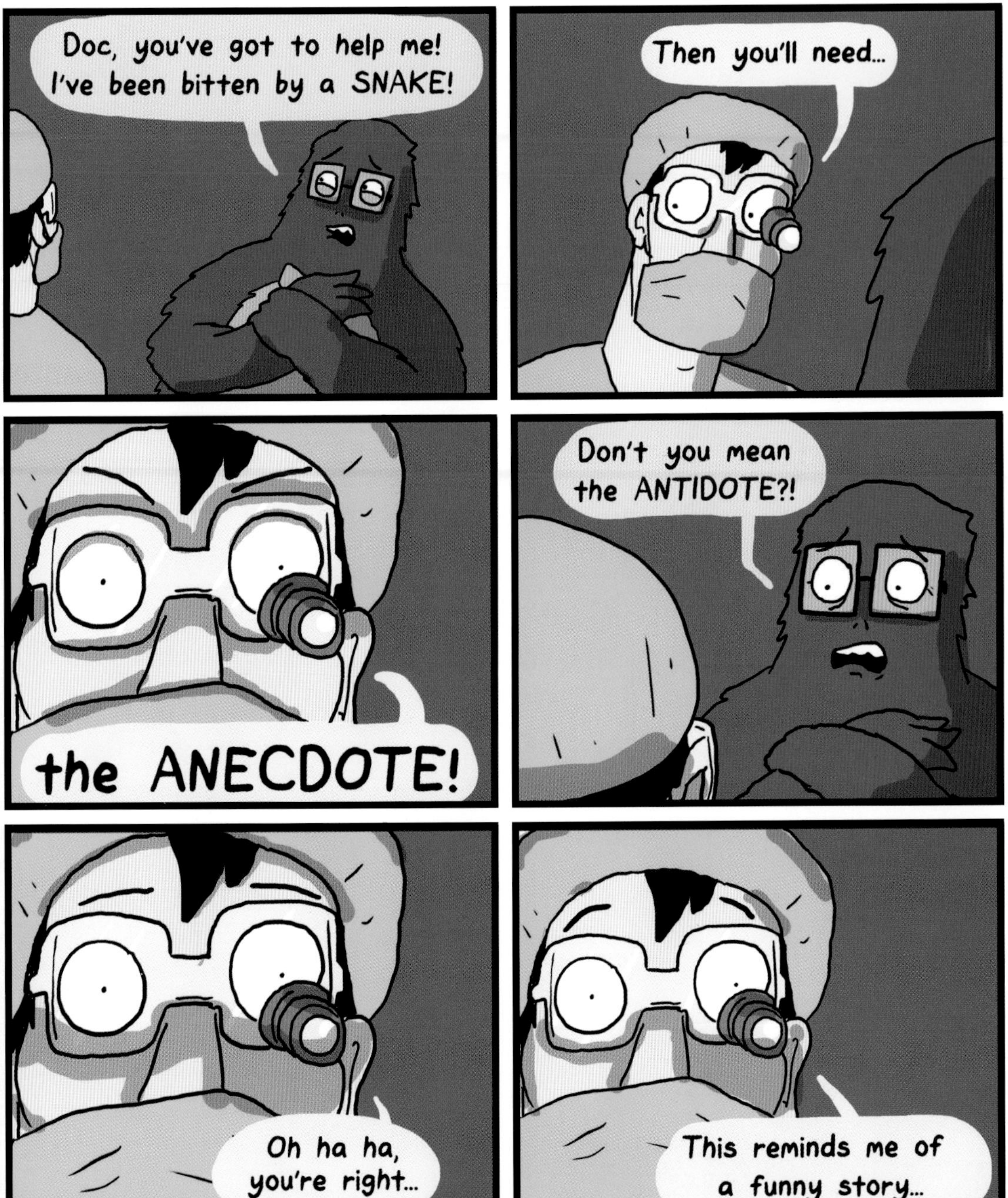
Doc, you've got to help me! I've been bitten by a SNAKE!
Then you'll need...
the ANECDOTE!
Don't you mean the ANTIDOTE?!
Oh ha ha, you're right...
This reminds me of a funny story...

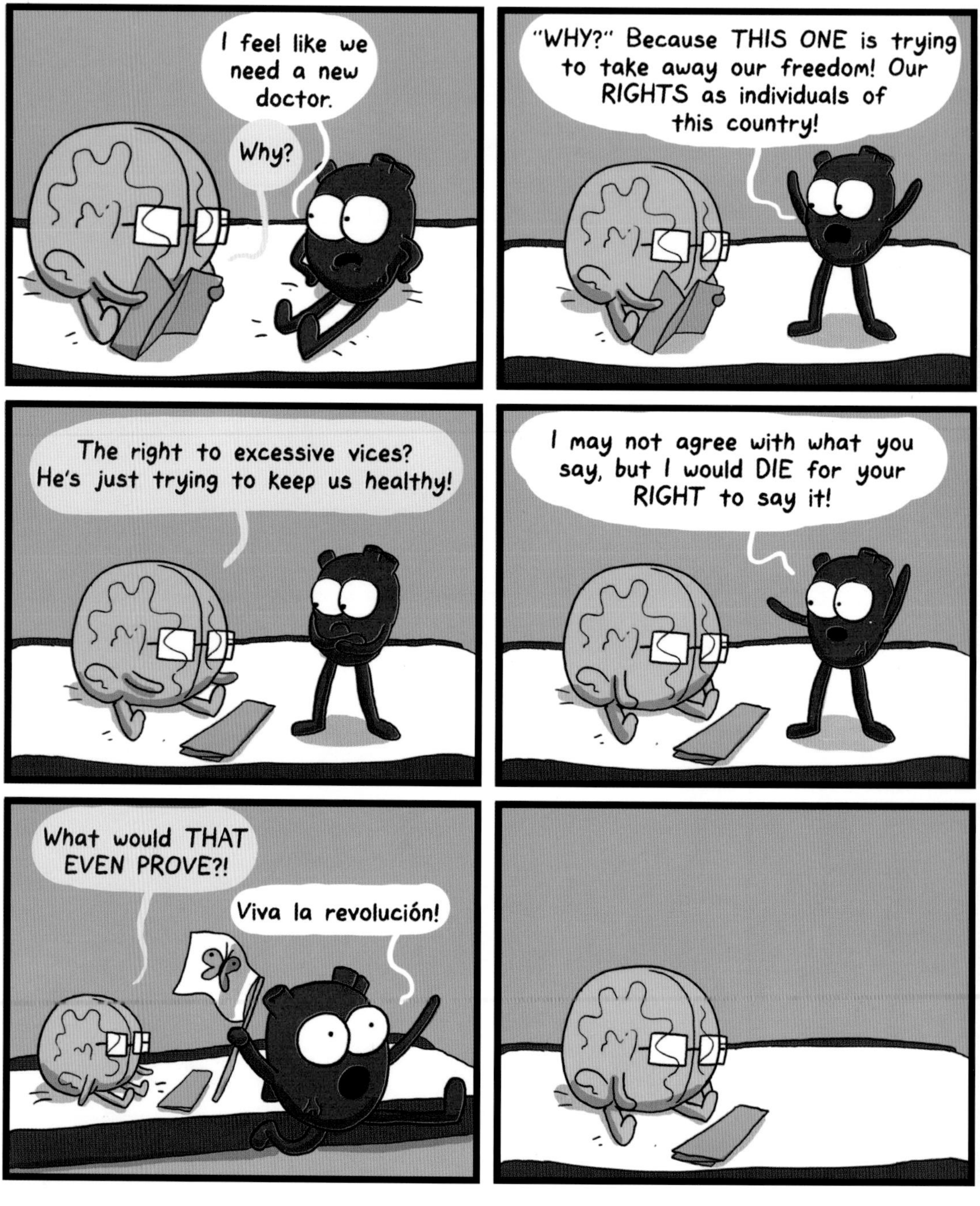
I feel like we need a new doctor.
Why?
"WHY?" Because THIS ONE is trying to take away our freedom! Our RIGHTS as individuals of this country!
The right to excessive vices? He's just trying to keep us healthy!
I may not agree with what you say, but I would DIE for your RIGHT to say it!
What would THAT EVEN PROVE?!
Viva la revolución!

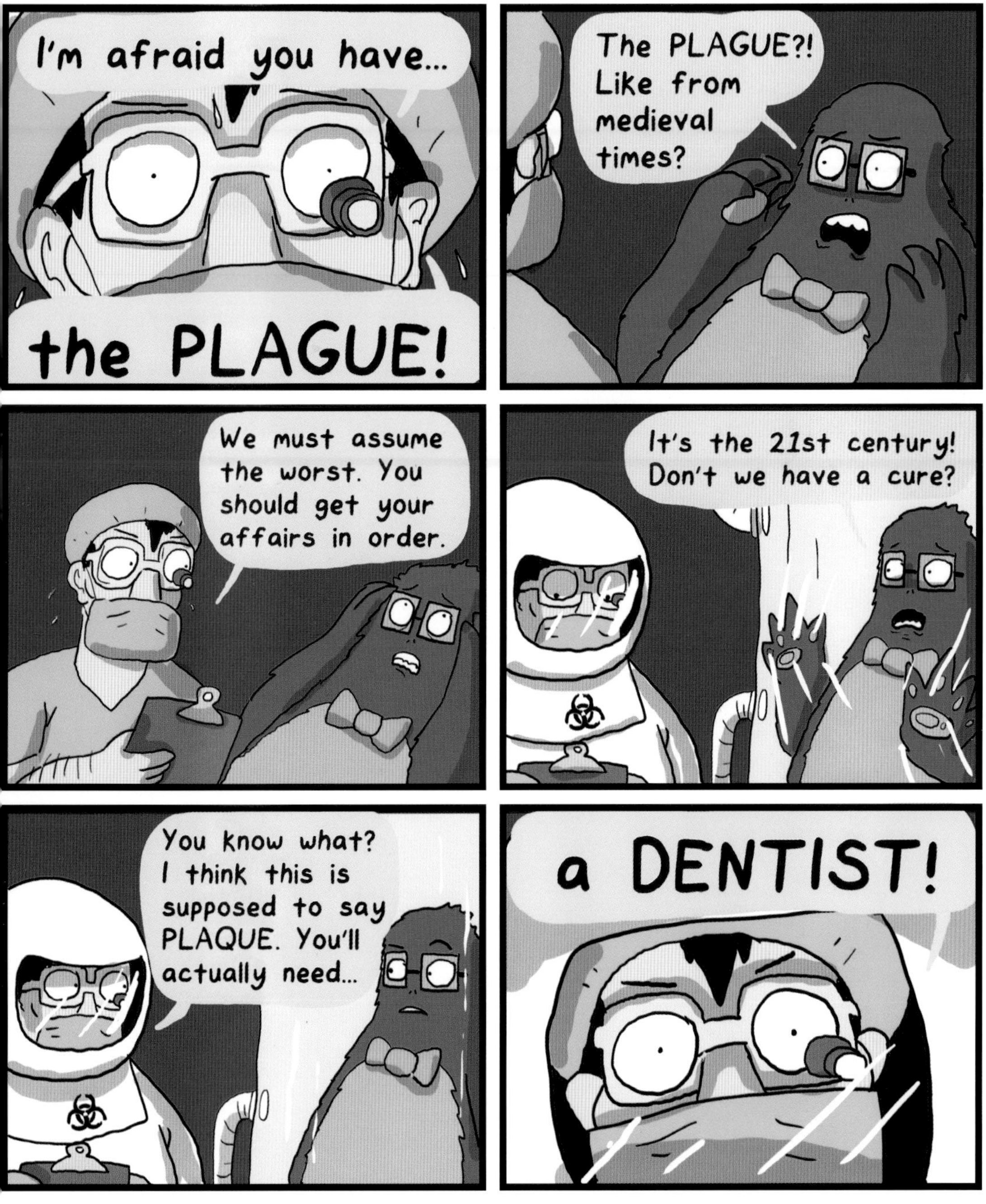
I'm afraid you have...
the PLAGUE!
The PLAGUE?! Like from medieval times?
We must assume the worst. You should get your affairs in order.
It's the 21st century! Don't we have a cure?
You know what? I think this is supposed to say PLAQUE. You'll actually need...
a DENTIST!

Whoa, NOSSSE, you SSsMELL!
No I don't!
You...don't SssMELL?
No...
SNIFF
WELL ISSSN'T THAT YOUR JOB?!
HAHA HAHA HA HA HA HAHAH HAAAAA
ON ACCOUNT OF THE FACT THAT YOU'RE A NOSSKE!
Please go away.

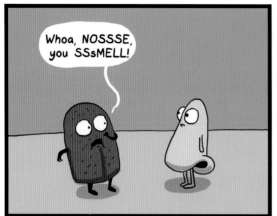

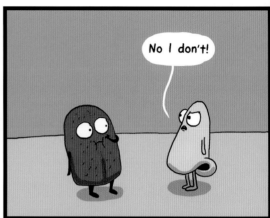

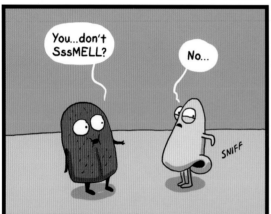

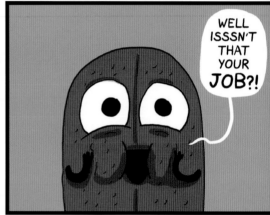

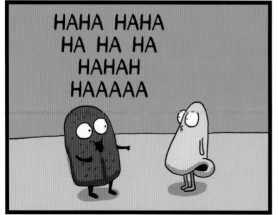

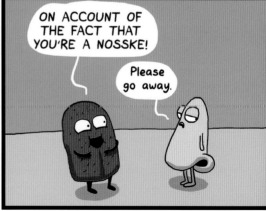

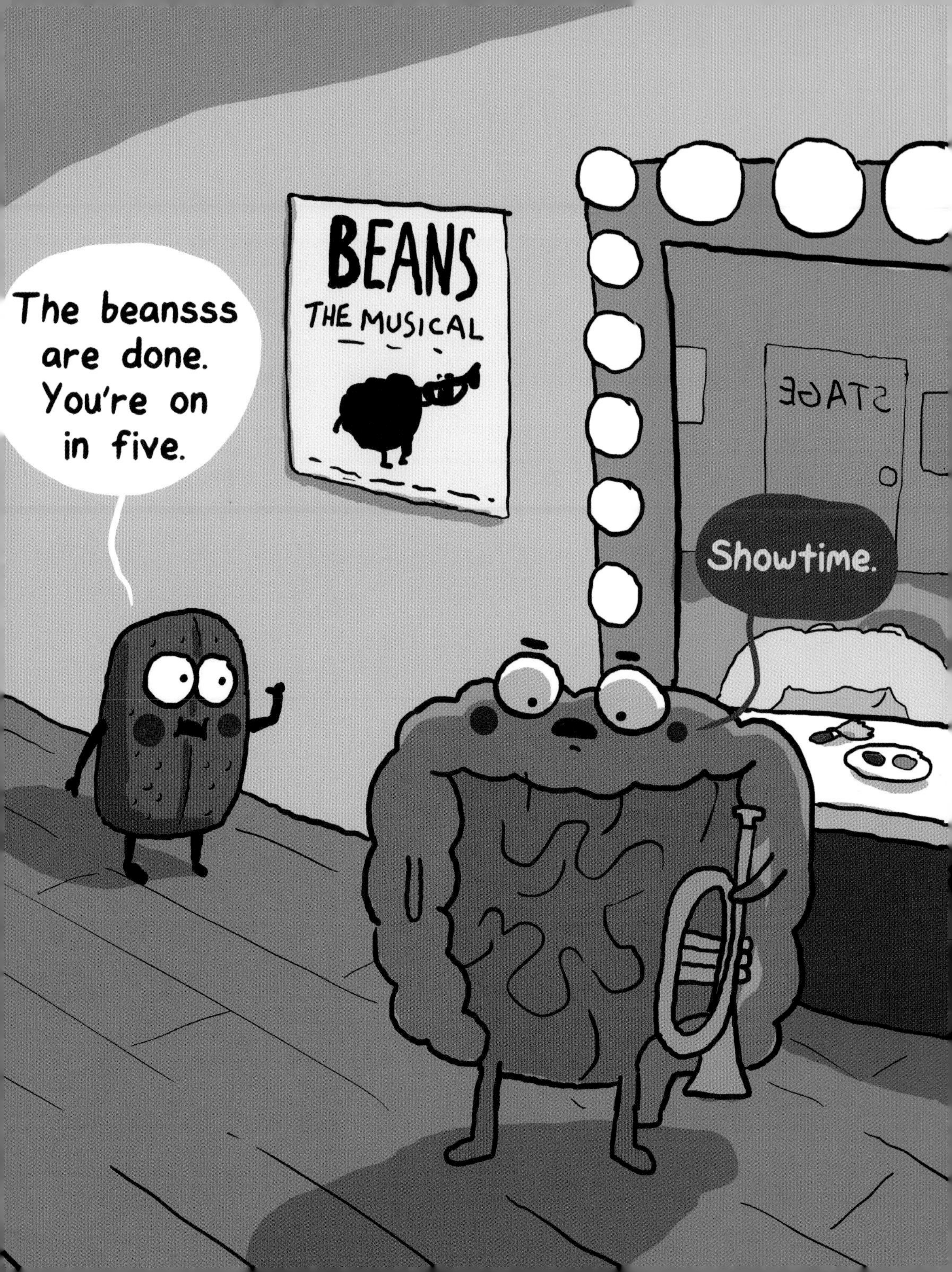

BEANS
THE MUSICAL
The beansss are done. You're on in five.
STAGE
Showtime.

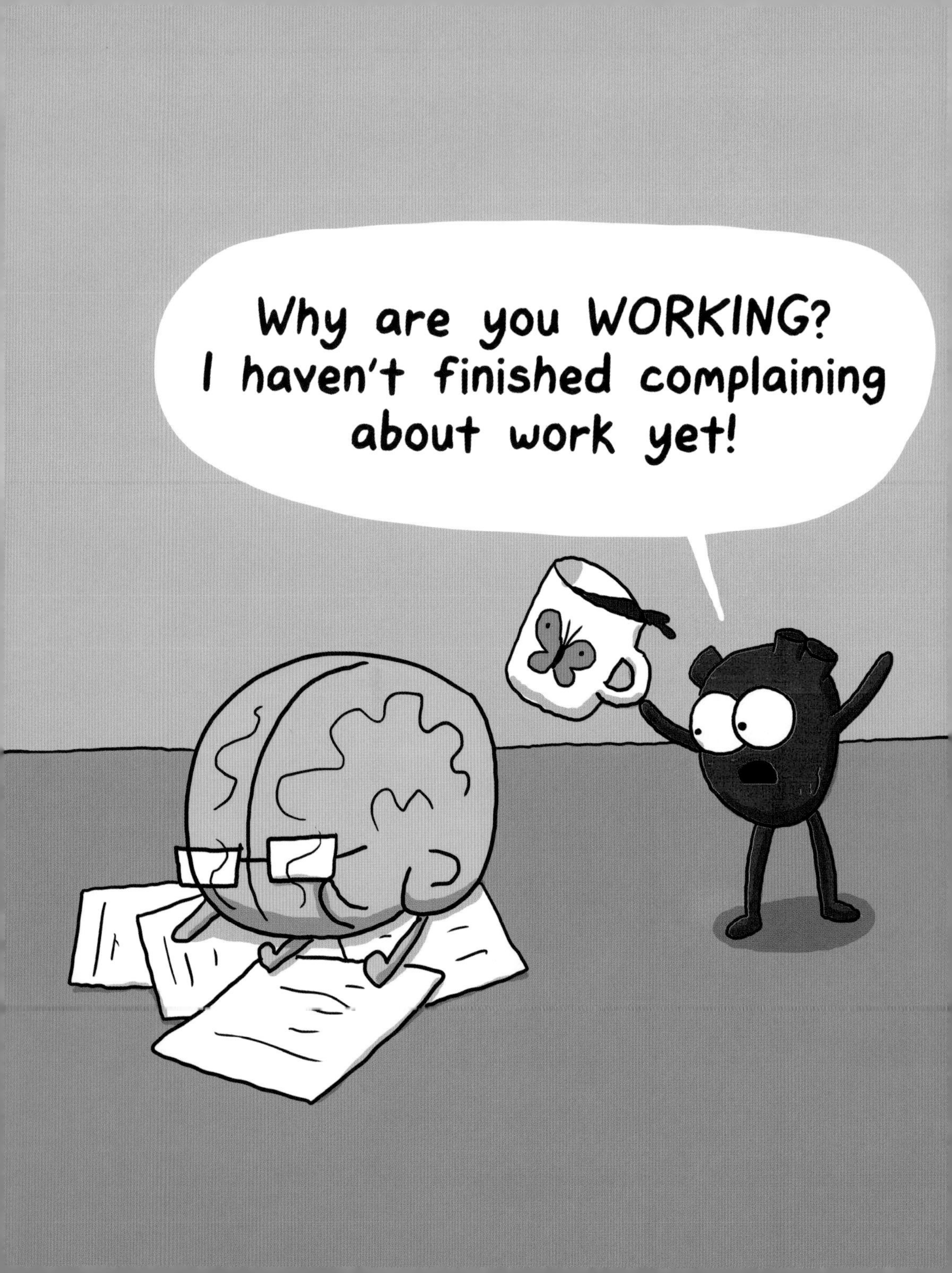
Why are you WORKING? I haven't finished complaining about work yet!

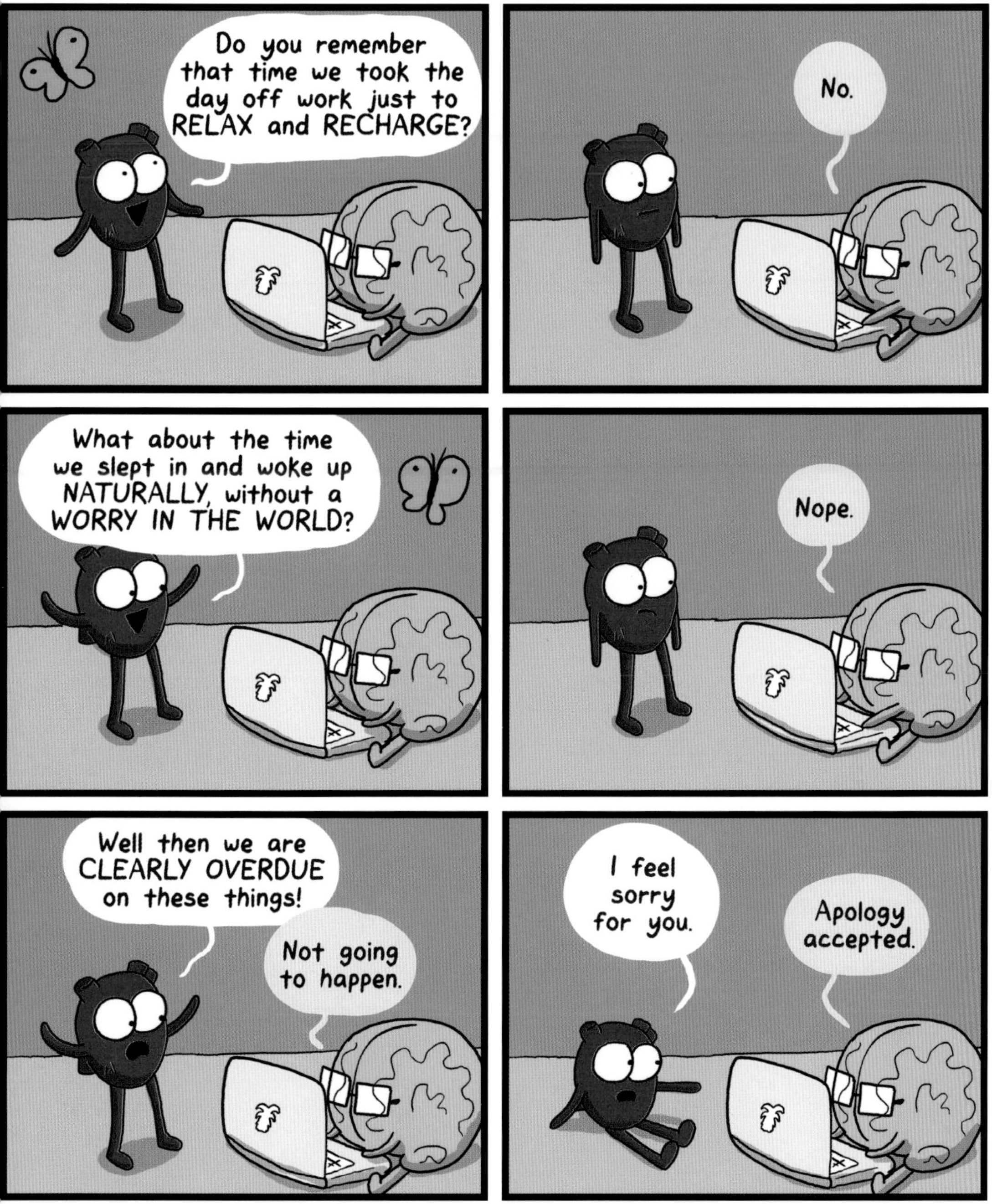
Do you remember that time we took the day off work just to RELAX and RECHARGE?
No.
What about the time we slept in and woke up NATURALLY, without a WORRY IN THE WORLD?
Nope.
Well then we are CLEARLY OVERDUE on these things!
Not going to happen.
I feel sorry for you.
Apology accepted.

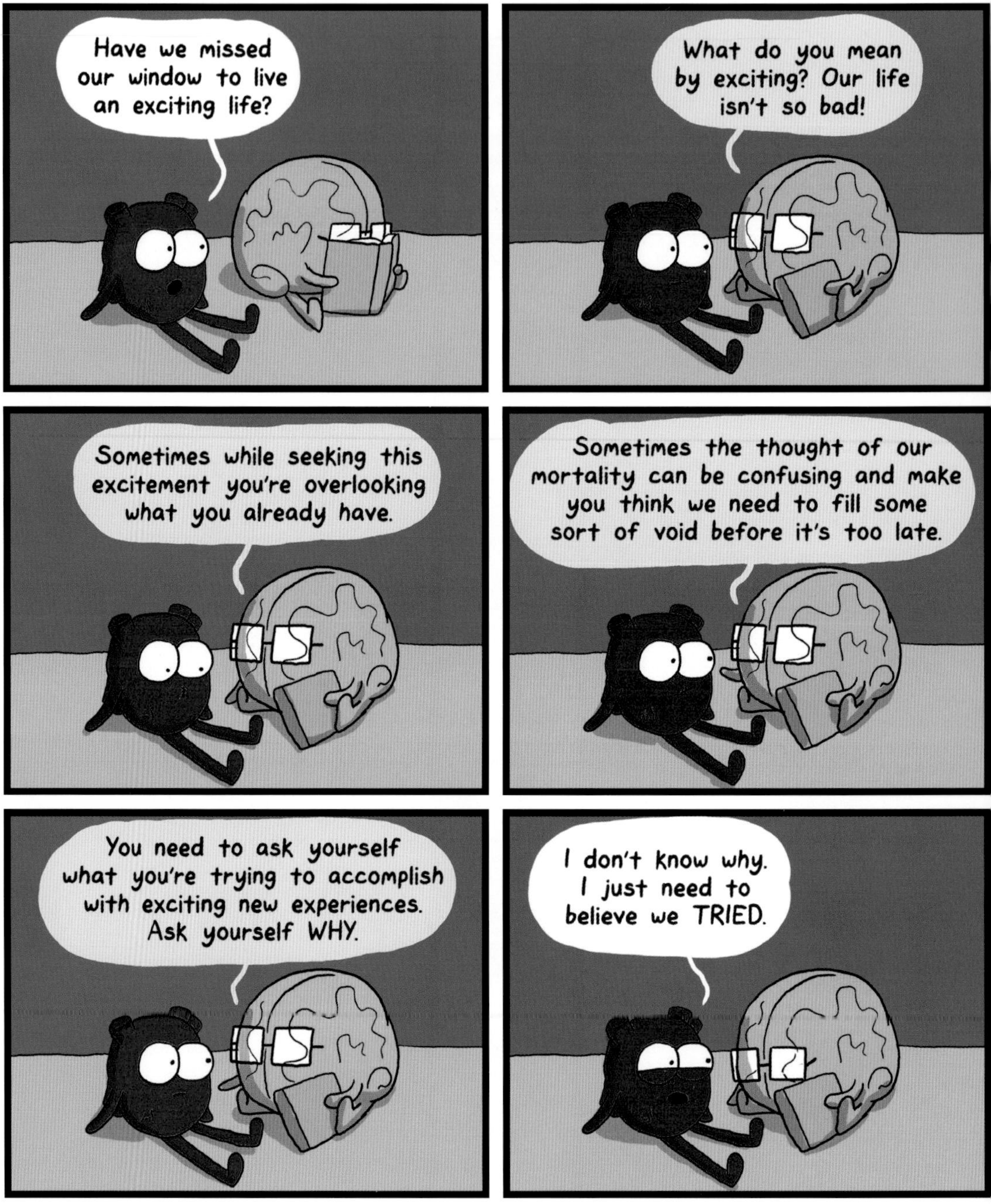
Have we missed our window to live an exciting life?
What do you mean by exciting? Our life isn't so bad!
Sometimes while seeking this excitement you're overlooking what you already have.
Sometimes the thought of our mortality can be confusing and make you think we need to fill some sort of void before it's too late.
You need to ask yourself what you're trying to accomplish with exciting new experiences. Ask yourself WHY.
I don't know why. I just need to believe we TRIED.

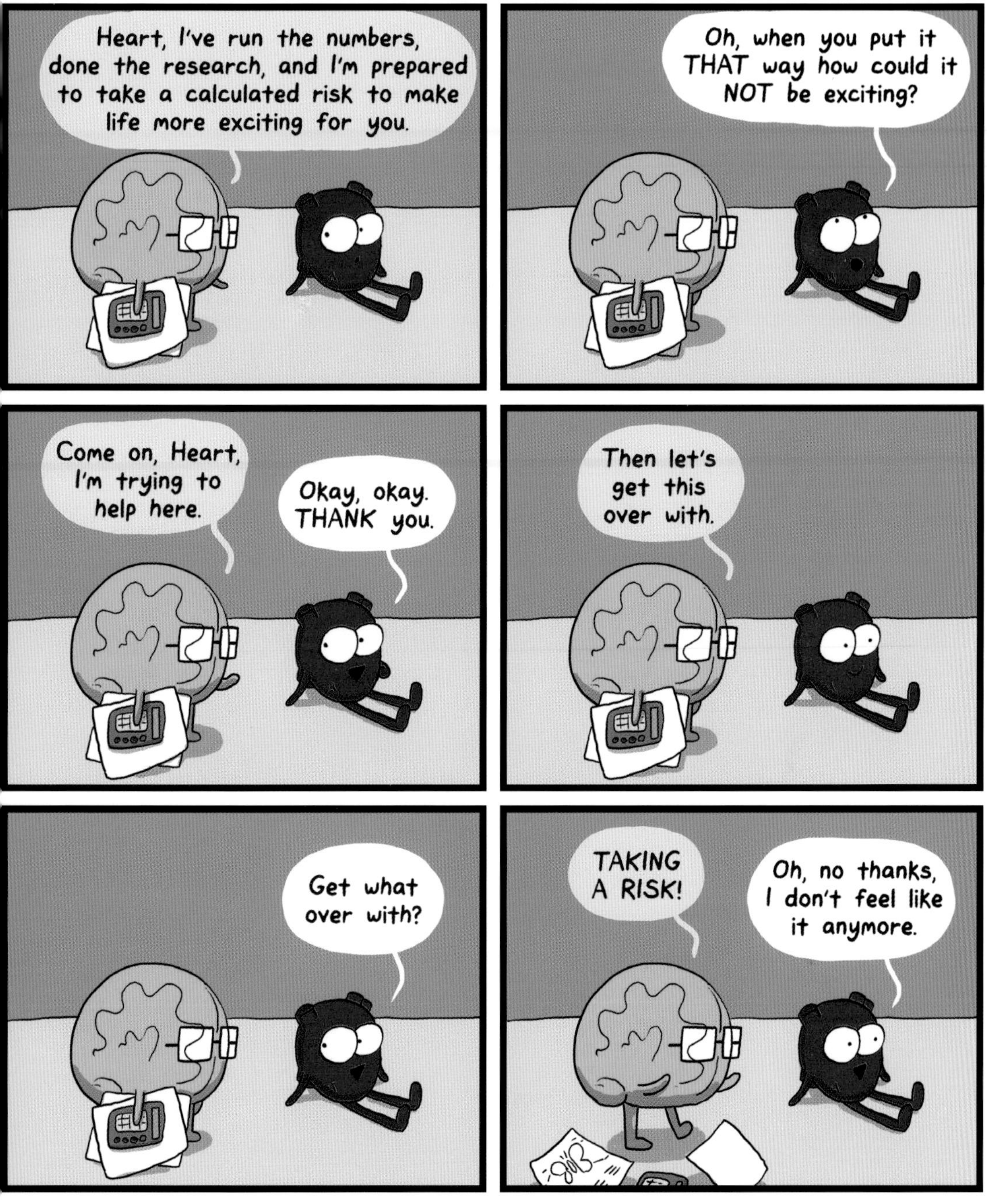
Heart, I've run the numbers, done the research, and I'm prepared to take a calculated risk to make life more exciting for you.
Oh, when you put it THAT way how could it NOT be exciting?
Come on, Heart, I'm trying to help here.
Okay, okay. THANK you.
Then let's get this over with.
Get what over with?
TAKING A RISK!
Oh, no thanks, I don't feel like it anymore.

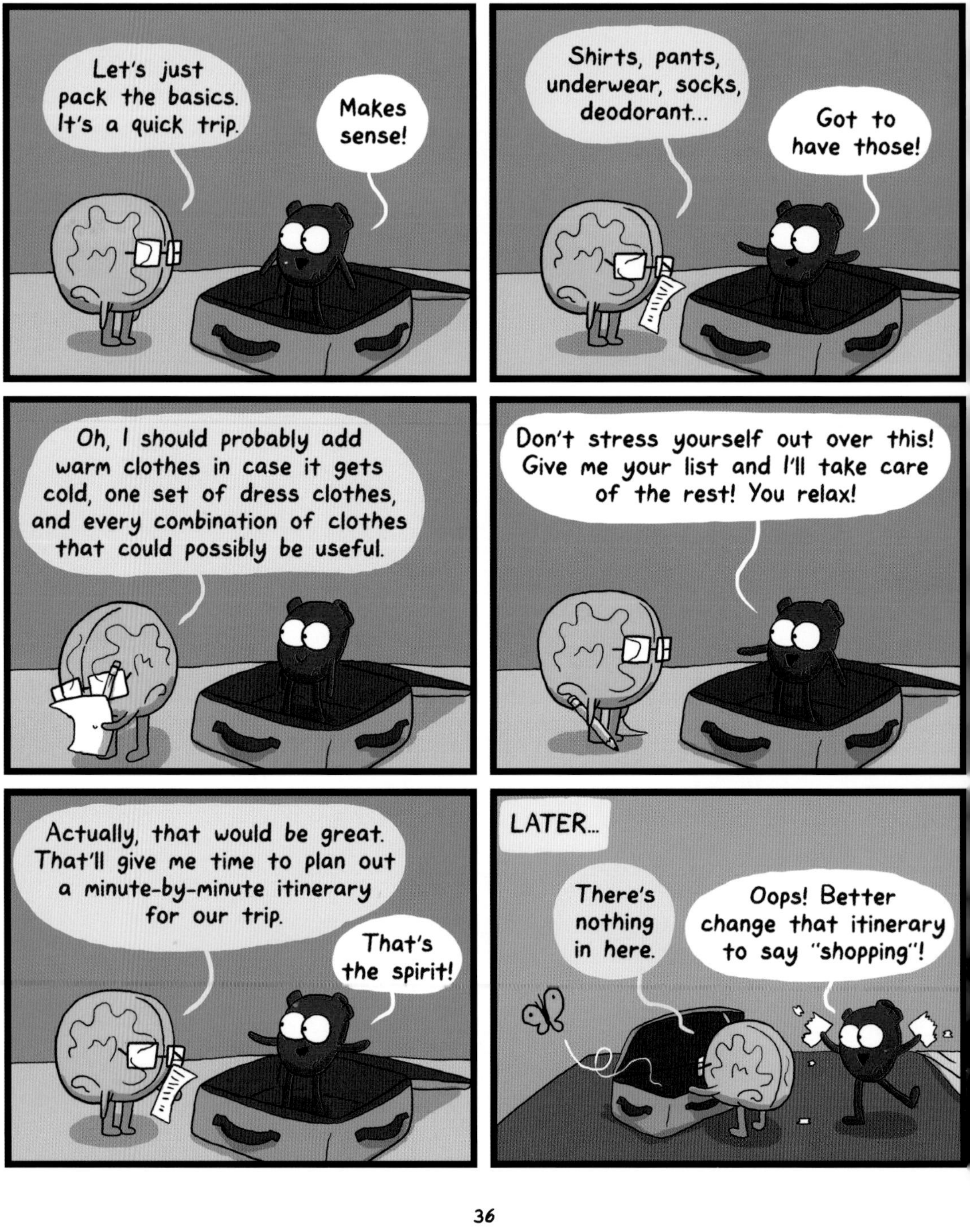
Let's just pack the basics. It's a quick trip.
Makes sense!
Shirts, pants, underwear, socks, deodorant...
Got to have those!
Oh, I should probably add warm clothes in case it gets cold, one set of dress clothes, and every combination of clothes that could possibly be useful.
Don't stress yourself out over this! Give me your list and I'll take care of the rest! You relax!
Actually, that would be great. That'll give me time to plan out a minute-by-minute itinerary for our trip.
That's the spirit!
LATER...
There's nothing in here.
Oops! Better change that itinerary to say "shopping"!

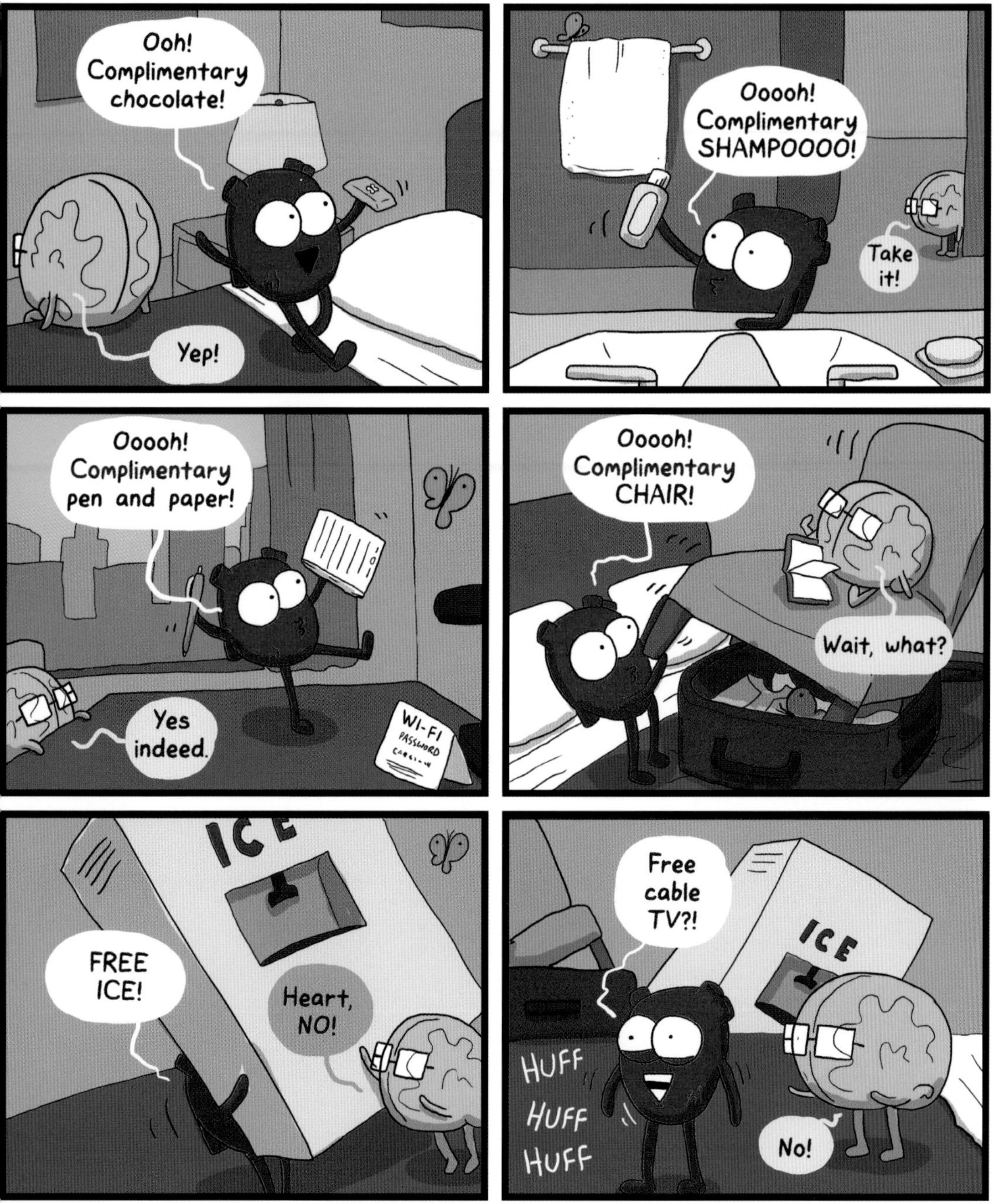
Ooh! Complimentary chocolate!
Yep!
Ooooh! Complimentary SHAMPOOOO!
Take it!
Ooooh! Complimentary pen and paper!
Yes indeed.
WI-FI PASSWORD
Ooooh! Complimentary CHAIR!
Wait, what?
ICE
FREE ICE!
Heart, NO!
Free cable TV?!
ICE
HUFF HUFF HUFF
No!

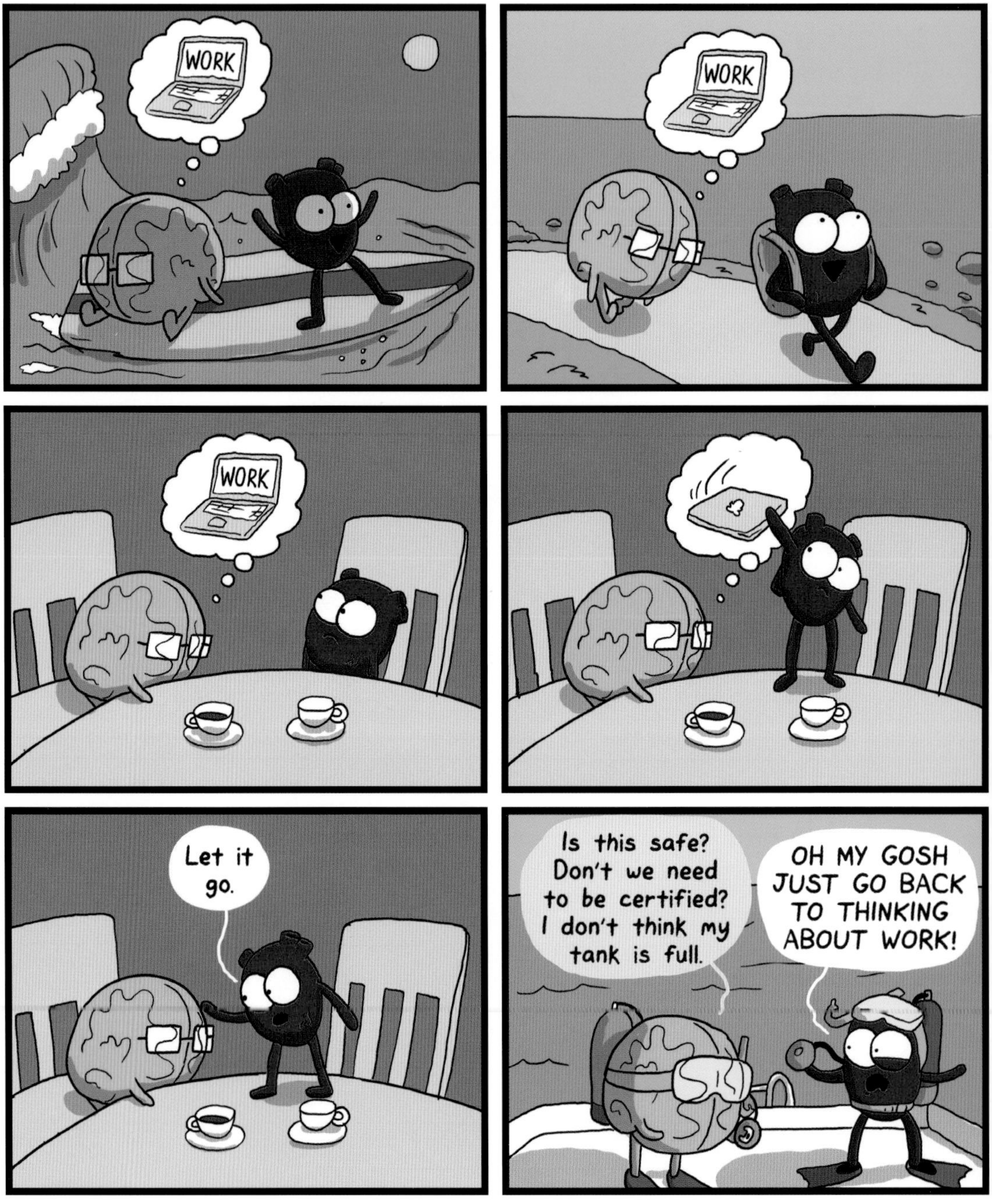
WORK
WORK
WORK
Let it go.
Is this safe? Don't we need to be certified? I don't think my tank is full.
OH MY GOSH JUST GO BACK TO THINKING ABOUT WORK!

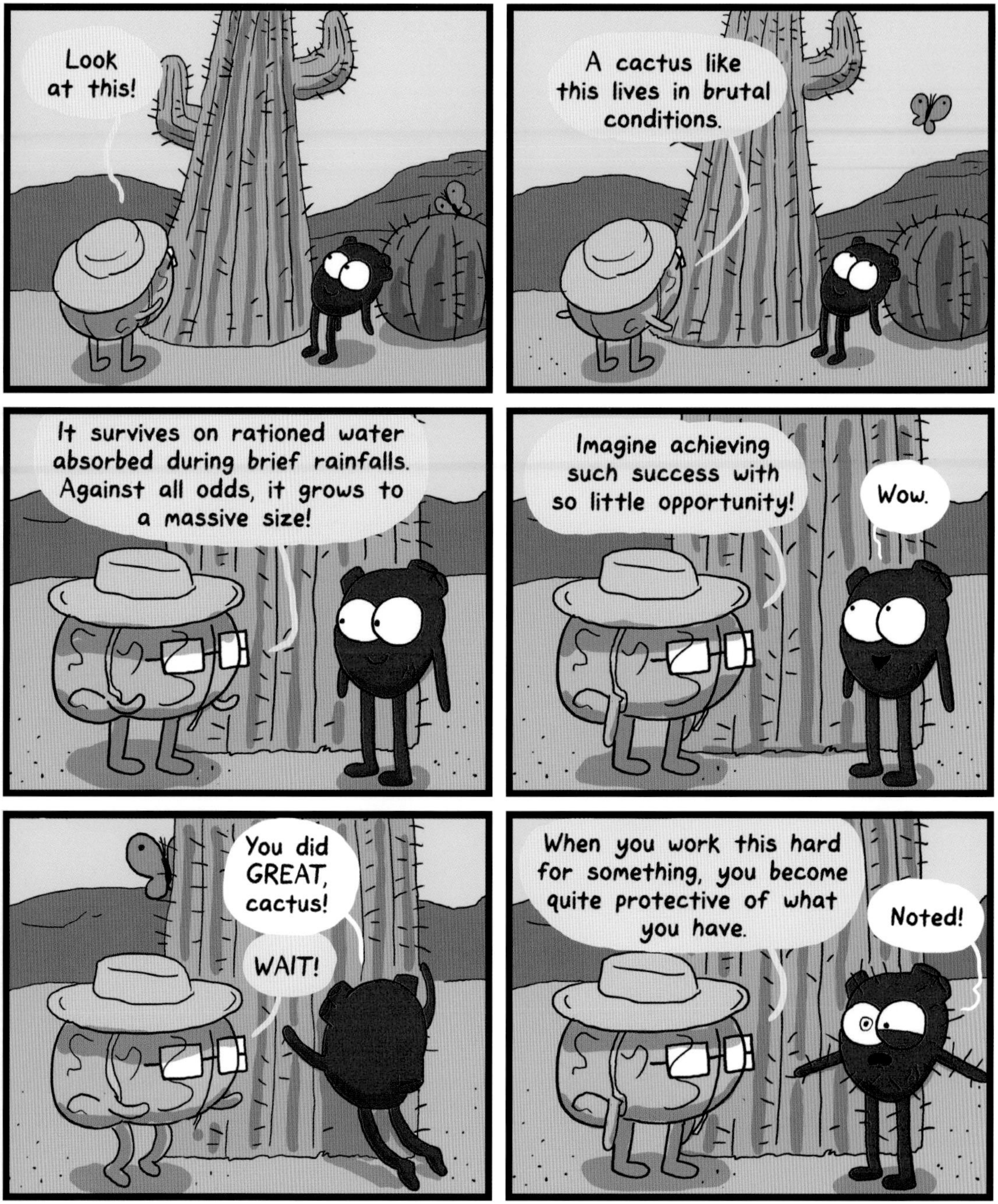
Look at this!
A cactus like this lives in brutal conditions.
It survives on rationed water absorbed during brief rainfalls. Against all odds, it grows to a massive size!
Imagine achieving such success with so little opportunity!
Wow.
You did GREAT, cactus!
WAIT!
When you work this hard for something, you become quite protective of what you have.
Noted!

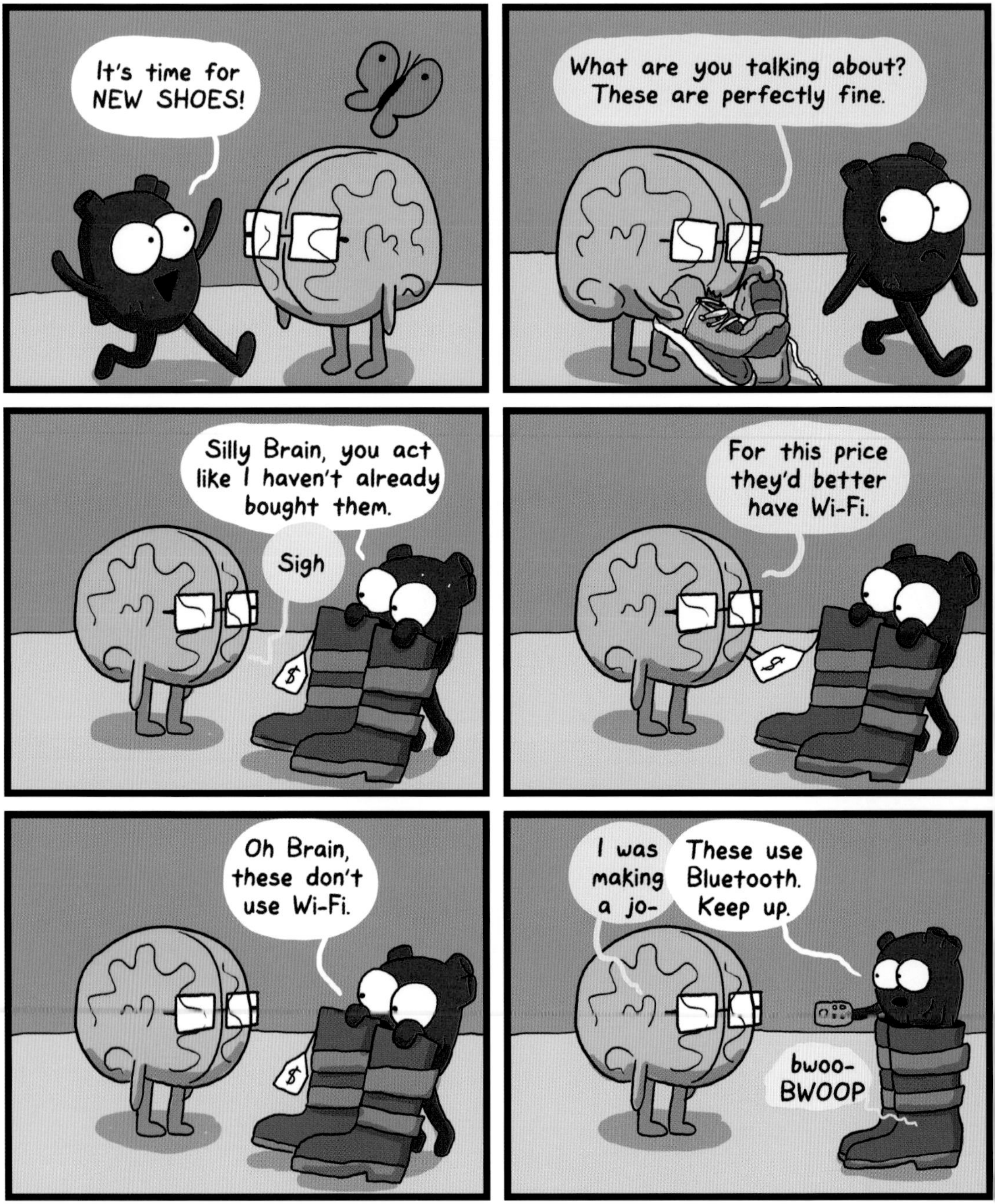

It's time for NEW SHOES!
What are you talking about? These are perfectly fine.
Silly Brain, you act like I haven't already bought them.
Sigh
For this price they'd better have Wi-Fi.
Oh Brain, these don't use Wi-Fi.
I was making a jo-
These use Bluetooth. Keep up.
bwoo-BWOOP

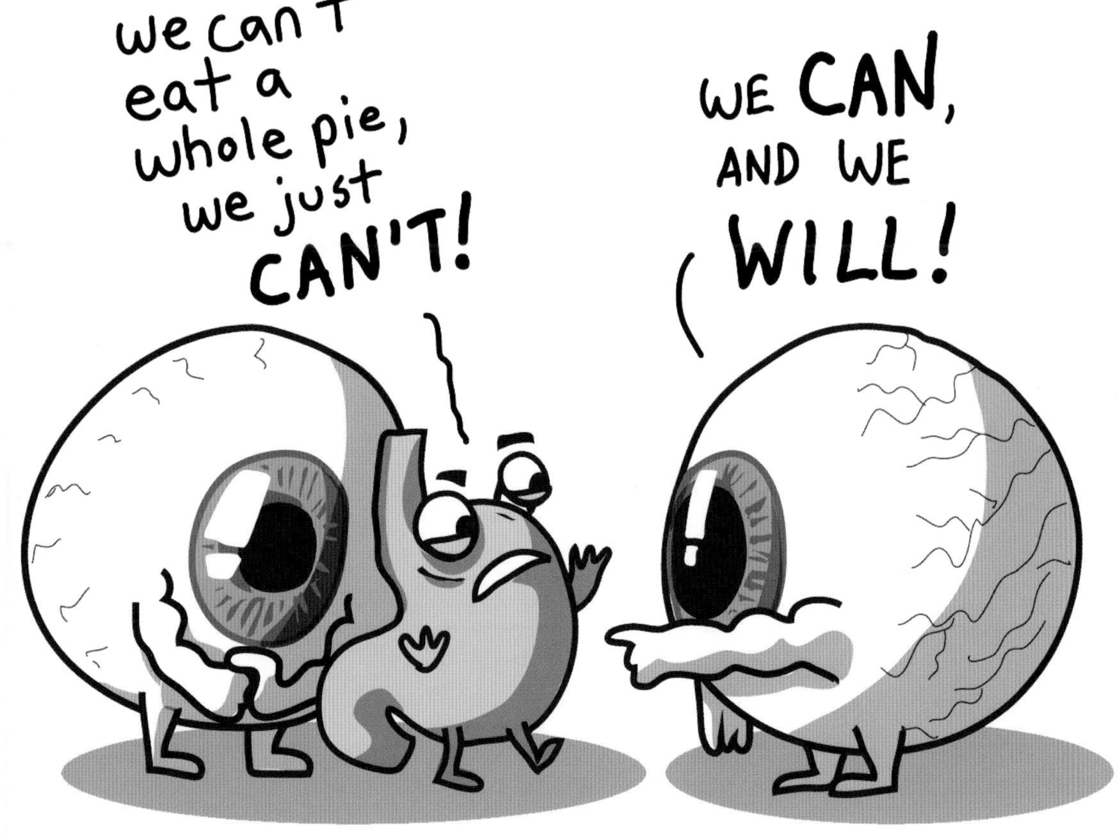
we can't eat a whole pie, we just CAN'T!
WE CAN, AND WE WILL!

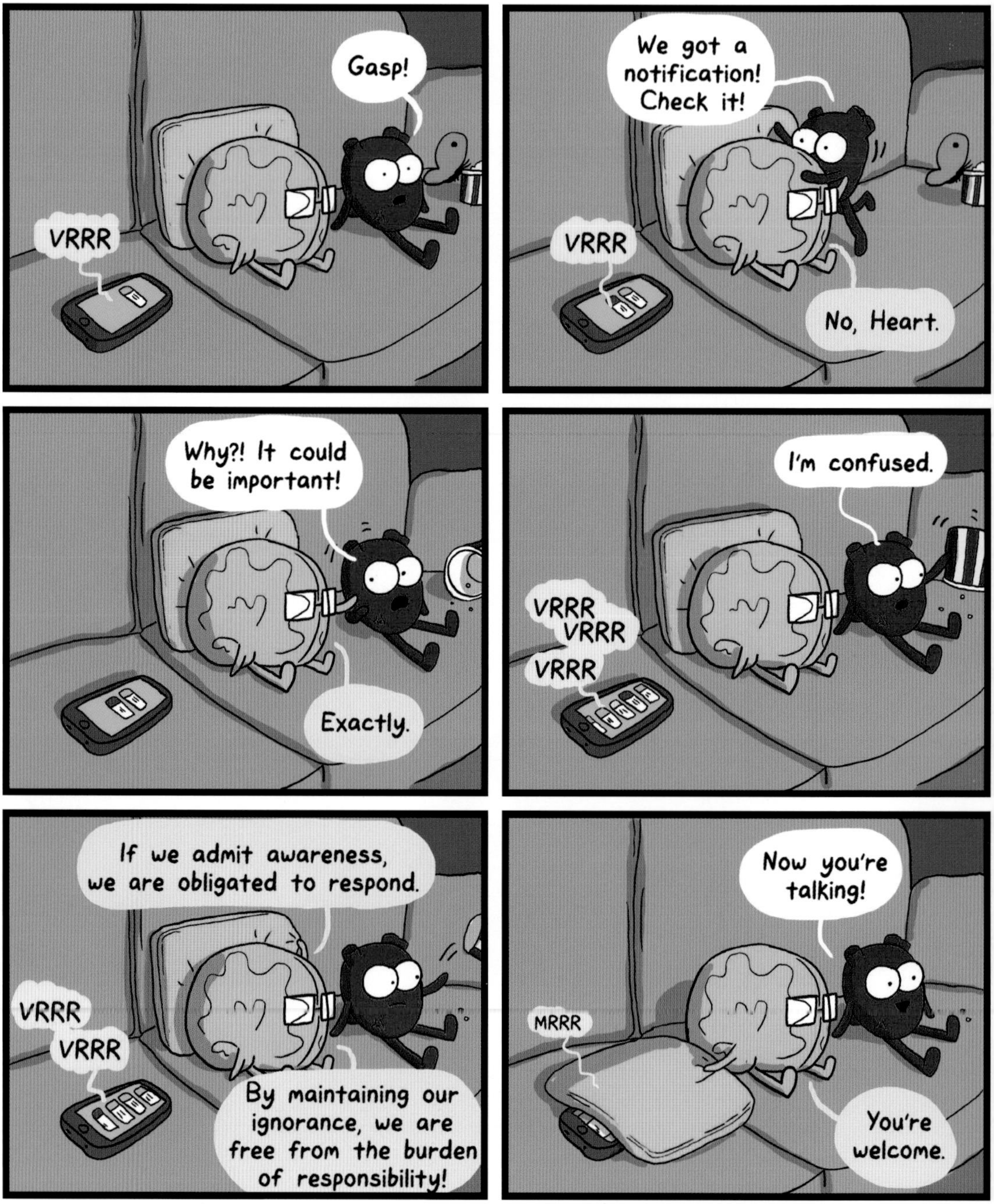

Gasp!
VRRR
We got a notification! Check it!
VRRR
No, Heart.
Why?! It could be important!
Exactly.
I'm confused.
VRRR
VRRR
VRRR
If we admit awareness, we are obligated to respond.
VRRR
VRRR
By maintaining our ignorance, we are free from the burden of responsibility!
Now you're talking!
MRRR
You're welcome.

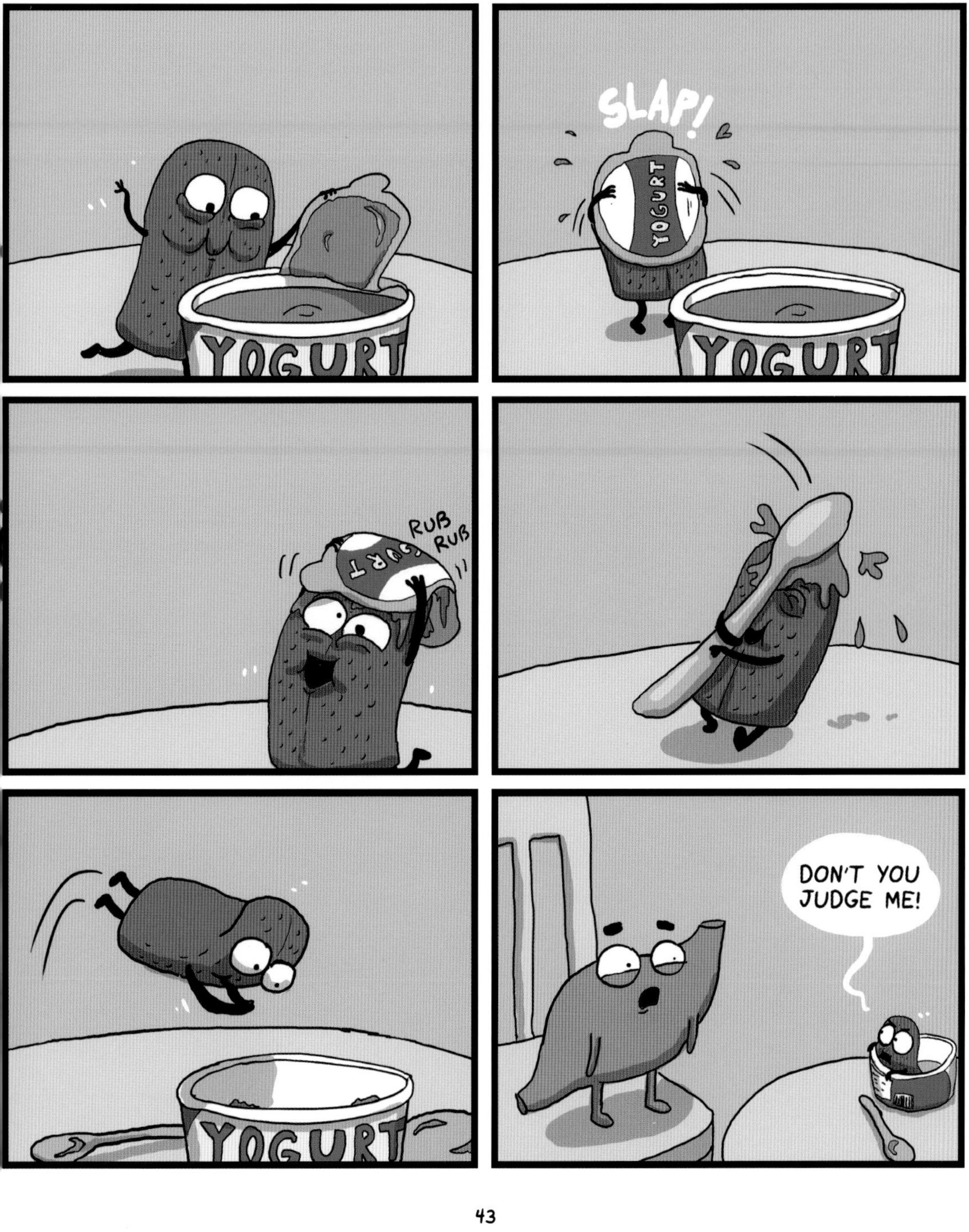
YOGURT
SLAP!
YOGURT
YOGURT
RUB
RUB
YOGURT
DON'T YOU JUDGE ME!

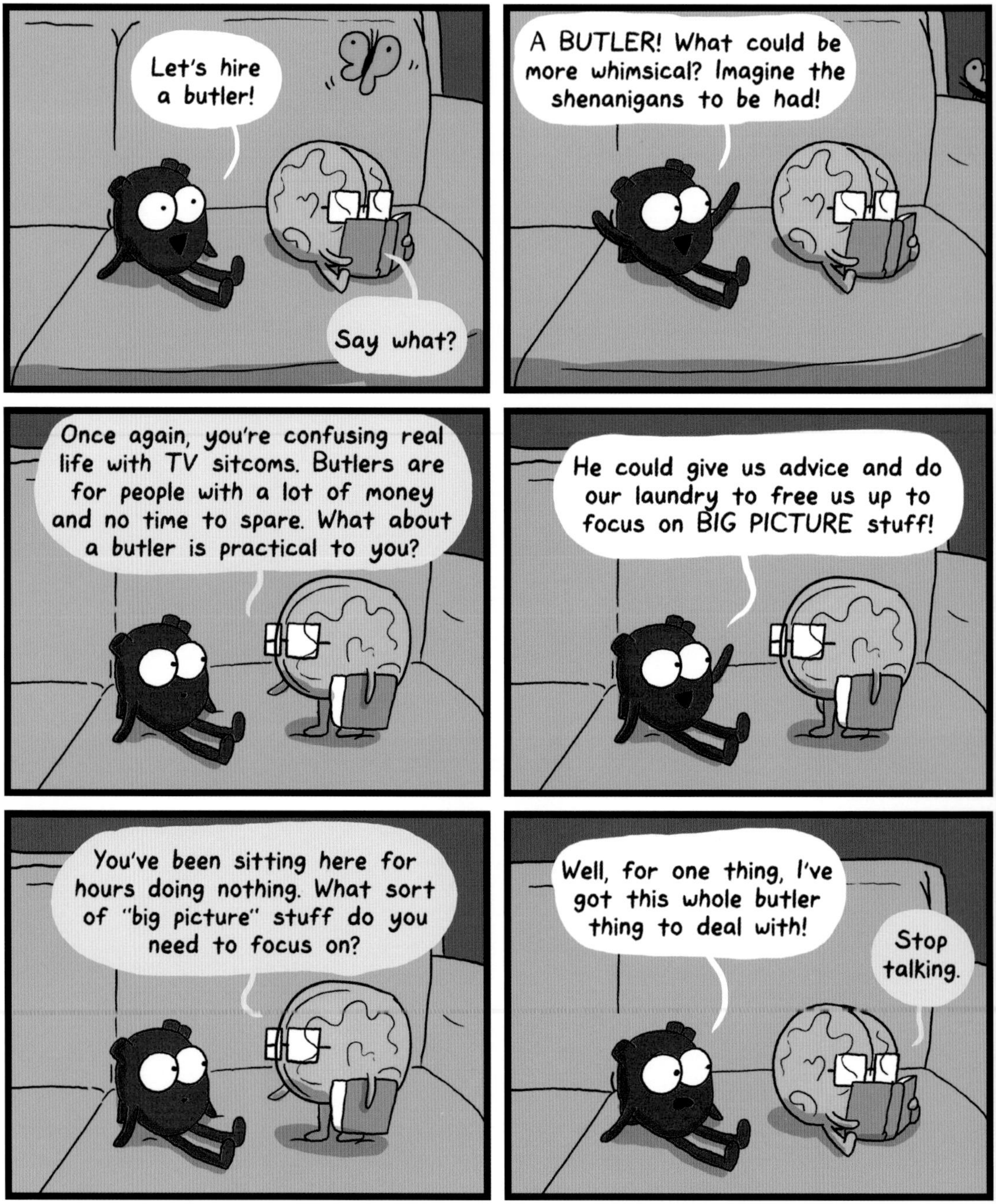
Let's hire a butler!
Say what?
A BUTLER! What could be more whimsical? Imagine the shenanigans to be had!
Once again, you're confusing real life with TV sitcoms. Butlers are for people with a lot of money and no time to spare. What about a butler is practical to you?
He could give us advice and do our laundry to free us up to focus on BIG PICTURE stuff!
You've been sitting here for hours doing nothing. What sort of "big picture" stuff do you need to focus on?
Well, for one thing, I've got this whole butler thing to deal with!
Stop talking.

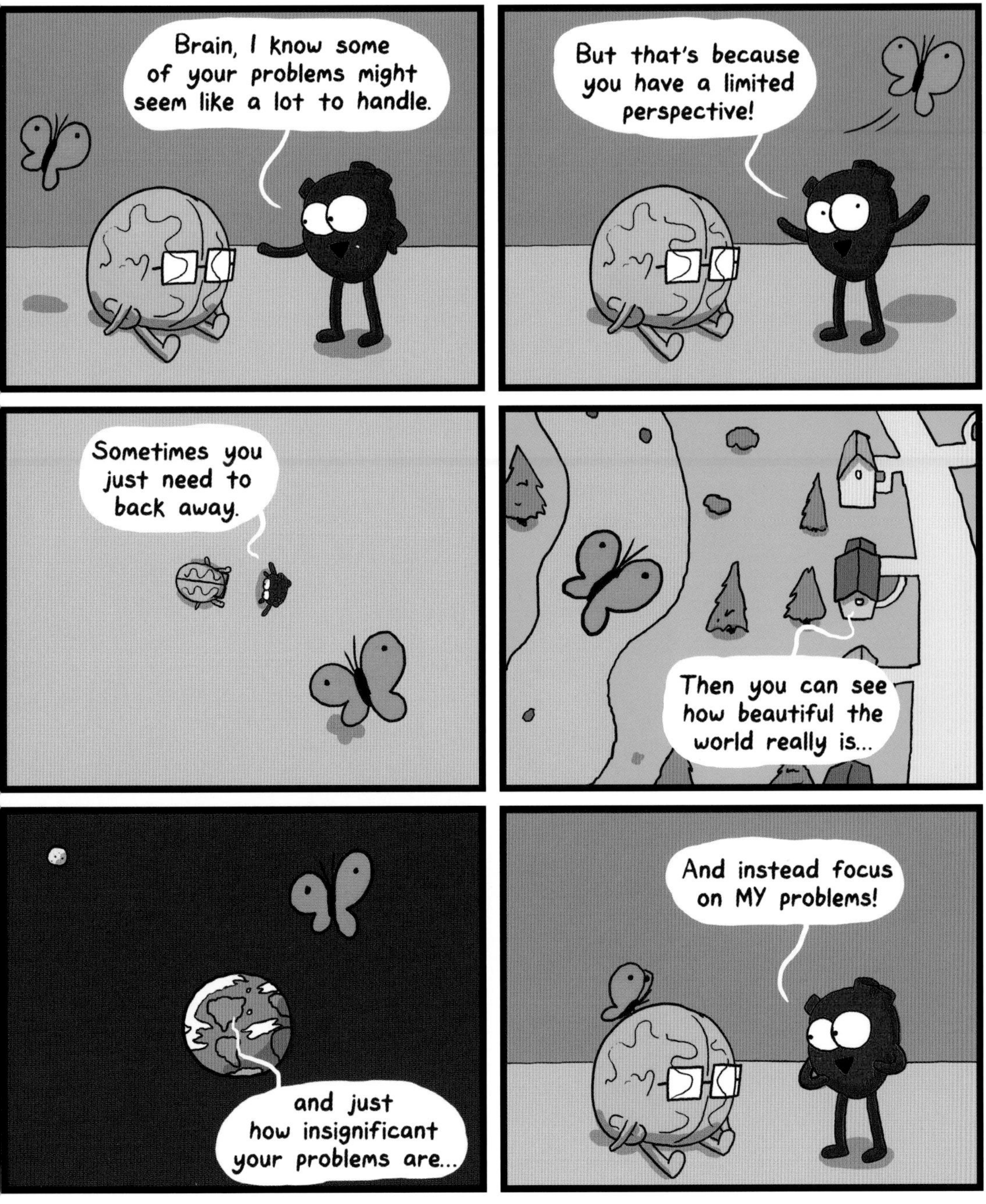
Brain, I know some of your problems might seem like a lot to handle.
But that's because you have a limited perspective!
Sometimes you just need to back away.
Then you can see how beautiful the world really is...
and just how insignificant your problems are...
And instead focus on MY problems!

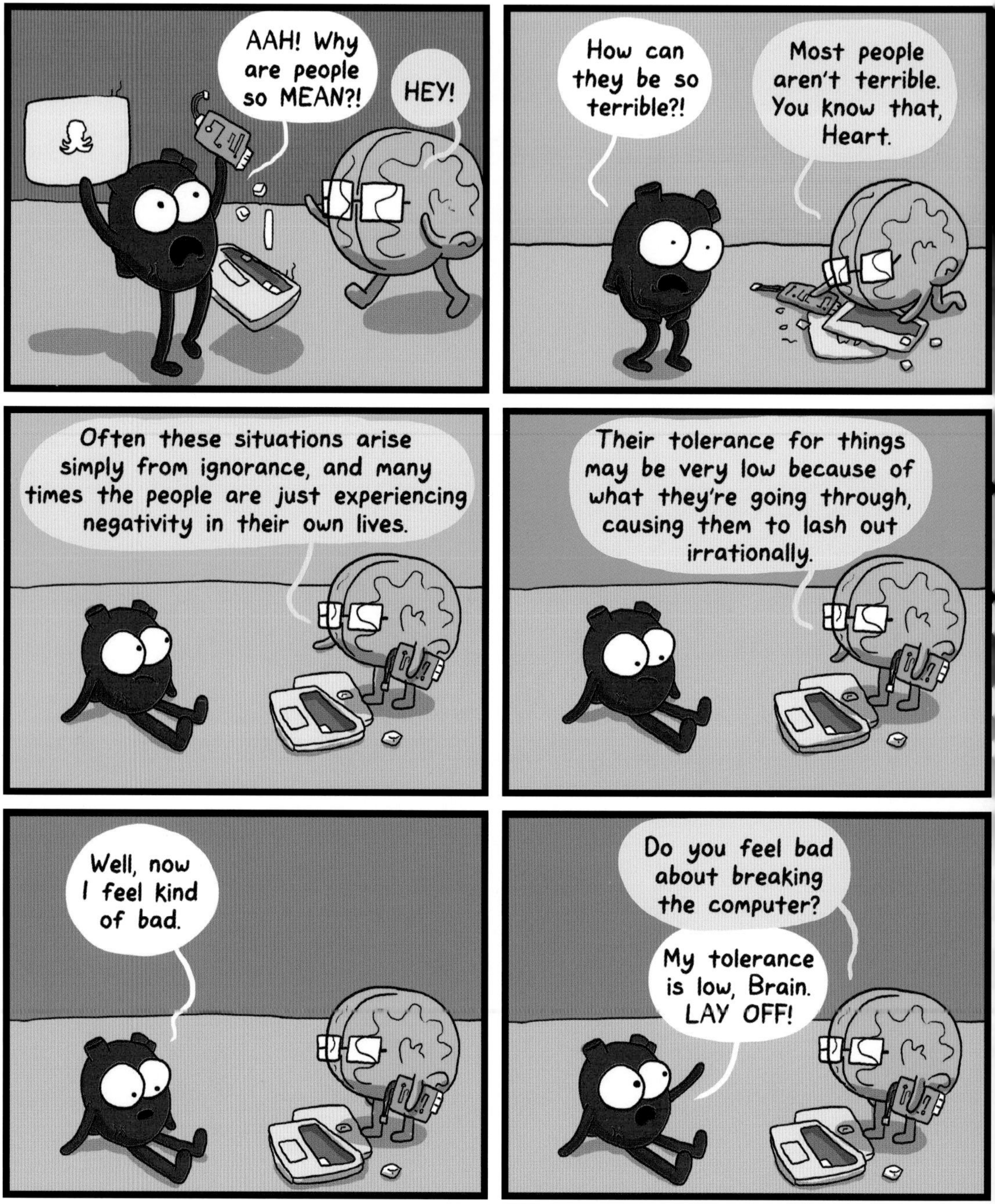
AAH! Why are people so MEAN?!
HEY!
How can they be so terrible?!
Most people aren't terrible. You know that, Heart.
Often these situations arise simply from ignorance, and many times the people are just experiencing negativity in their own lives.
Their tolerance for things may be very low because of what they're going through, causing them to lash out irrationally.
Well, now I feel kind of bad.
Do you feel bad about breaking the computer?
My tolerance is low, Brain. LAY OFF!

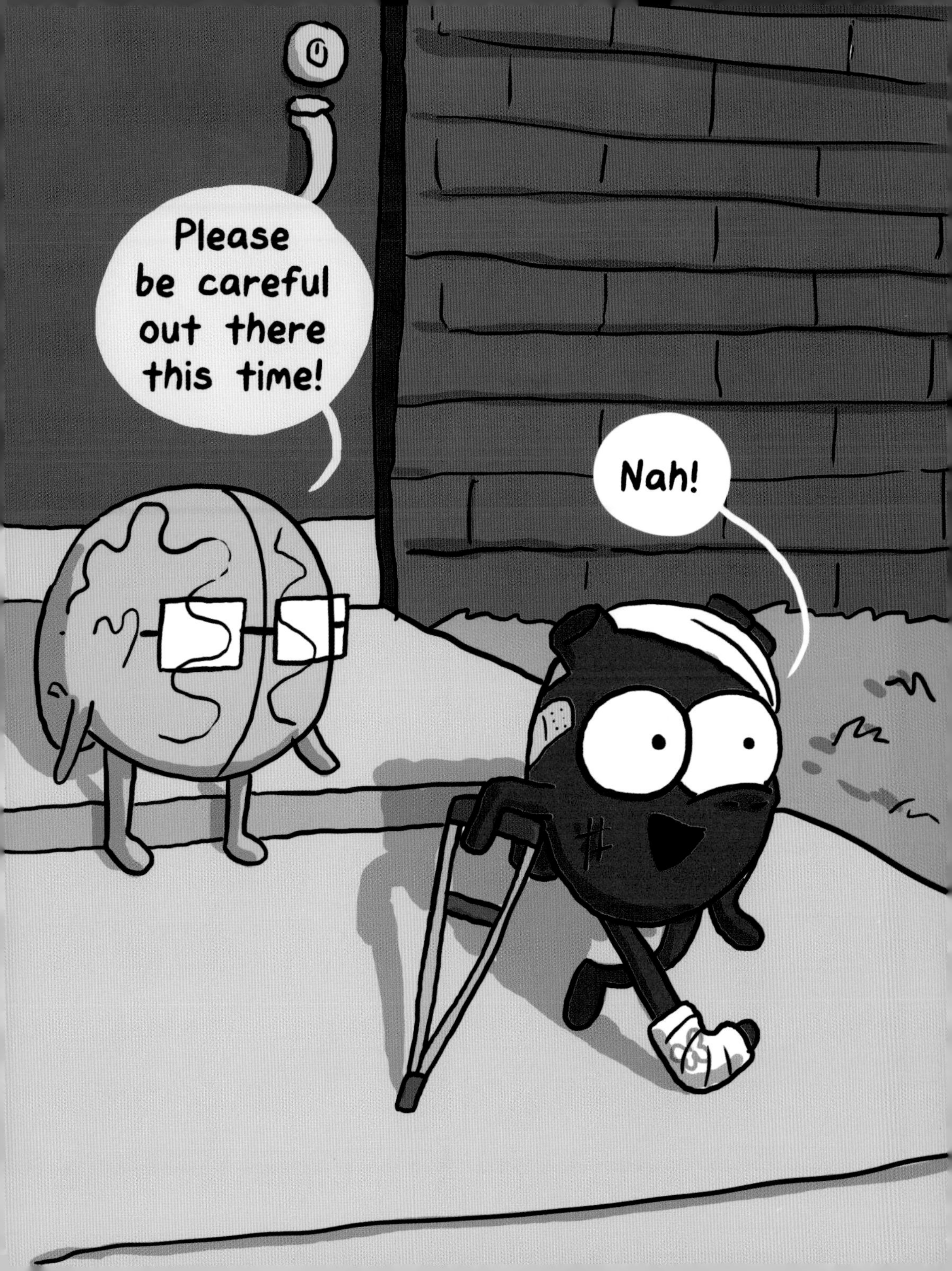
Please be careful out there this time!
Nah!

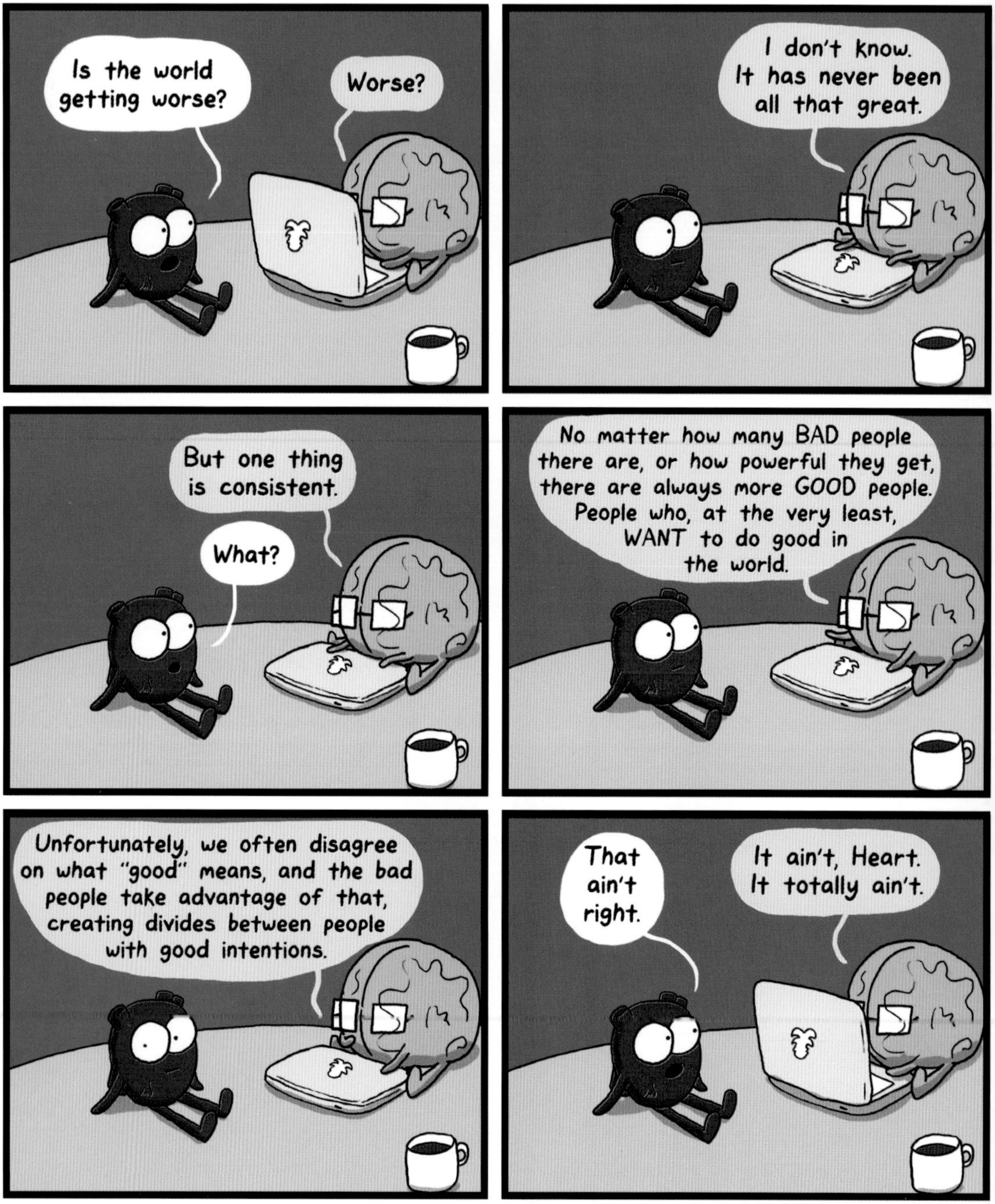
Is the world getting worse?
Worse?
I don't know. It has never been all that great.
But one thing is consistent.
What?
No matter how many BAD people there are, or how powerful they get, there are always more GOOD people. People who, at the very least, WANT to do good in the world.
Unfortunately, we often disagree on what "good" means, and the bad people take advantage of that, creating divides between people with good intentions.
That ain't right.
It ain't, Heart. It totally ain't.

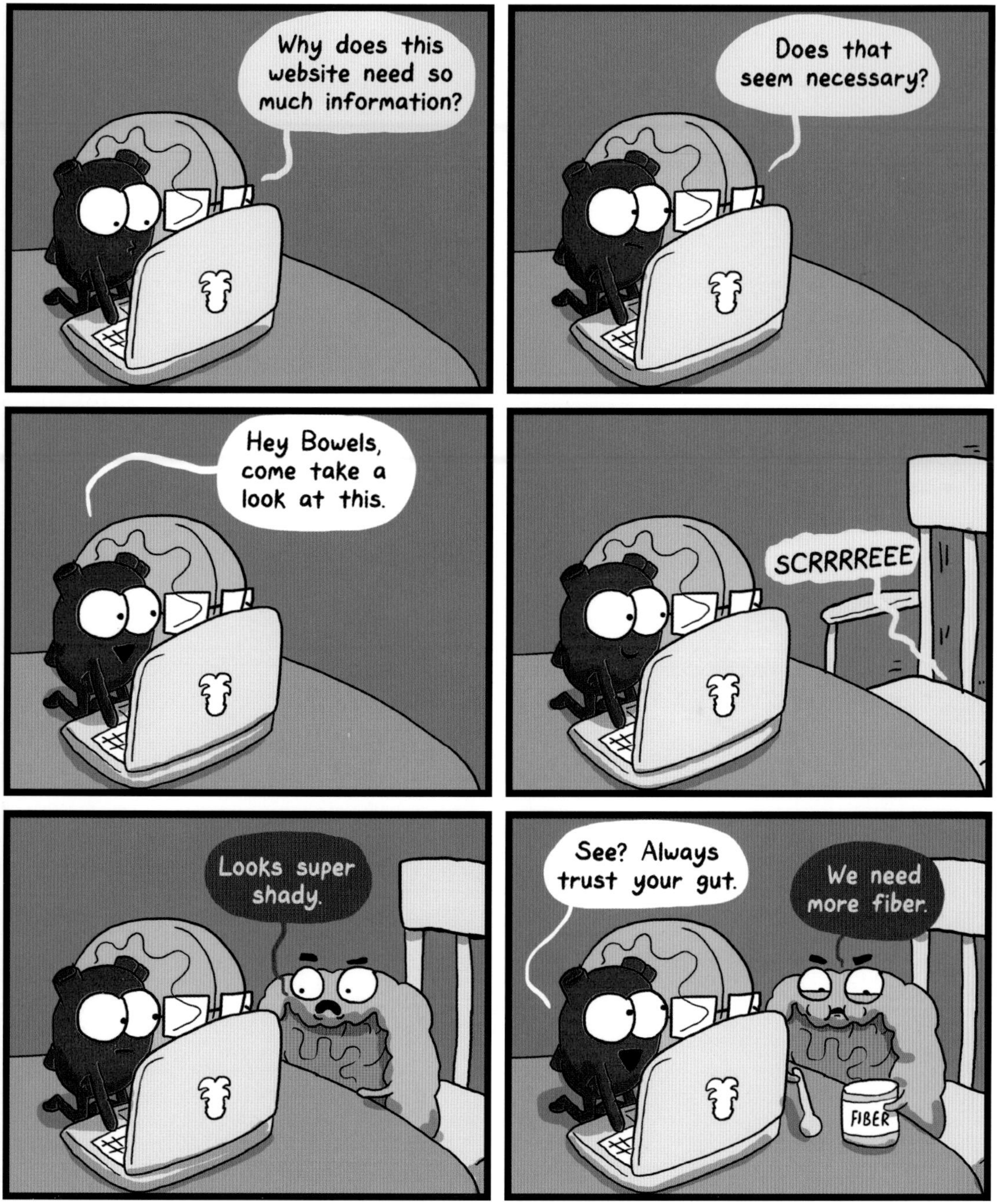

Why does this website need so much information?
Does that seem necessary?
Hey Bowels, come take a look at this.
SCRRRREEE
Looks super shady.
See? Always trust your gut.
We need more fiber.
FIBER

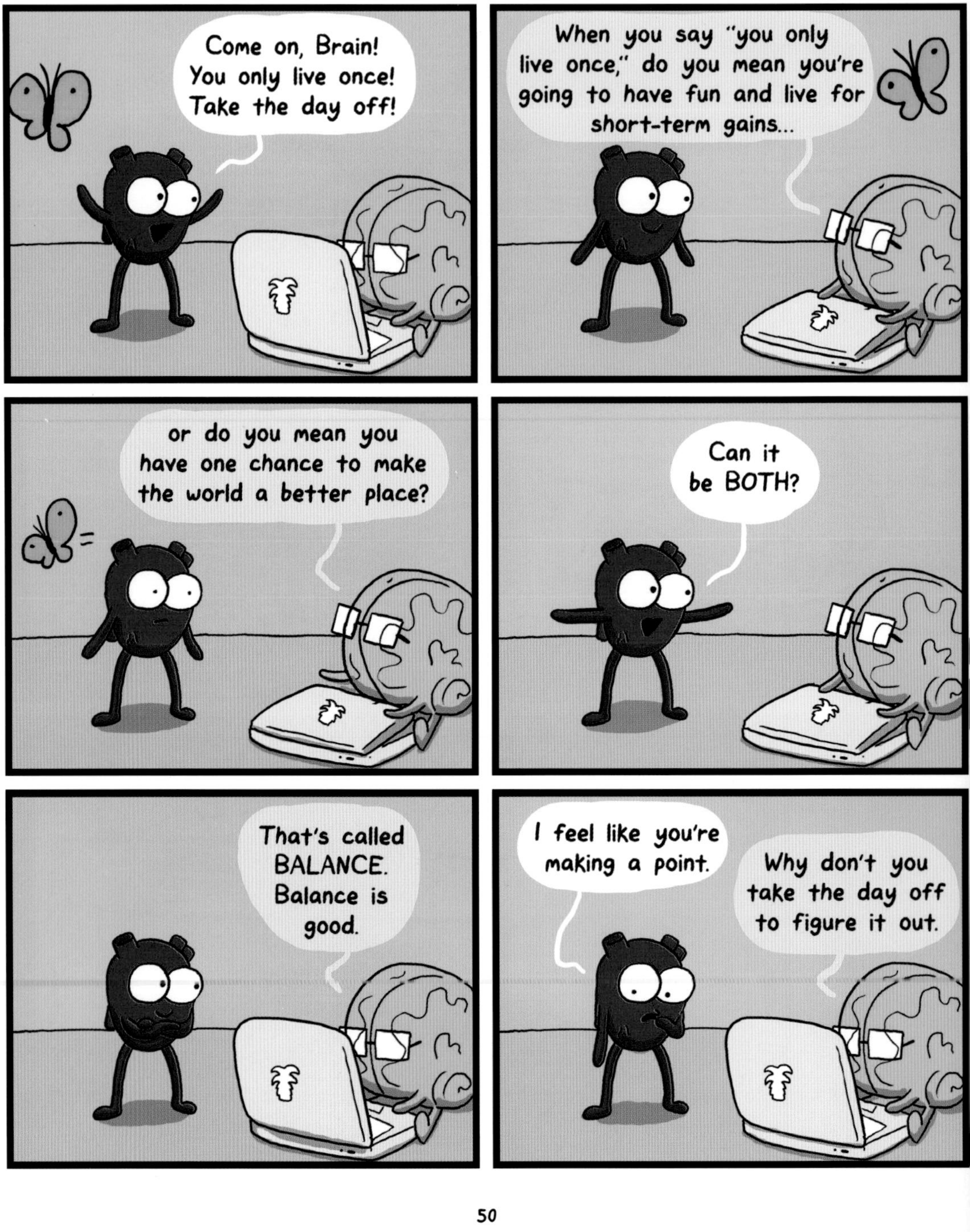
Come on, Brain! You only live once! Take the day off!
When you say "you only live once," do you mean you're going to have fun and live for short-term gains...
or do you mean you have one chance to make the world a better place?
Can it be BOTH?
That's called BALANCE. Balance is good.
I feel like you're making a point.
Why don't you take the day off to figure it out.

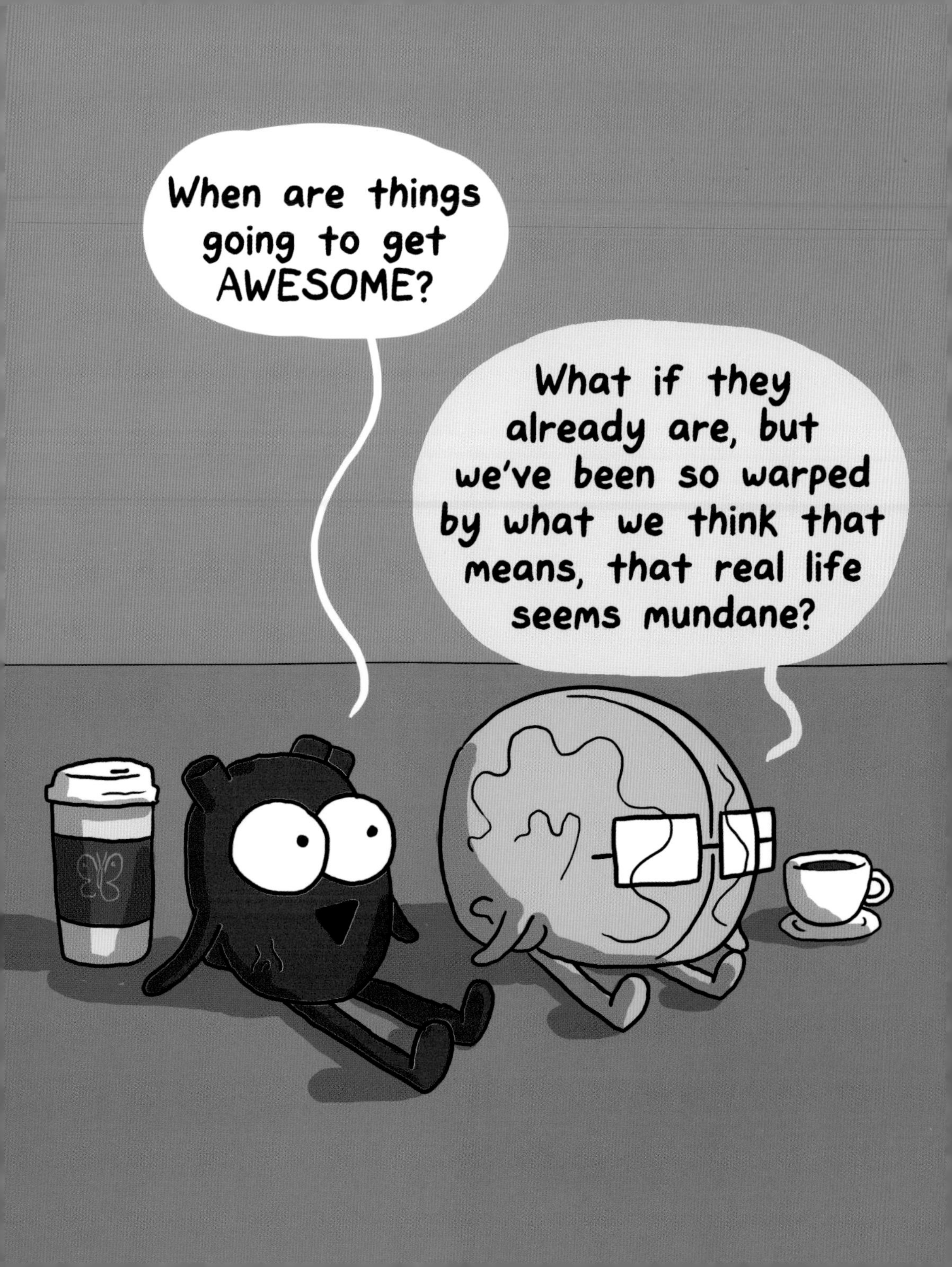
When are things going to get AWESOME?
What if they already are, but we've been so warped by what we think that means, that real life seems mundane?

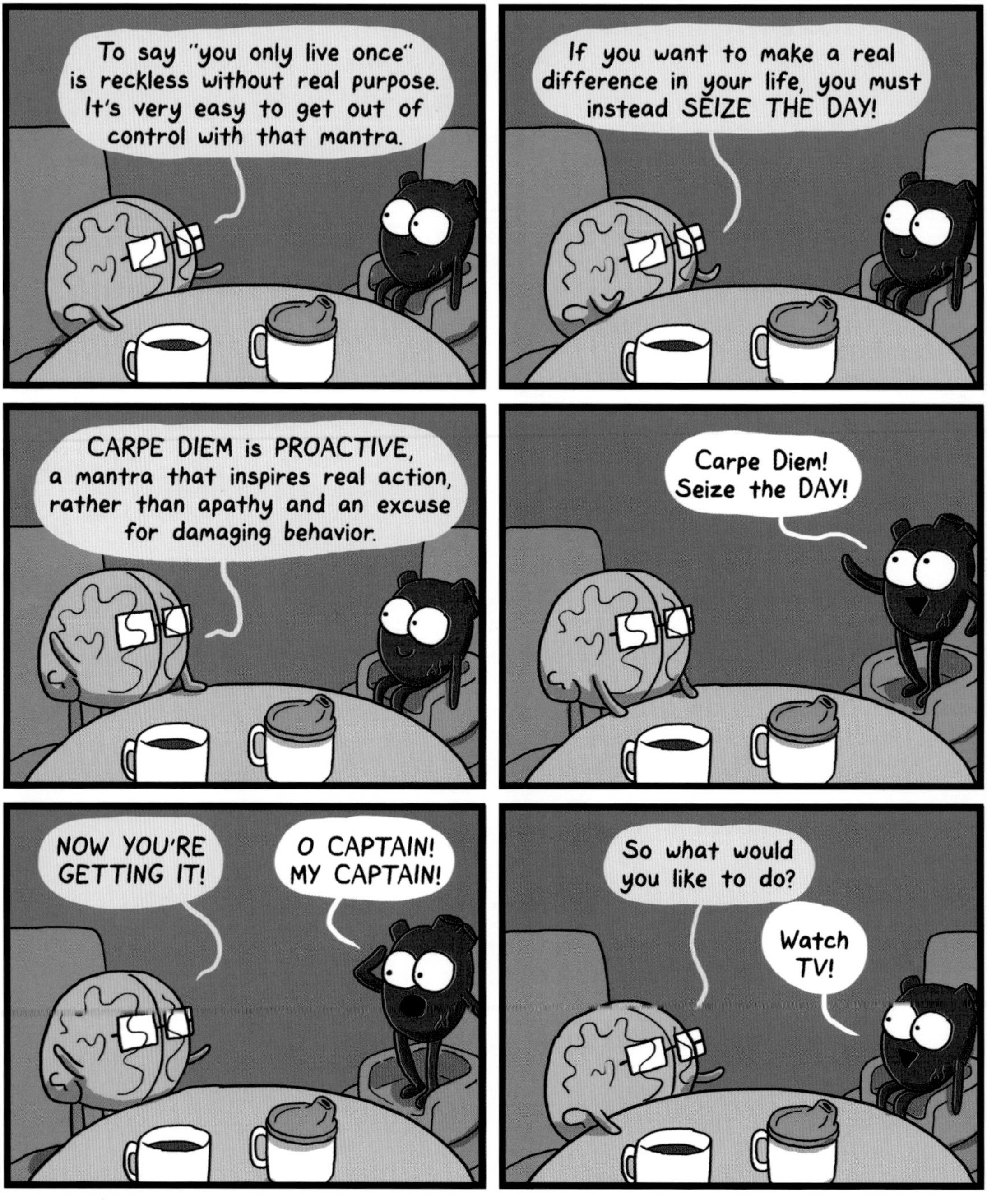
To say "you only live once" is reckless without real purpose. It's very easy to get out of control with that mantra.
If you want to make a real difference in your life, you must instead SEIZE THE DAY!
CARPE DIEM is PROACTIVE, a mantra that inspires real action, rather than apathy and an excuse for damaging behavior.
Carpe Diem! Seize the DAY!
NOW YOU'RE GETTING IT!
O CAPTAIN! MY CAPTAIN!
So what would you like to do?
Watch TV!

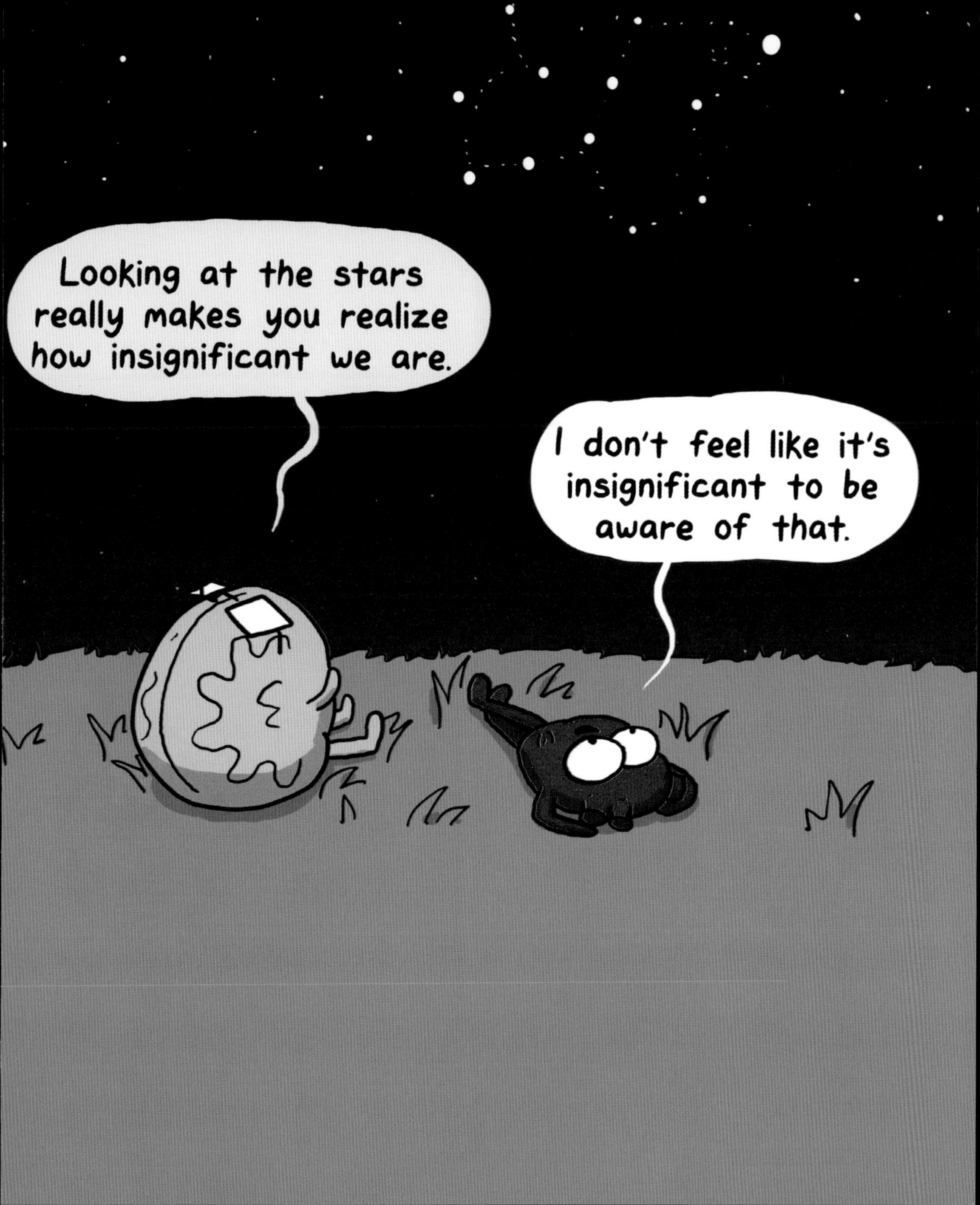
Looking at the stars really makes you realize how insignificant we are.
I don't feel like it's insignificant to be aware of that.

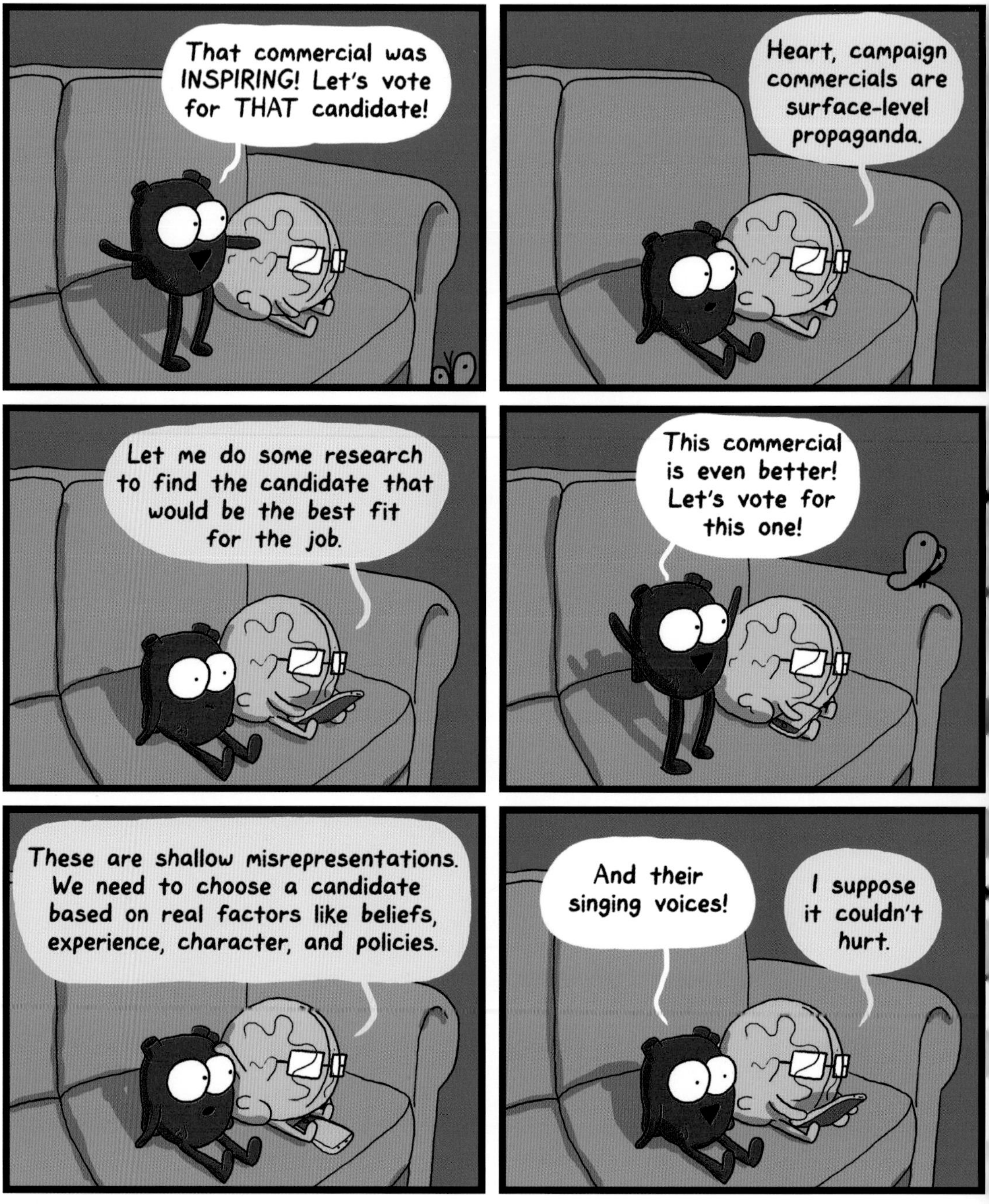

That commercial was INSPIRING! Let's vote for THAT candidate!
Heart, campaign commercials are surface-level propaganda.
Let me do some research to find the candidate that would be the best fit for the job.
This commercial is even better! Let's vote for this one!
These are shallow misrepresentations. We need to choose a candidate based on real factors like beliefs, experience, character, and policies.
And their singing voices!
I suppose it couldn't hurt.

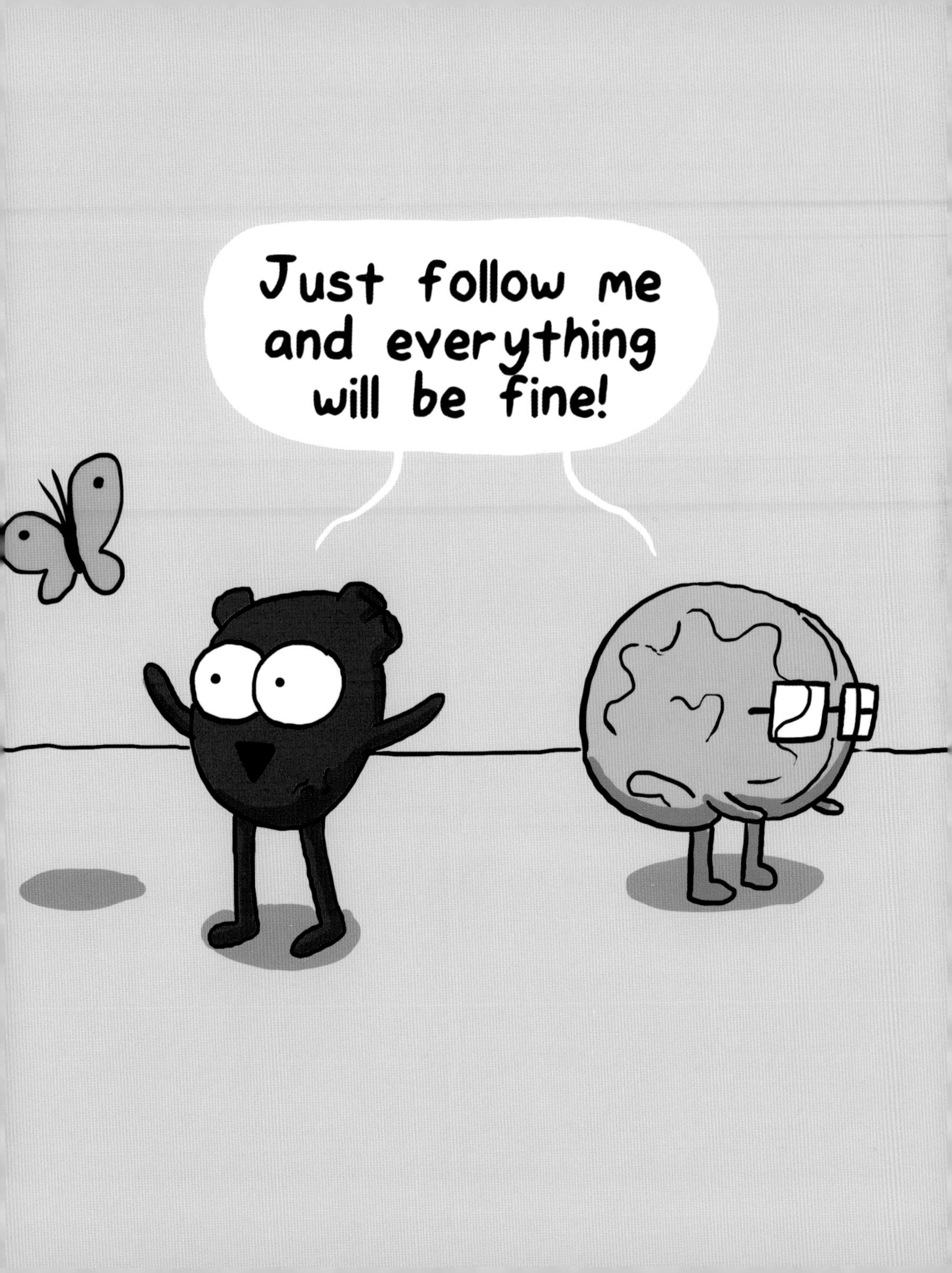
Just follow me and everything will be fine!

HEY! YOU GOT MORE THAN ME!

Heart, true compassion comes from ensuring that everyone has the chance to have what you have, not making sure YOU have MORE!

I guess you're right. Sorry.

However, there are those who would EXPLOIT that very compassion and use it for their OWN personal gain!

How do I know the difference between someone who needs it and someone who's being greedy?

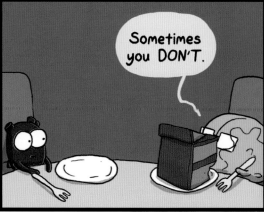

Sometimes you DON'T.

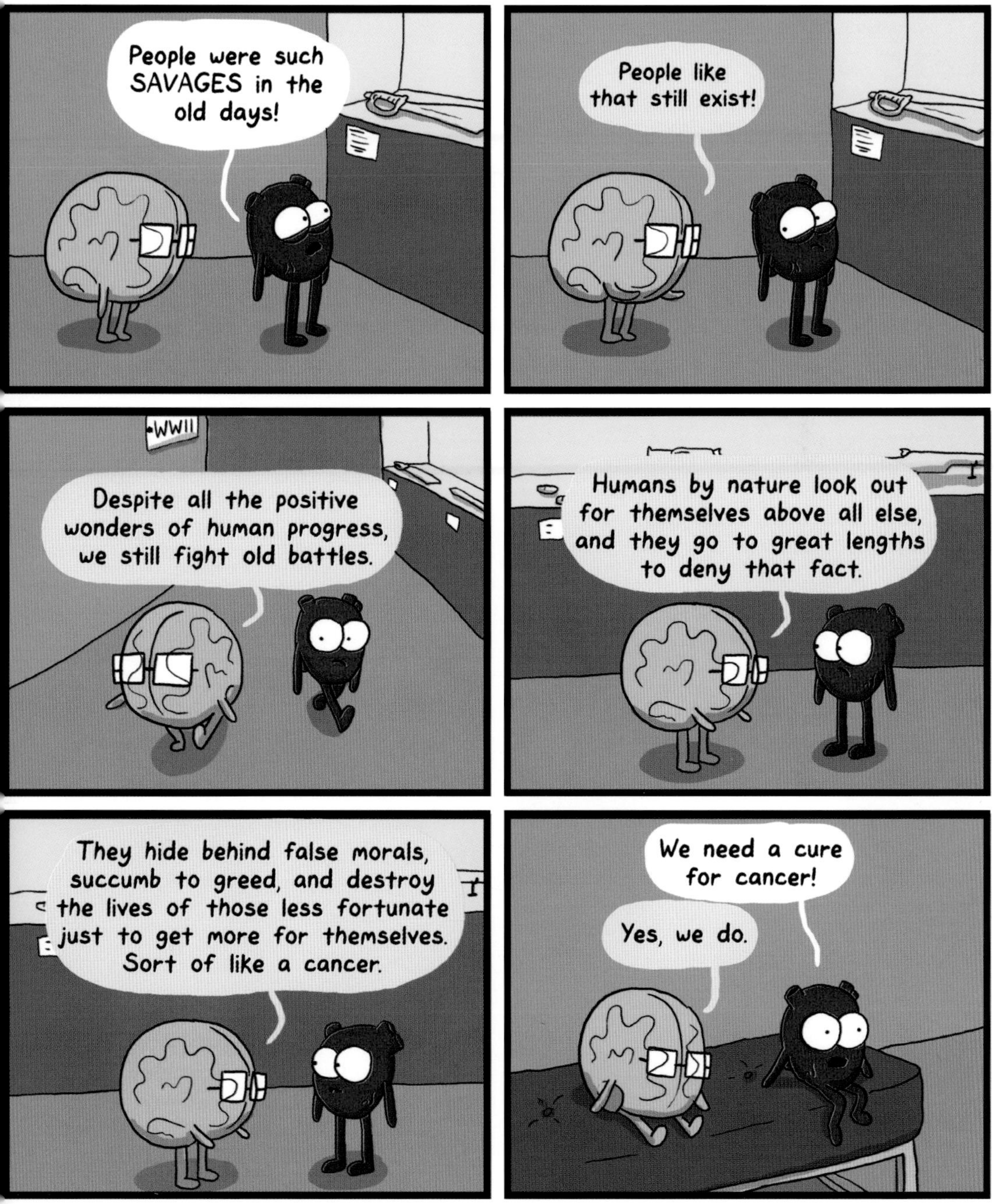
People were such SAVAGES in the old days!
People like that still exist!
•WWII
Despite all the positive wonders of human progress, we still fight old battles.
Humans by nature look out for themselves above all else, and they go to great lengths to deny that fact.
They hide behind false morals, succumb to greed, and destroy the lives of those less fortunate just to get more for themselves. Sort of like a cancer.
We need a cure for cancer!
Yes, we do.

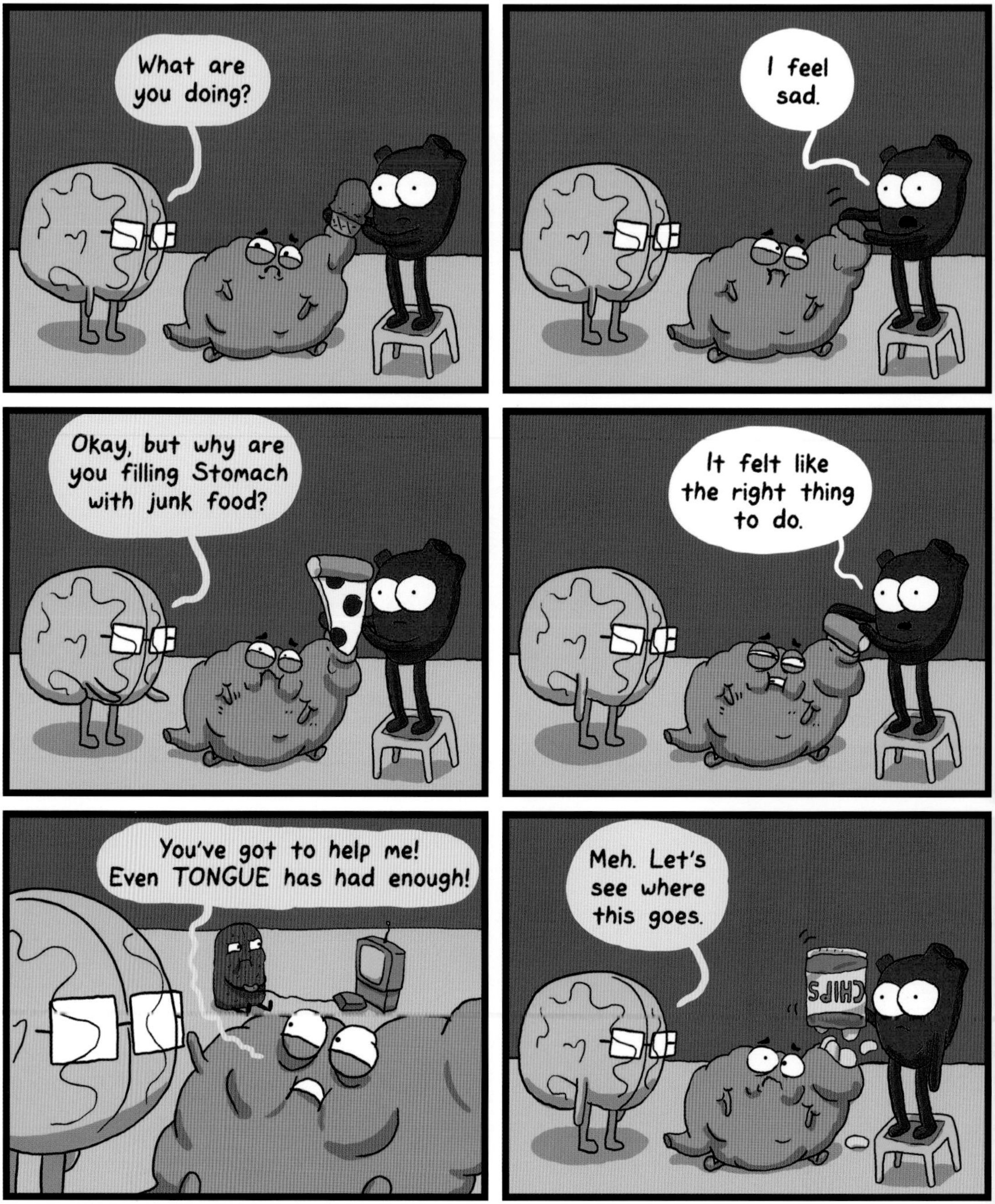
What are you doing?
I feel sad.
Okay, but why are you filling Stomach with junk food?
It felt like the right thing to do.
You've got to help me! Even TONGUE has had enough!
Meh. Let's see where this goes.
CHIPS

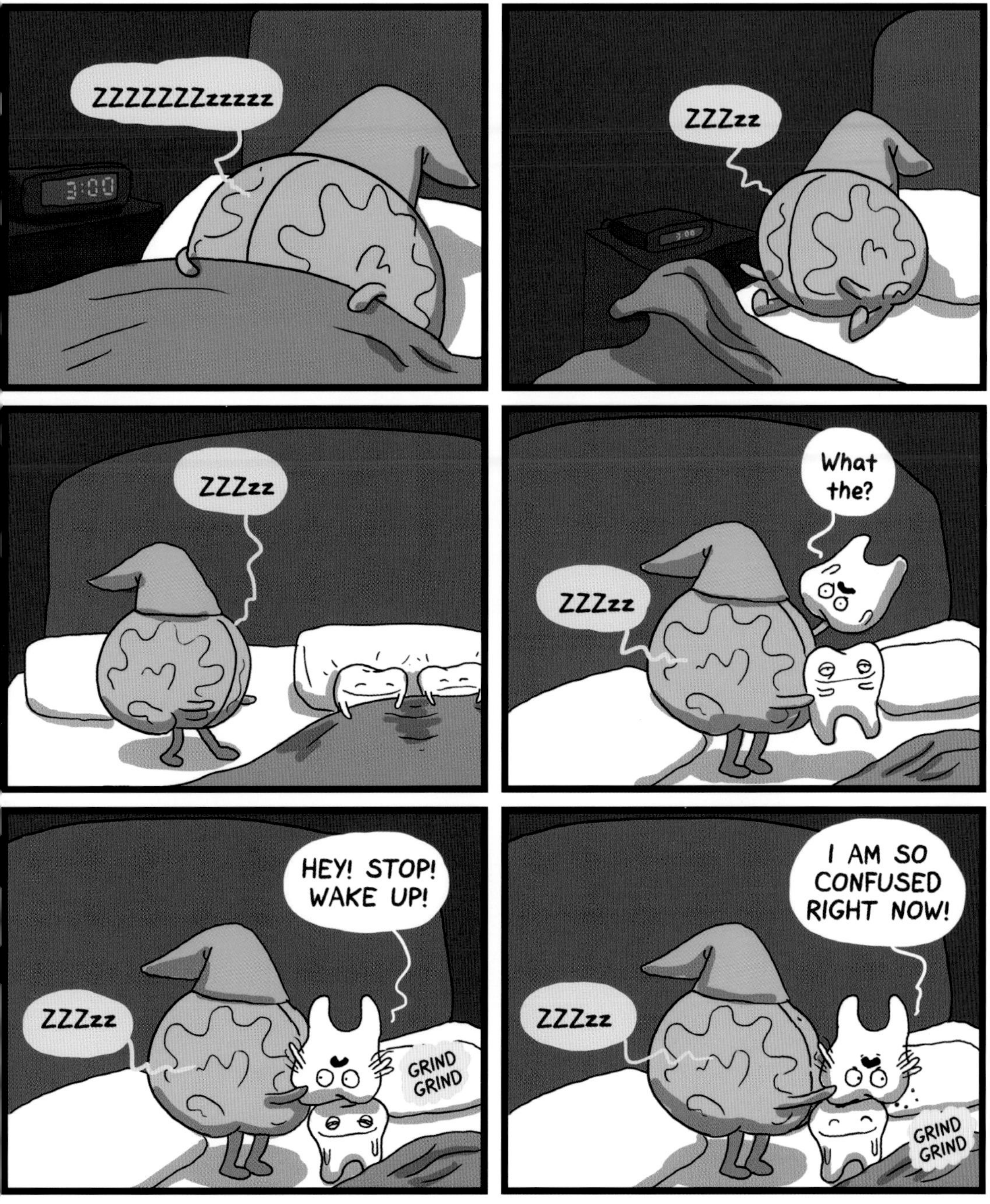
ZZZZZZZzzzzz
3:00
ZZZzz
ZZZzz
What the?
ZZZzz
HEY! STOP! WAKE UP!
ZZZzz
GRIND GRIND
I AM SO CONFUSED RIGHT NOW!
ZZZzz
GRIND GRIND

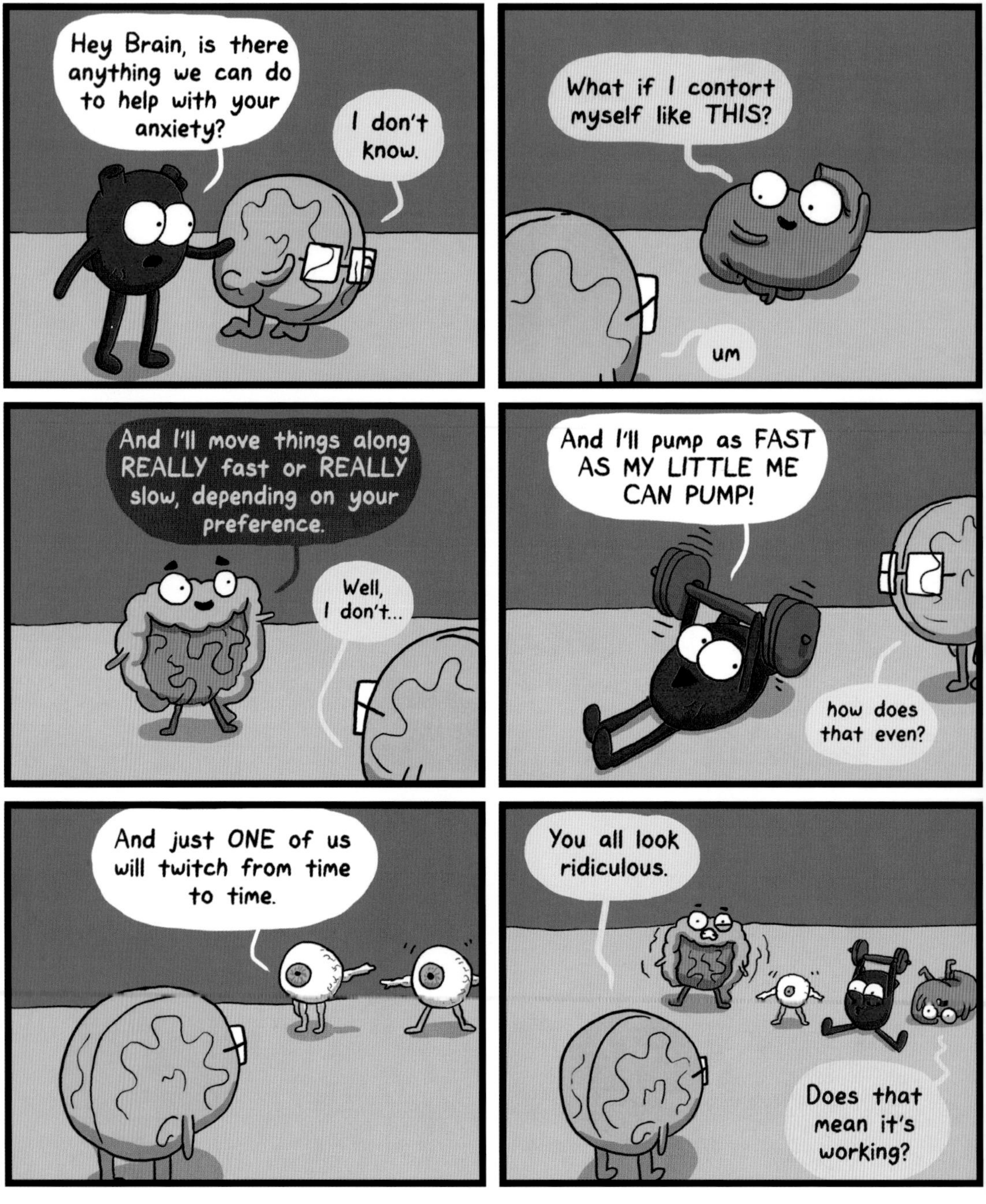
Hey Brain, is there anything we can do to help with your anxiety?
I don't know.
What if I contort myself like THIS?
um
And I'll move things along REALLY fast or REALLY slow, depending on your preference.
Well, I don't...
And I'll pump as FAST AS MY LITTLE ME CAN PUMP!
how does that even?
And just ONE of us will twitch from time to time.
You all look ridiculous.
Does that mean it's working?

What's going on here?
Brain is anxious, sent you to us for modification.
For WHAT?
MODIFICATION
RRRIIIP
YAAAAHH!
COUGH
I just...I don't understand WHY!
MODIFICATION

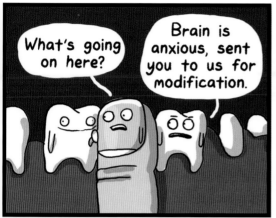

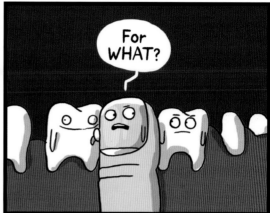

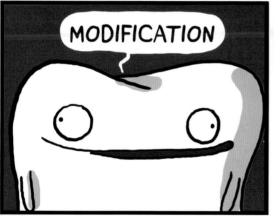

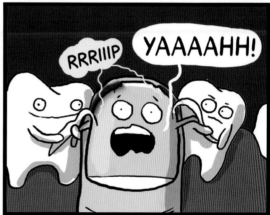

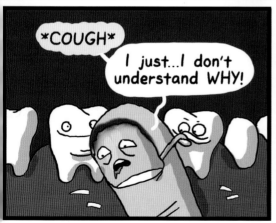

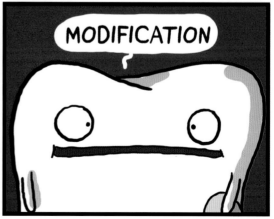

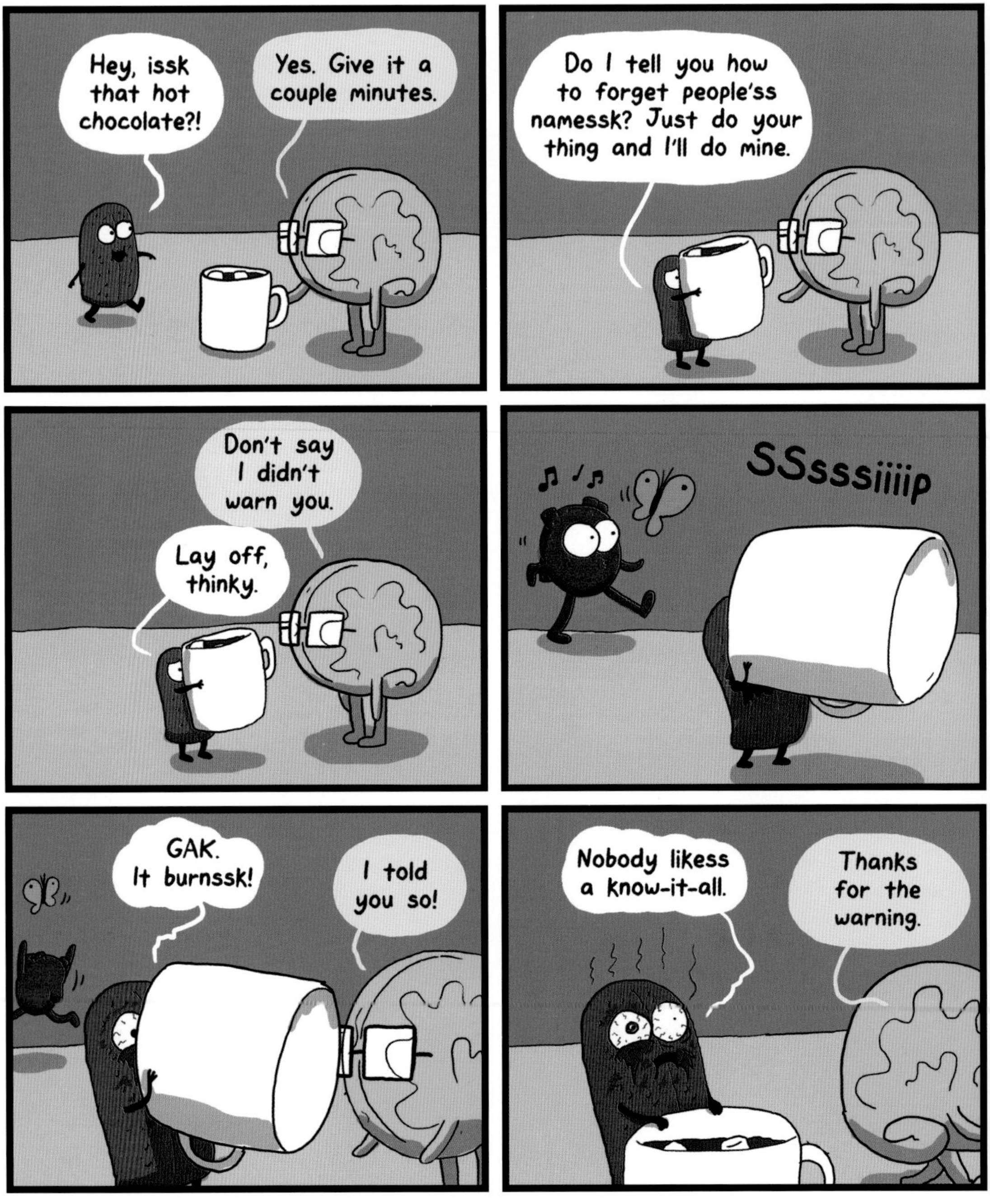
Hey, issk that hot chocolate?!
Yes. Give it a couple minutes.
Do I tell you how to forget people'ss namessk? Just do your thing and I'll do mine.
Don't say I didn't warn you.
Lay off, thinky.
SSsssiiiip
GAK. It burnssk!
I told you so!
Nobody likess a know-it-all.
Thanks for the warning.

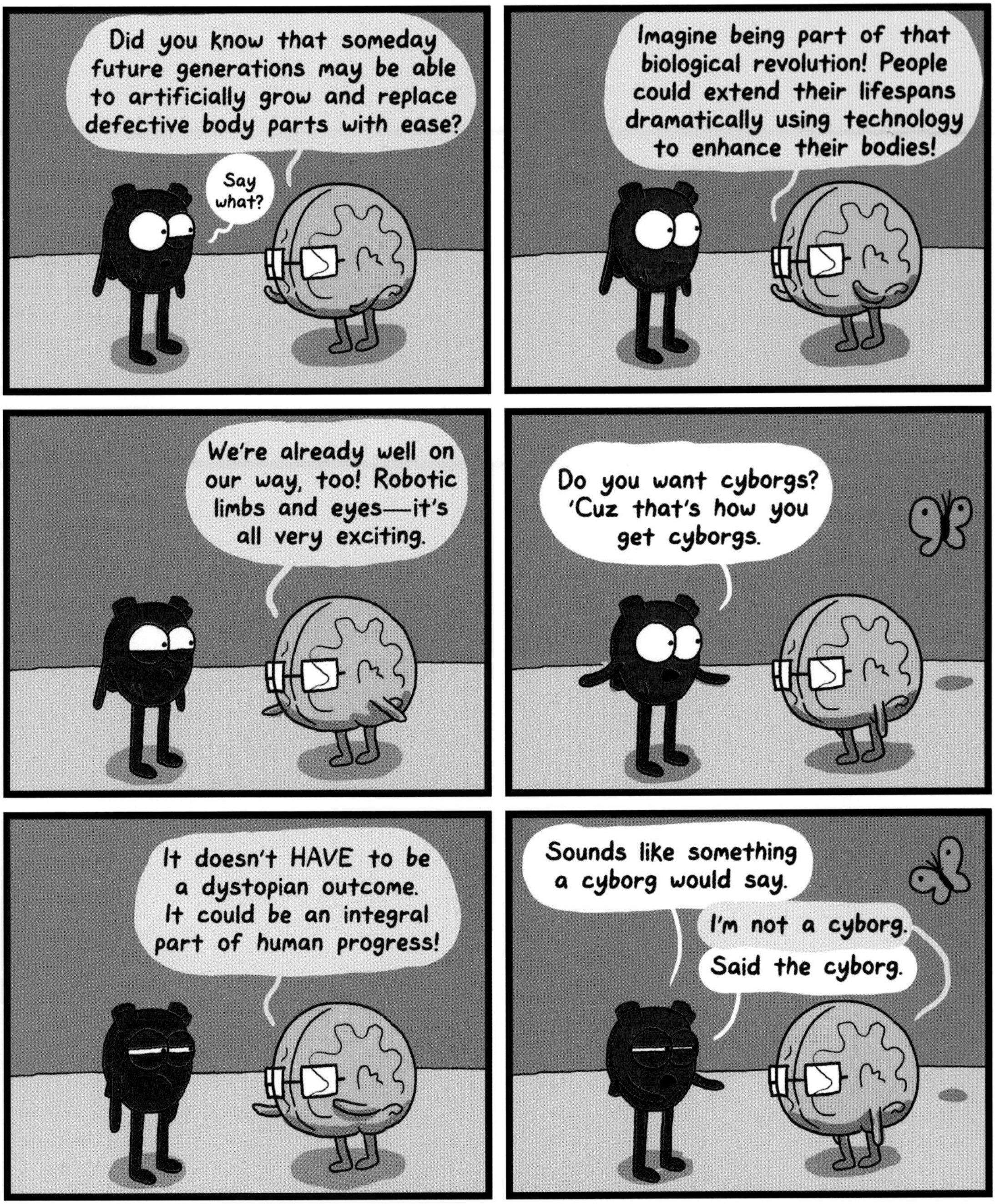
Did you know that someday future generations may be able to artificially grow and replace defective body parts with ease?
Say what?
Imagine being part of that biological revolution! People could extend their lifespans dramatically using technology to enhance their bodies!
We're already well on our way, too! Robotic limbs and eyes—it's all very exciting.
Do you want cyborgs? 'Cuz that's how you get cyborgs.
It doesn't HAVE to be a dystopian outcome. It could be an integral part of human progress!
Sounds like something a cyborg would say.
I'm not a cyborg.
Said the cyborg.

Achieving Your Dreams with Caffeine

Step 1

Drink a strong caffeinated beverage

Step 2

Make plans to change the world

Step 3

Take a break for more caffeine

Step 4

Crash and dream

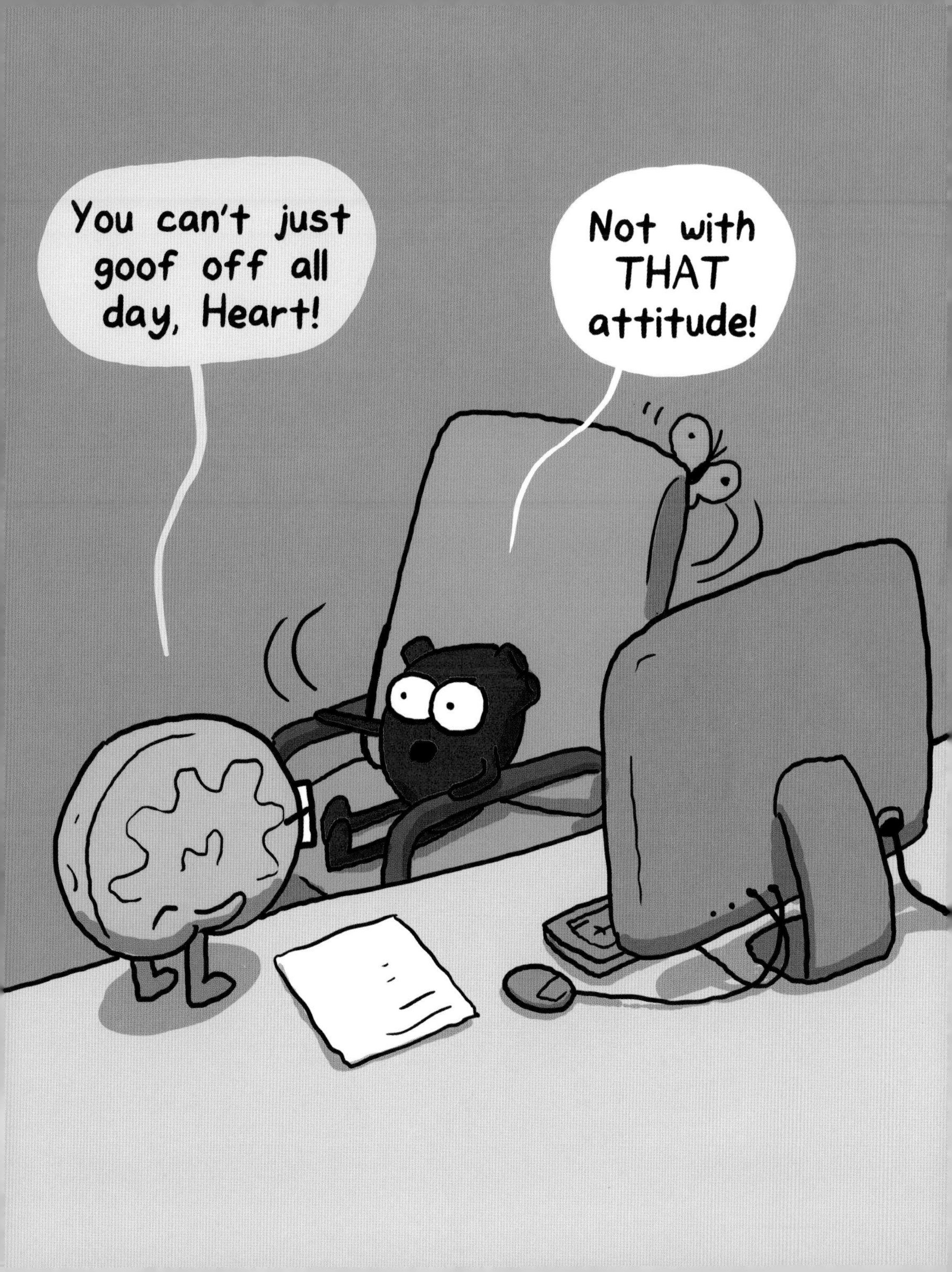
You can't just goof off all day, Heart!
Not with THAT attitude!

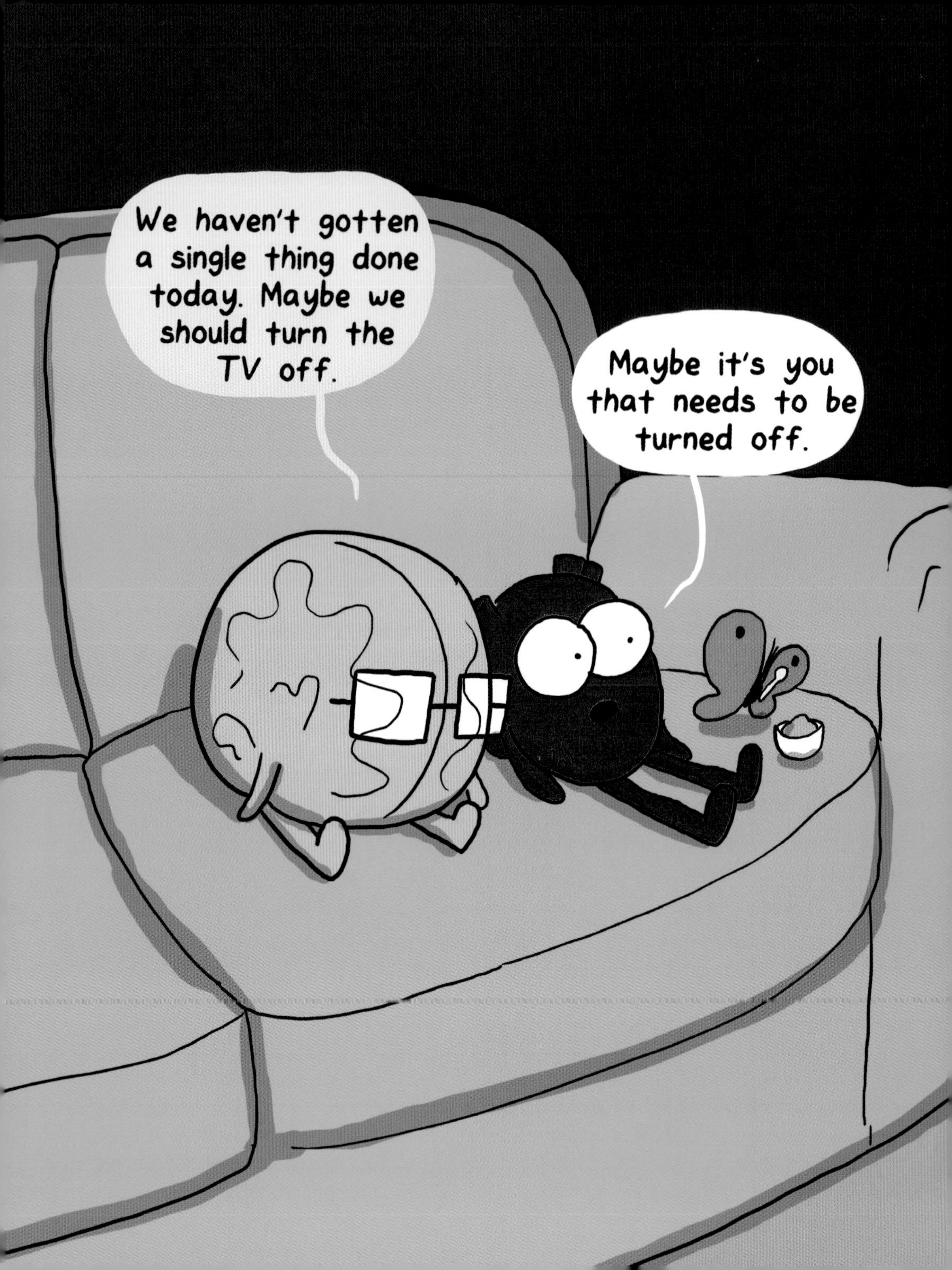
We haven't gotten a single thing done today. Maybe we should turn the TV off.
Maybe it's you that needs to be turned off.

Could you hold on to this? I might need it later. Keep it safe, please.
FACT
FACT
Here's another one.
FACT
FACT
Hey, could I see that first one again? I need to reference it for this next part.
You lost it, didn't you?
Yeah, let's go with that.

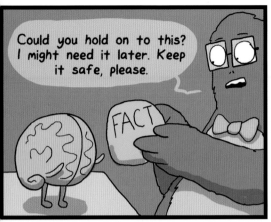

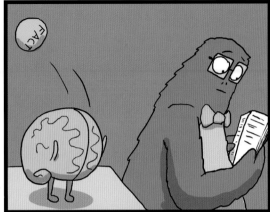

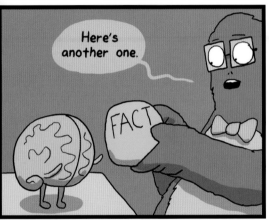

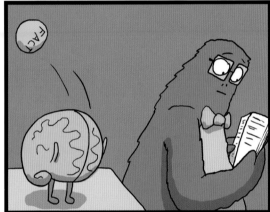

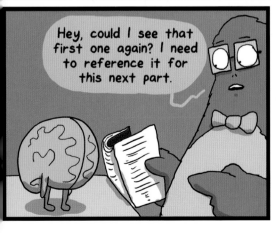

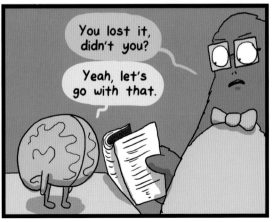

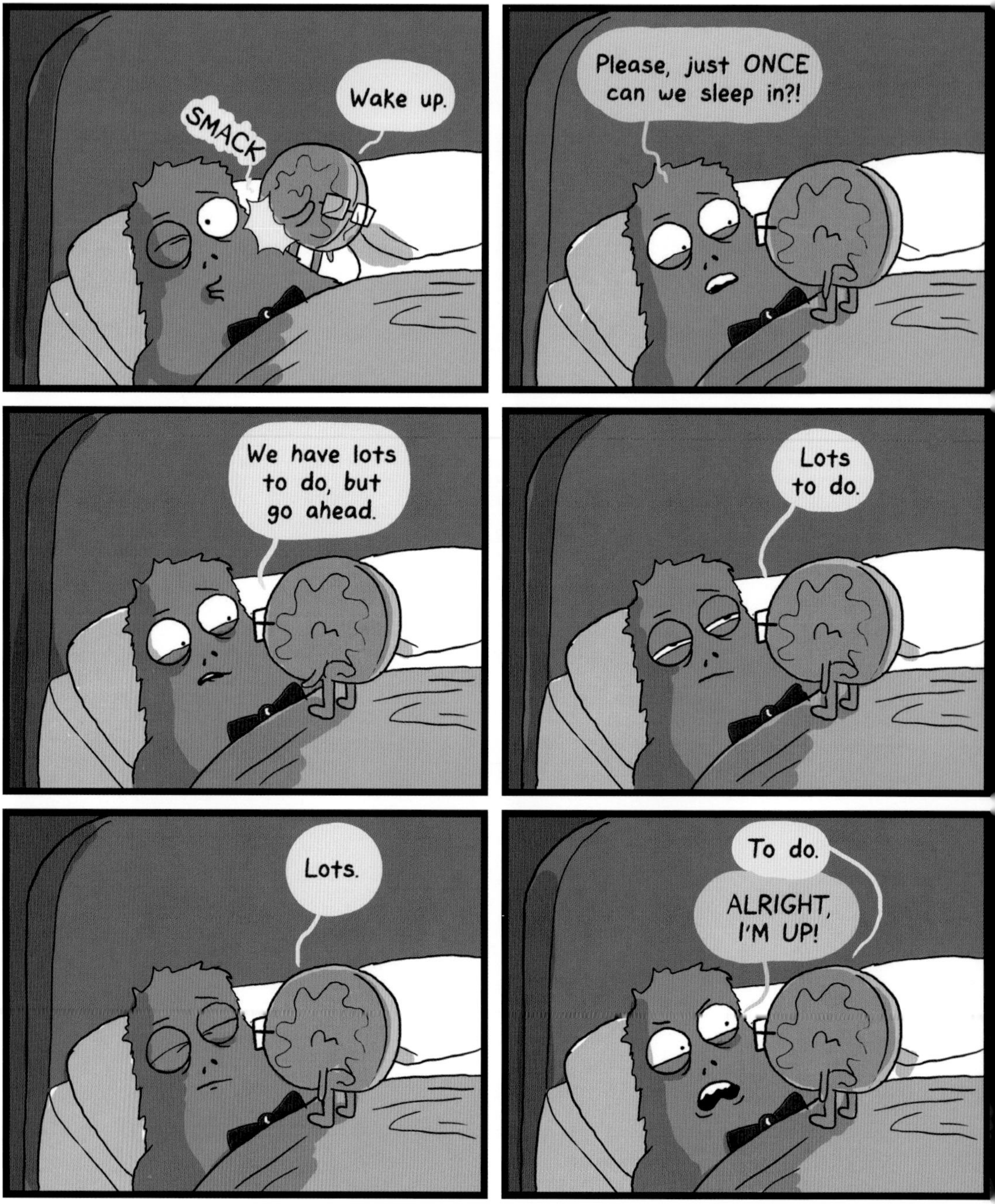

SMACK
Wake up.
Please, just ONCE can we sleep in?!
We have lots to do, but go ahead.
Lots to do.
Lots.
To do.
ALRIGHT, I'M UP!

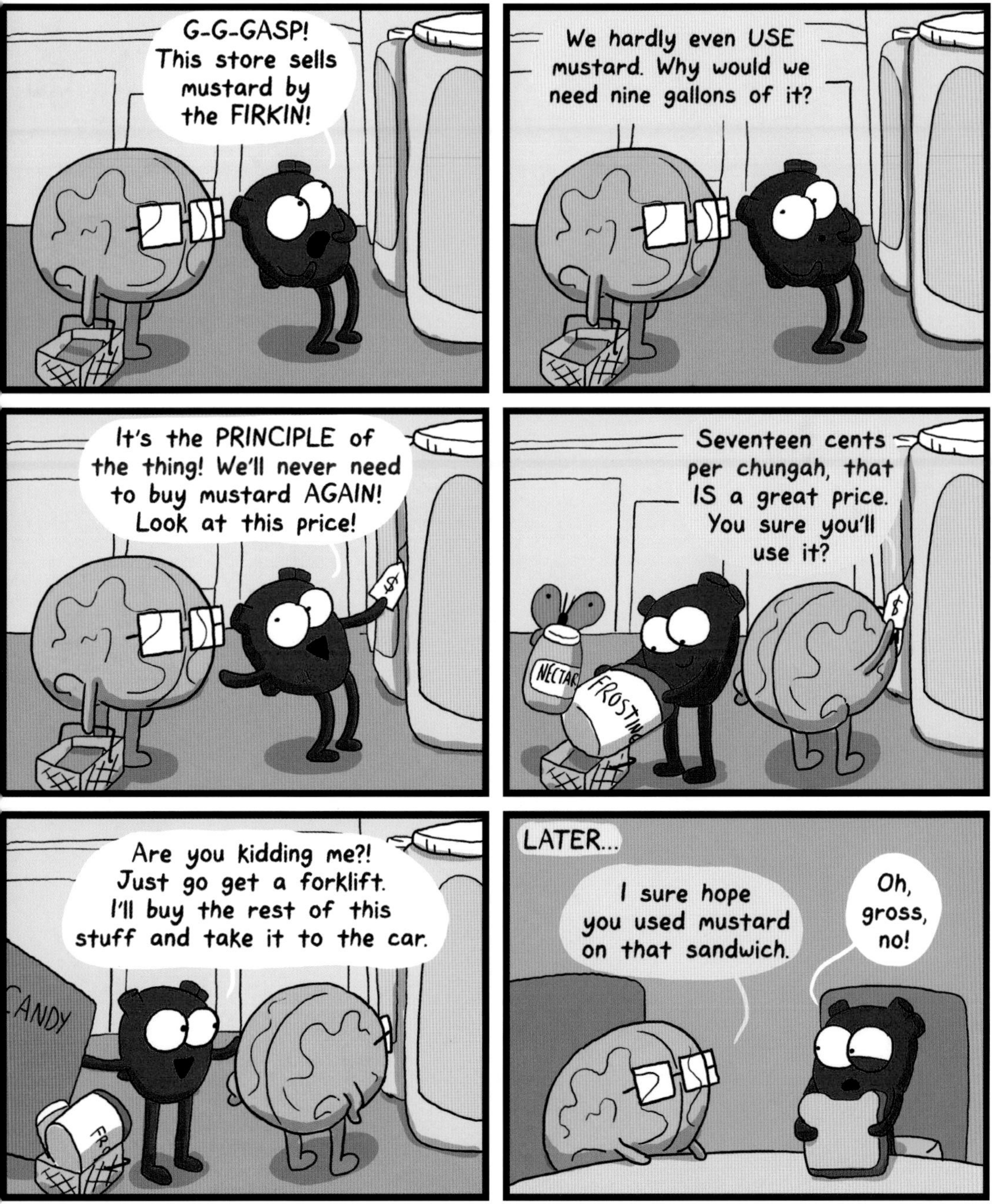
G-G-GASP! This store sells mustard by the FIRKIN!
We hardly even USE mustard. Why would we need nine gallons of it?
It's the PRINCIPLE of the thing! We'll never need to buy mustard AGAIN! Look at this price!
NECTAR
FROSTING
Seventeen cents per chungah, that IS a great price. You sure you'll use it?
Are you kidding me?! Just go get a forklift. I'll buy the rest of this stuff and take it to the car.
CANDY
LATER...
I sure hope you used mustard on that sandwich.
Oh, gross, no!

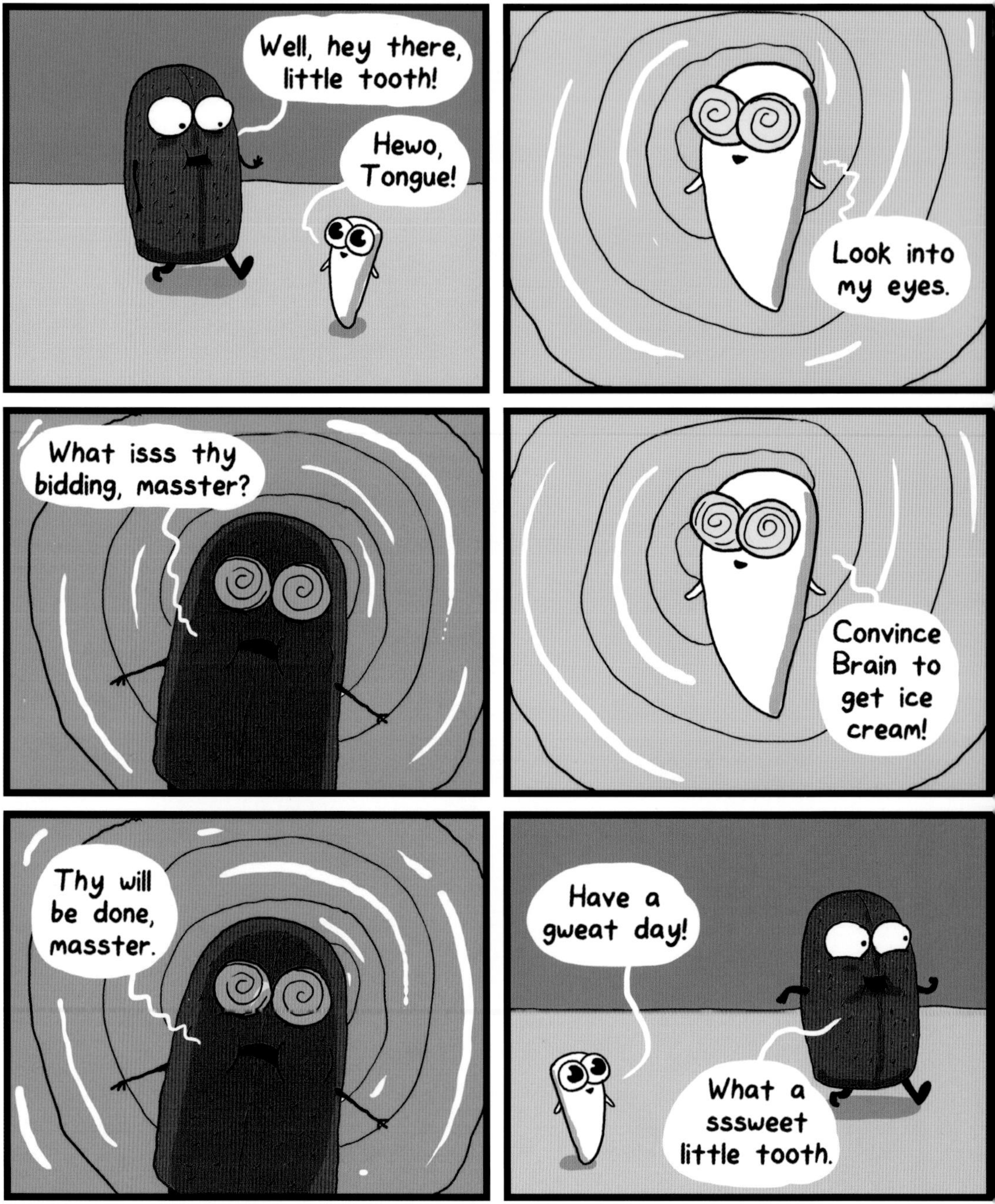
Well, hey there, little tooth!
Hewo, Tongue!
Look into my eyes.
What isss thy bidding, masster?
Convince Brain to get ice cream!
Thy will be done, masster.
Have a gweat day!
What a sssweet little tooth.

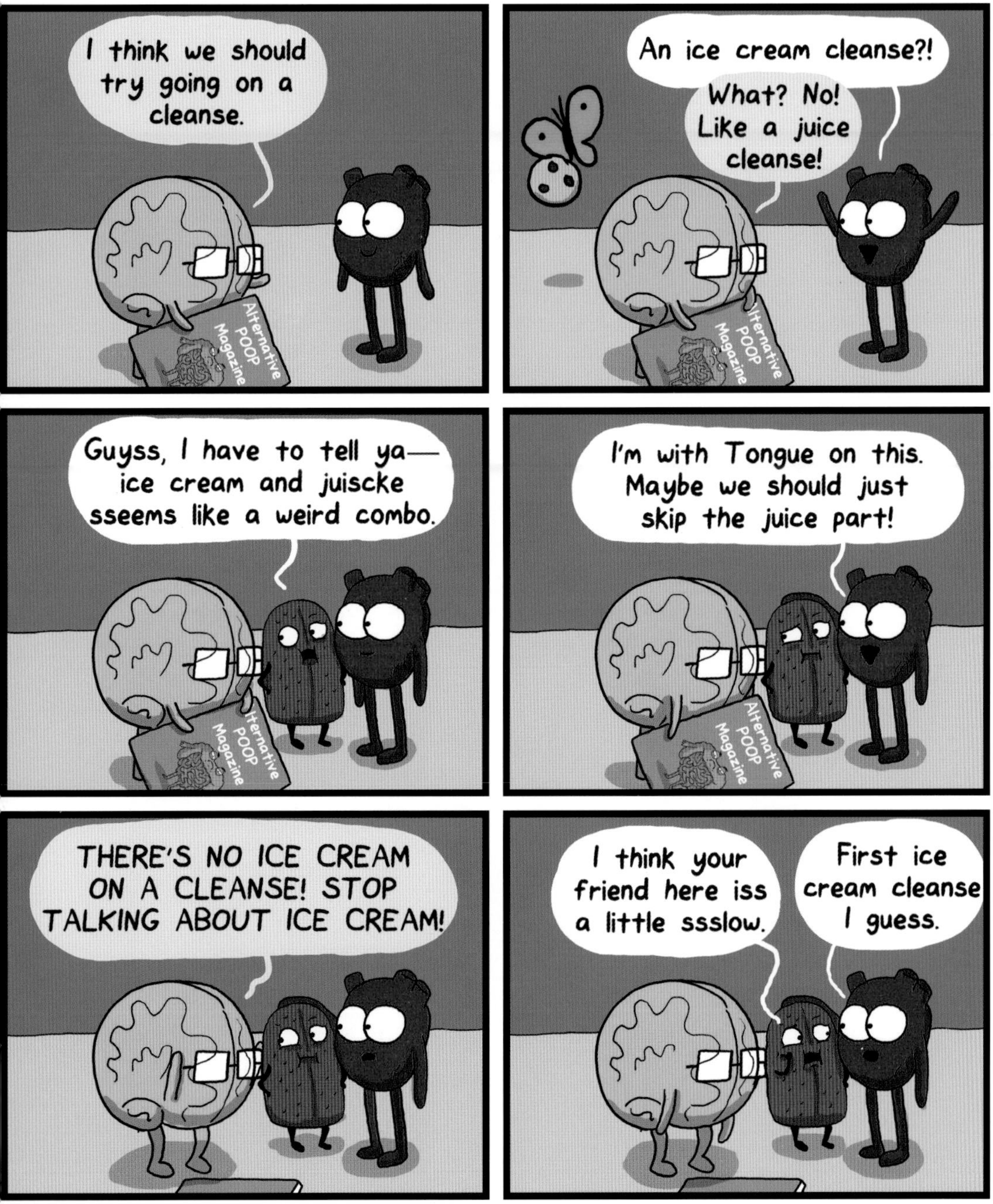
I think we should try going on a cleanse.
An ice cream cleanse?!
What? No! Like a juice cleanse!
Alternative POOP Magazine
Guyss, I have to tell ya— ice cream and juiscke sseems like a weird combo.
I'm with Tongue on this. Maybe we should just skip the juice part!
THERE'S NO ICE CREAM ON A CLEANSE! STOP TALKING ABOUT ICE CREAM!
I think your friend here iss a little ssslow.
First ice cream cleanse I guess.

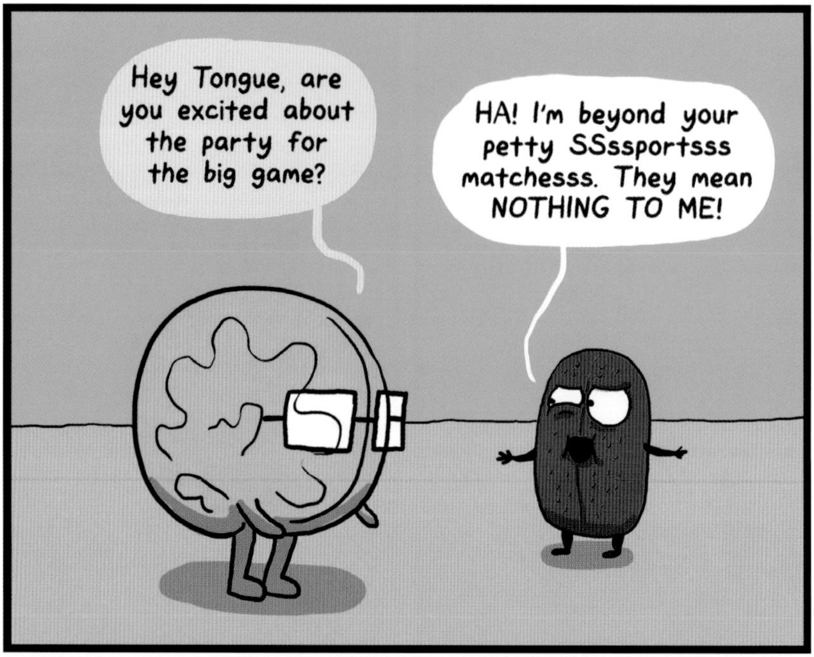
Hey Tongue, are you excited about the party for the big game?
HA! I'm beyond your petty SSssportsss matchesss. They mean NOTHING TO ME!

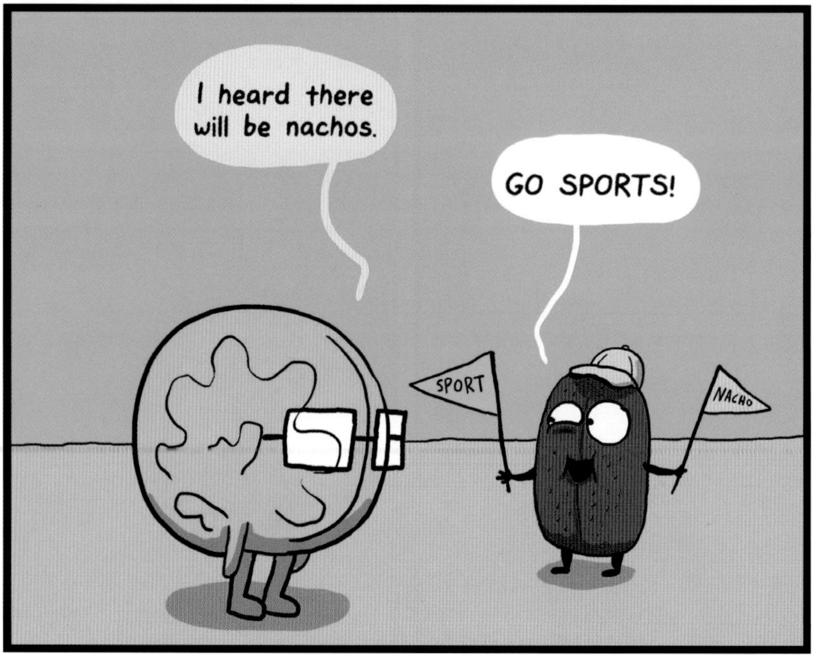
I heard there will be nachos.
GO SPORTS!
SPORT
NACHO

Hey bro, you want to watch some tennis?
You even need to ask? Let's do this!
SLAP

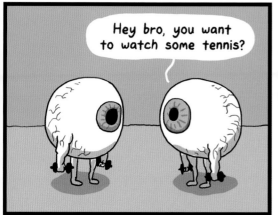

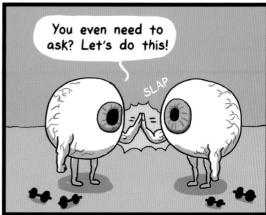

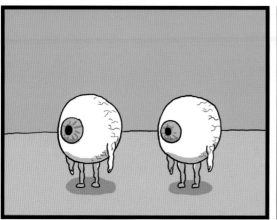

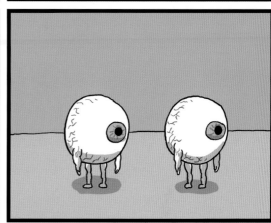

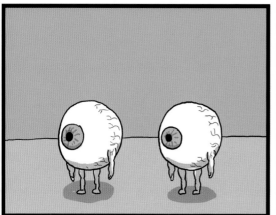

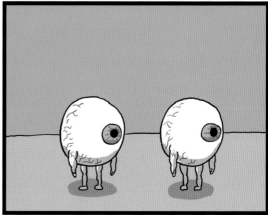

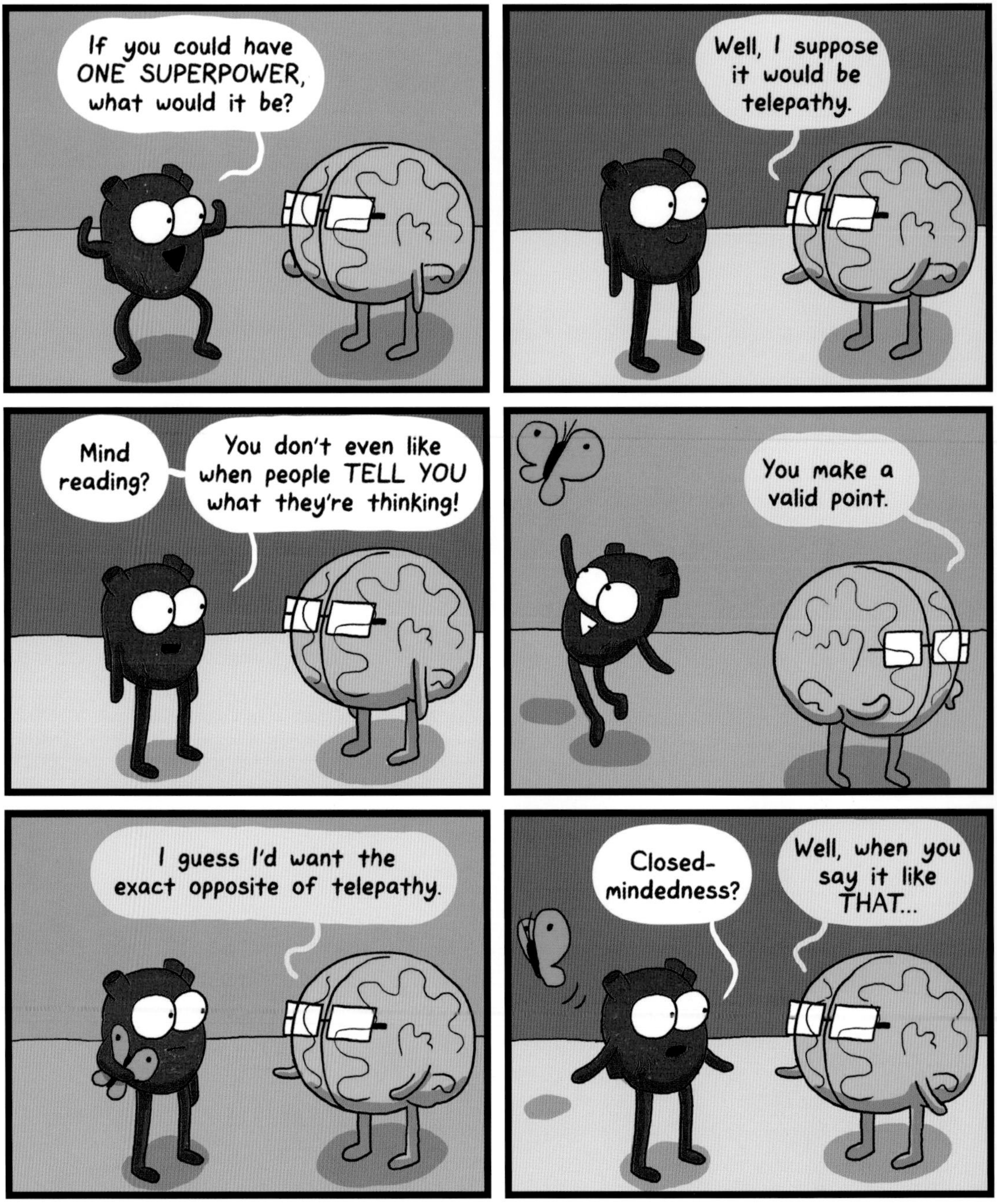
If you could have ONE SUPERPOWER, what would it be?
Well, I suppose it would be telepathy.
Mind reading?
You don't even like when people TELL YOU what they're thinking!
You make a valid point.
I guess I'd want the exact opposite of telepathy.
Closed-mindedness?
Well, when you say it like THAT...

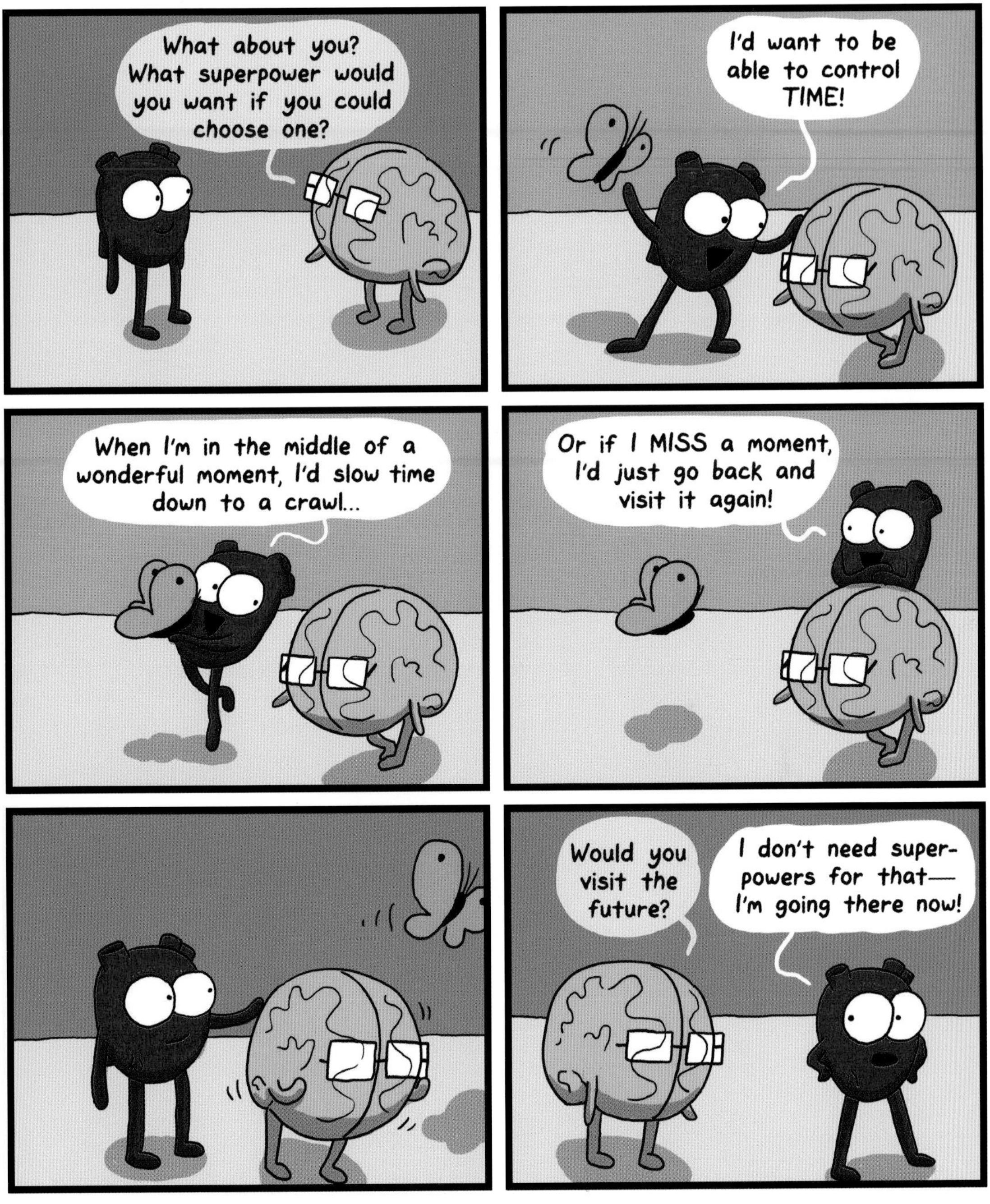
What about you? What superpower would you want if you could choose one?
I'd want to be able to control TIME!
When I'm in the middle of a wonderful moment, I'd slow time down to a crawl...
Or if I MISS a moment, I'd just go back and visit it again!
Would you visit the future?
I don't need super-powers for that— I'm going there now!

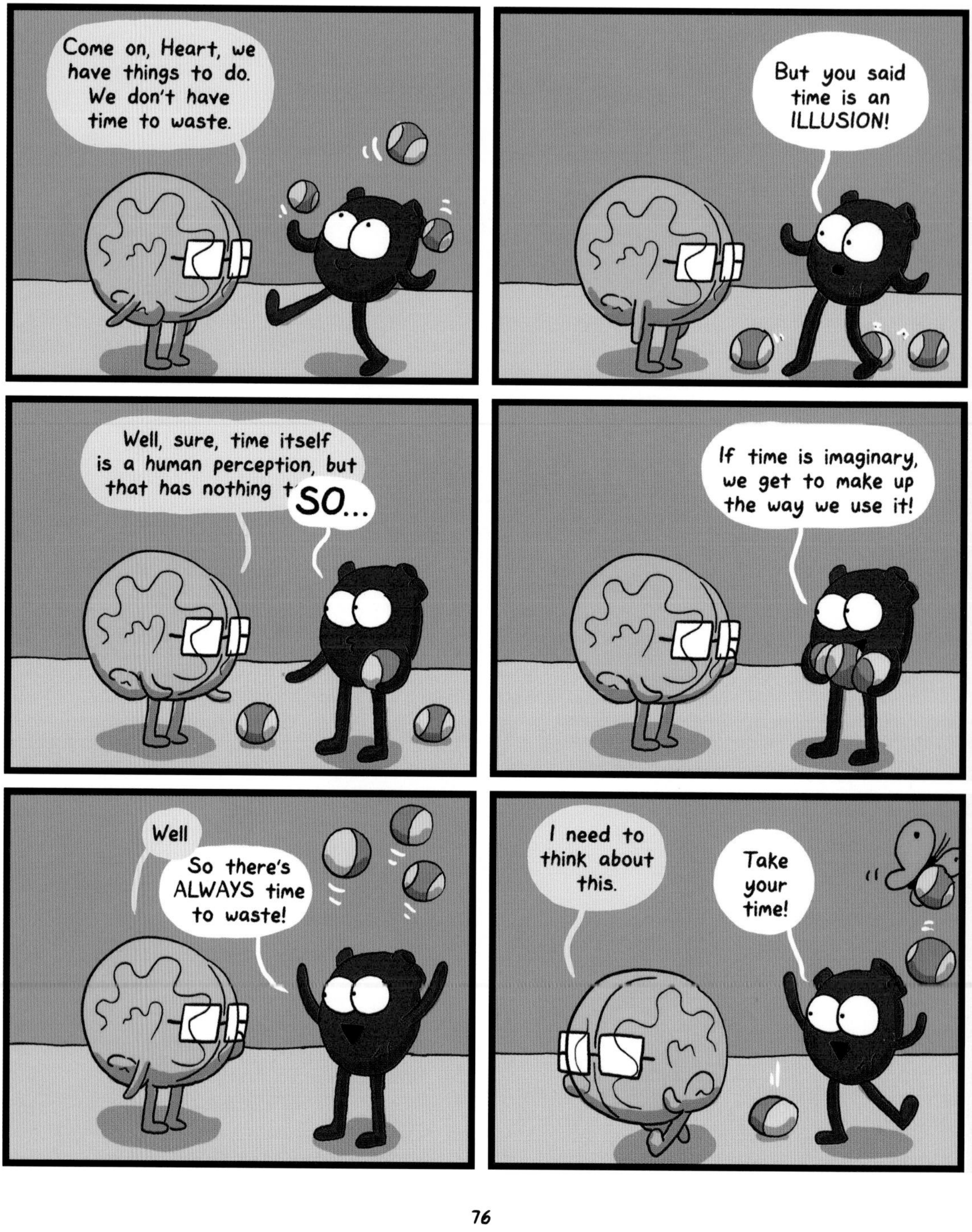
Come on, Heart, we have things to do. We don't have time to waste.
But you said time is an ILLUSION!
Well, sure, time itself is a human perception, but that has nothing t
SO...
If time is imaginary, we get to make up the way we use it!
Well
So there's ALWAYS time to waste!
I need to think about this.
Take your time!

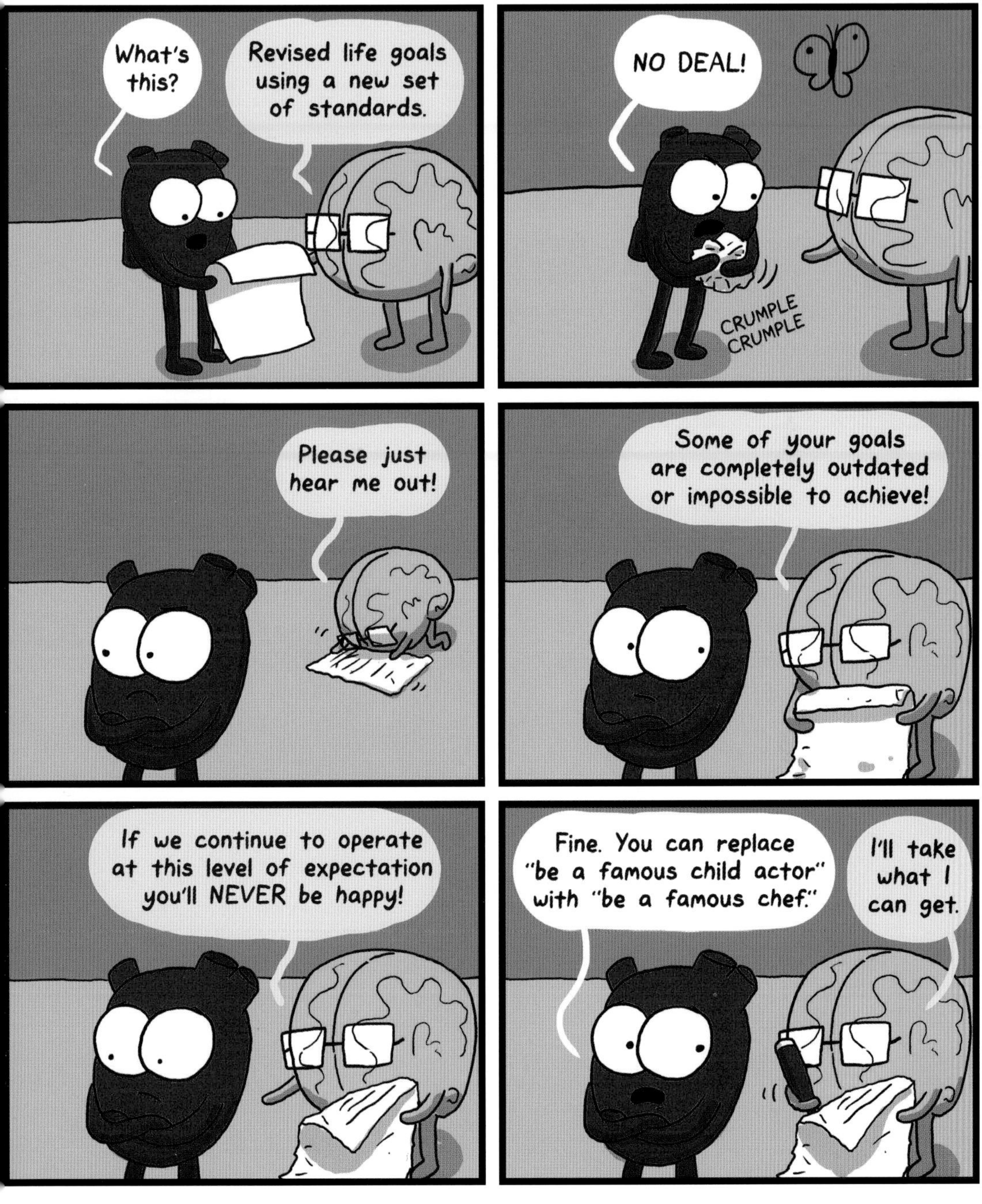
What's this?
Revised life goals using a new set of standards.
NO DEAL!
CRUMPLE CRUMPLE
Please just hear me out!
Some of your goals are completely outdated or impossible to achieve!
If we continue to operate at this level of expectation you'll NEVER be happy!
Fine. You can replace "be a famous child actor" with "be a famous chef."
I'll take what I can get.

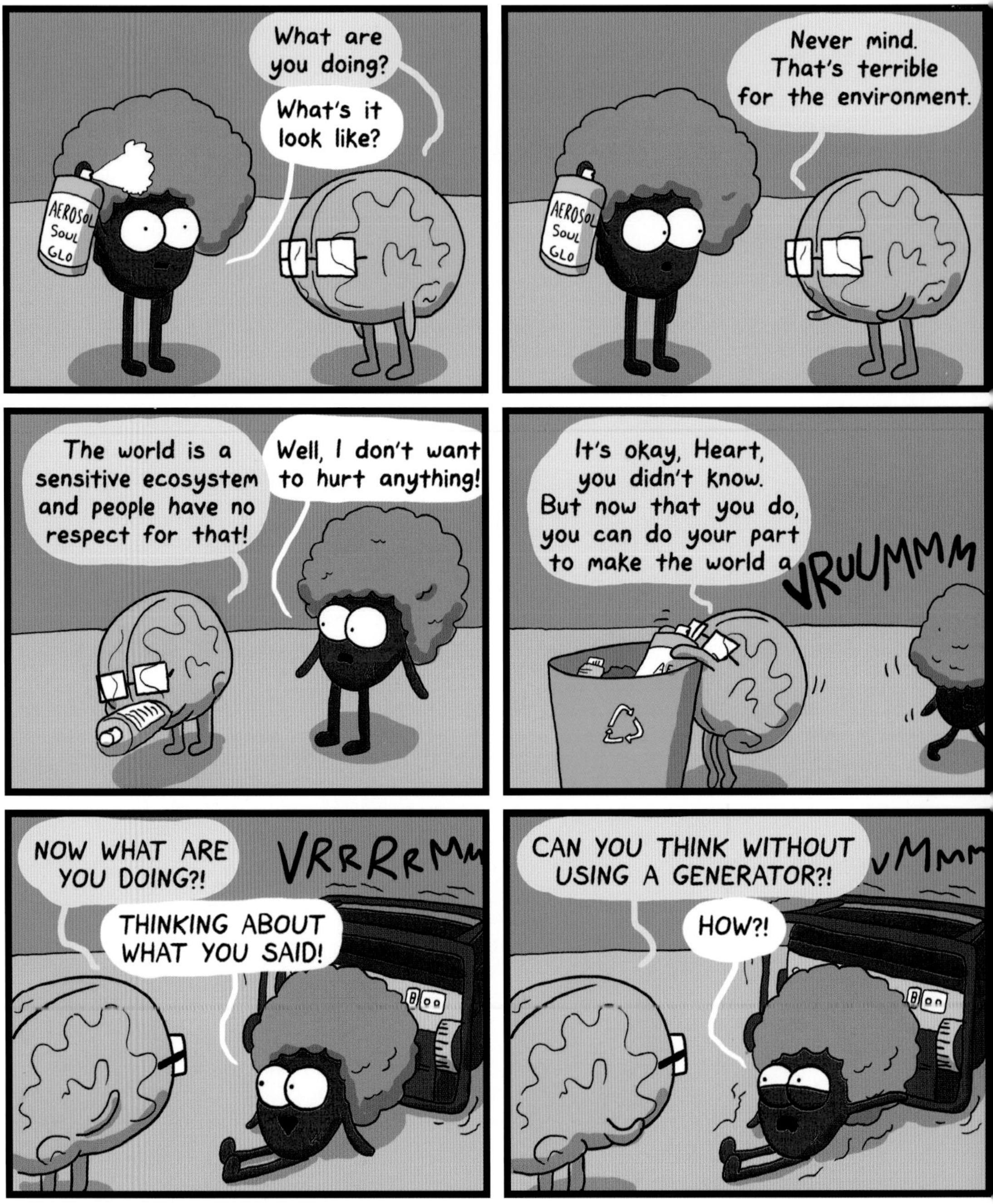
What are you doing?
What's it look like?
AEROSOL SOUL GLO
Never mind. That's terrible for the environment.
The world is a sensitive ecosystem and people have no respect for that!
Well, I don't want to hurt anything!
It's okay, Heart, you didn't know. But now that you do, you can do your part to make the world a
VRUUMMM
NOW WHAT ARE YOU DOING?!
VRRRRRMM
THINKING ABOUT WHAT YOU SAID!
CAN YOU THINK WITHOUT USING A GENERATOR?!
VMMM
HOW?!

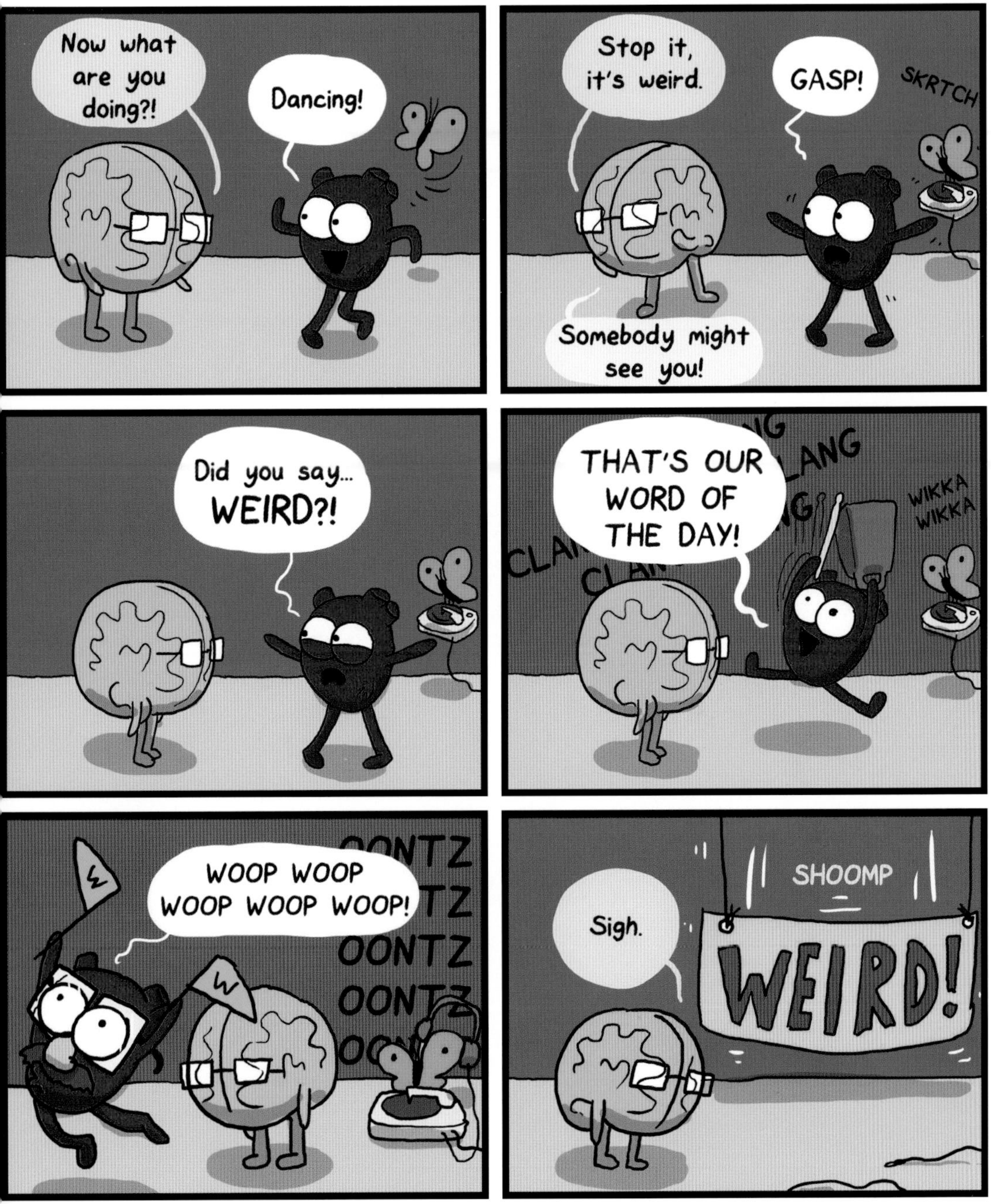
Now what are you doing?!
Dancing!
Stop it, it's weird.
Somebody might see you!
GASP!
SKRTCH
Did you say... WEIRD?!
THAT'S OUR WORD OF THE DAY!
WIKKA WIKKA
WOOP WOOP WOOP WOOP WOOP!
OONTZ
OONTZ
Sigh.
SHOOMP
WEIRD!

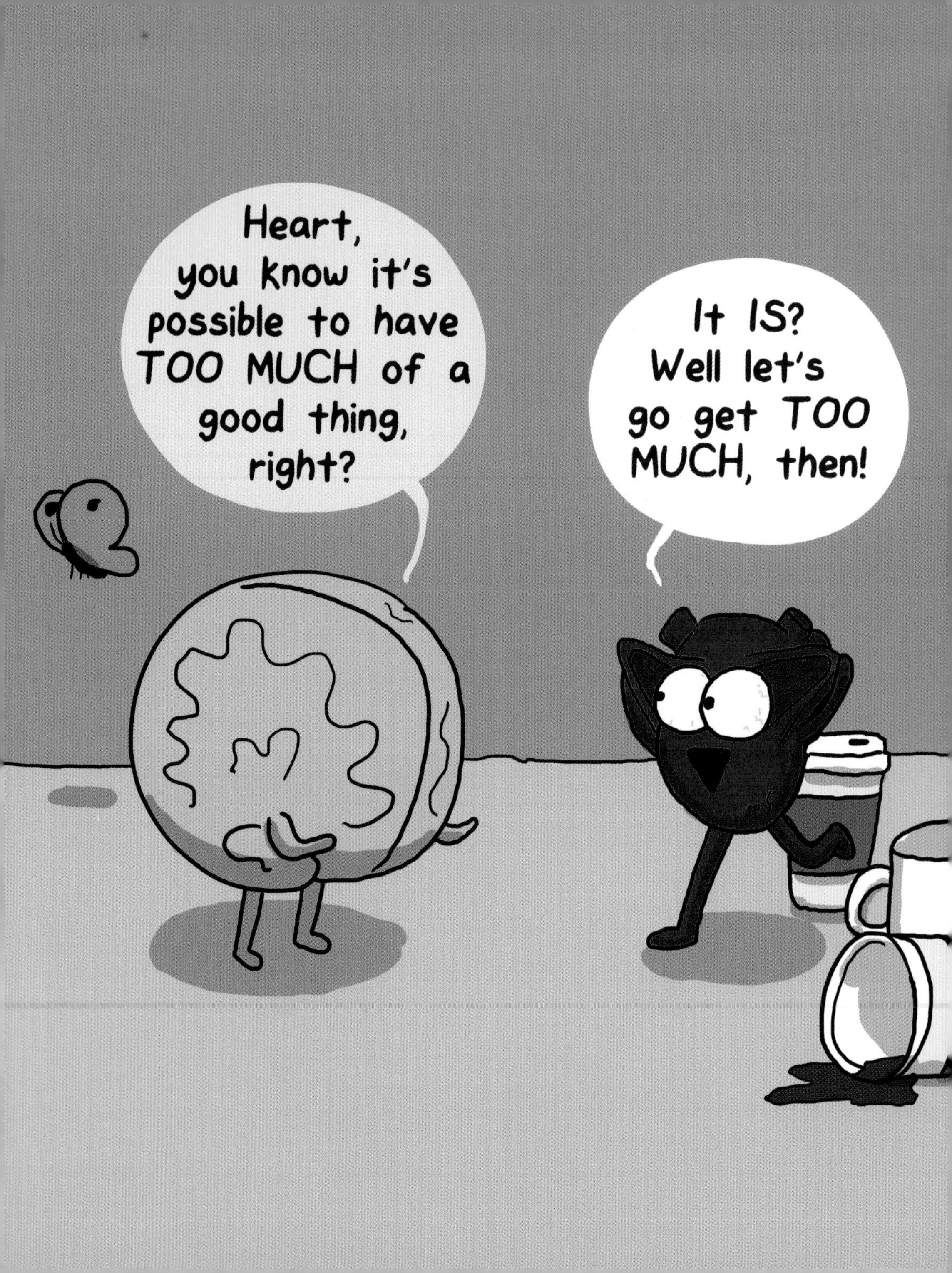

Heart, you know it's possible to have TOO MUCH of a good thing, right?
It IS? Well let's go get TOO MUCH, then!

Life is GREAT! I can't wait to see what TOMORROW brings!
Heart, while I appreciate your positivity, I wonder if it only sets you up for failure, and well, heartbreak.
NONSENSE! If things are good now, then all I need is for things to remain equally awesome or better forever!
AWESOME
TIME
But life WON'T always be awesome. Life is mostly "okay." If you always expect "awesome," then by contrast, "okay" will feel terrible to you.
HAPPINESS
TIME
You need to appreciate the great times, but be prepared for the okay times. Then you'll be better equipped to handle the bad times, too.
What are you so happy about NOW?
After that boring speech there's nowhere to go but UP!

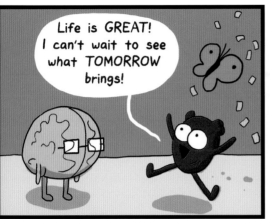

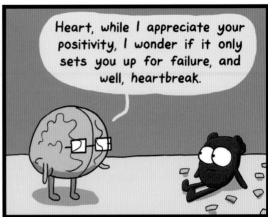

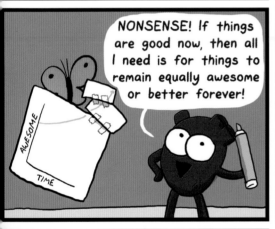

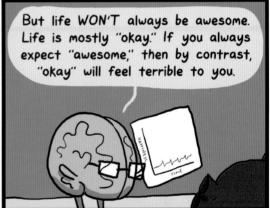

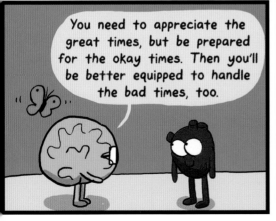

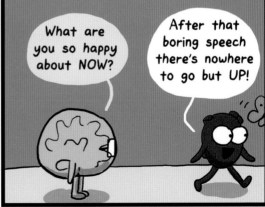

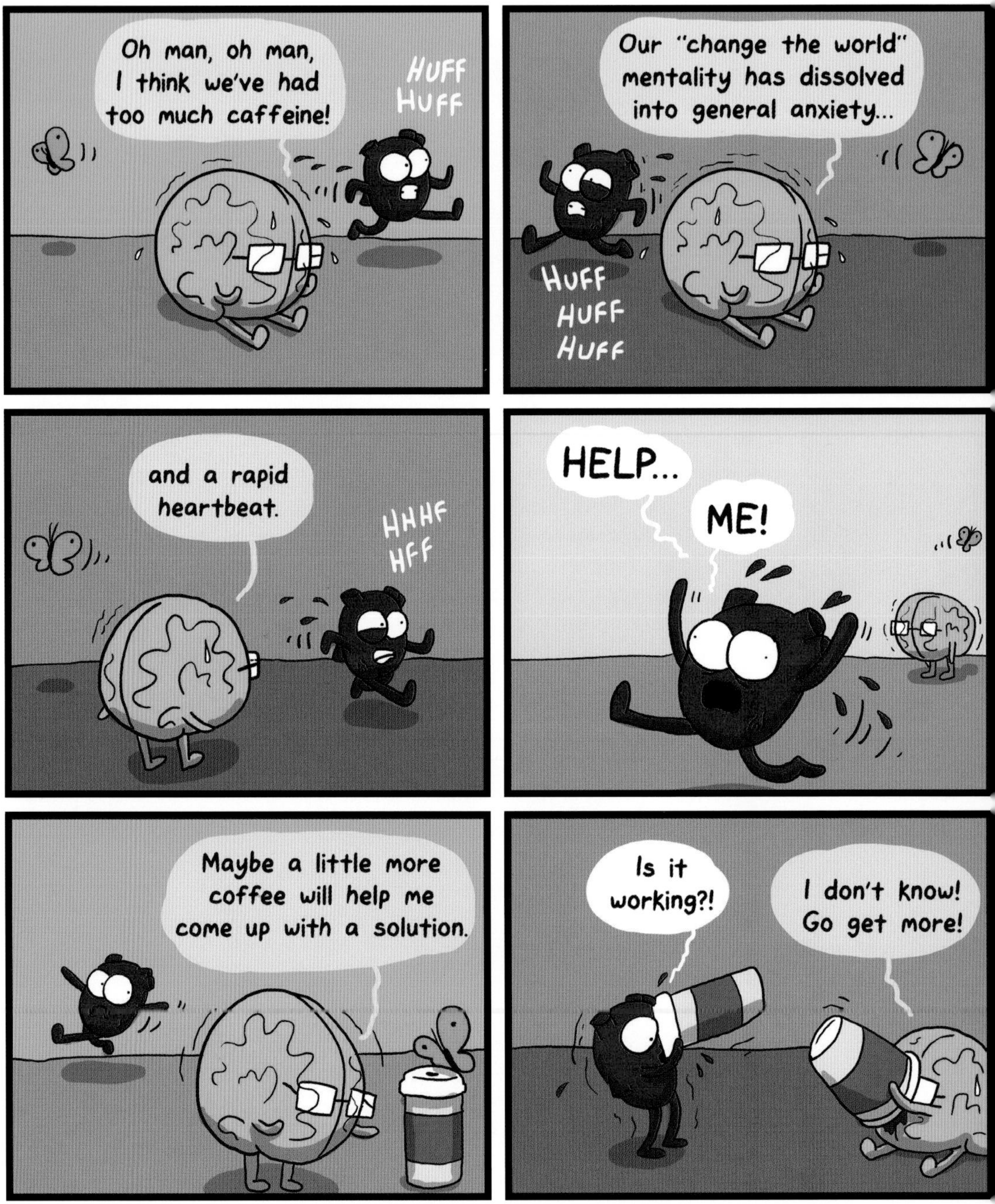
Oh man, oh man, I think we've had too much caffeine!
HUFF HUFF
Our "change the world" mentality has dissolved into general anxiety...
HUFF HUFF HUFF
and a rapid heartbeat.
HHHF HFF
HELP...
ME!
Maybe a little more coffee will help me come up with a solution.
Is it working?!
I don't know! Go get more!

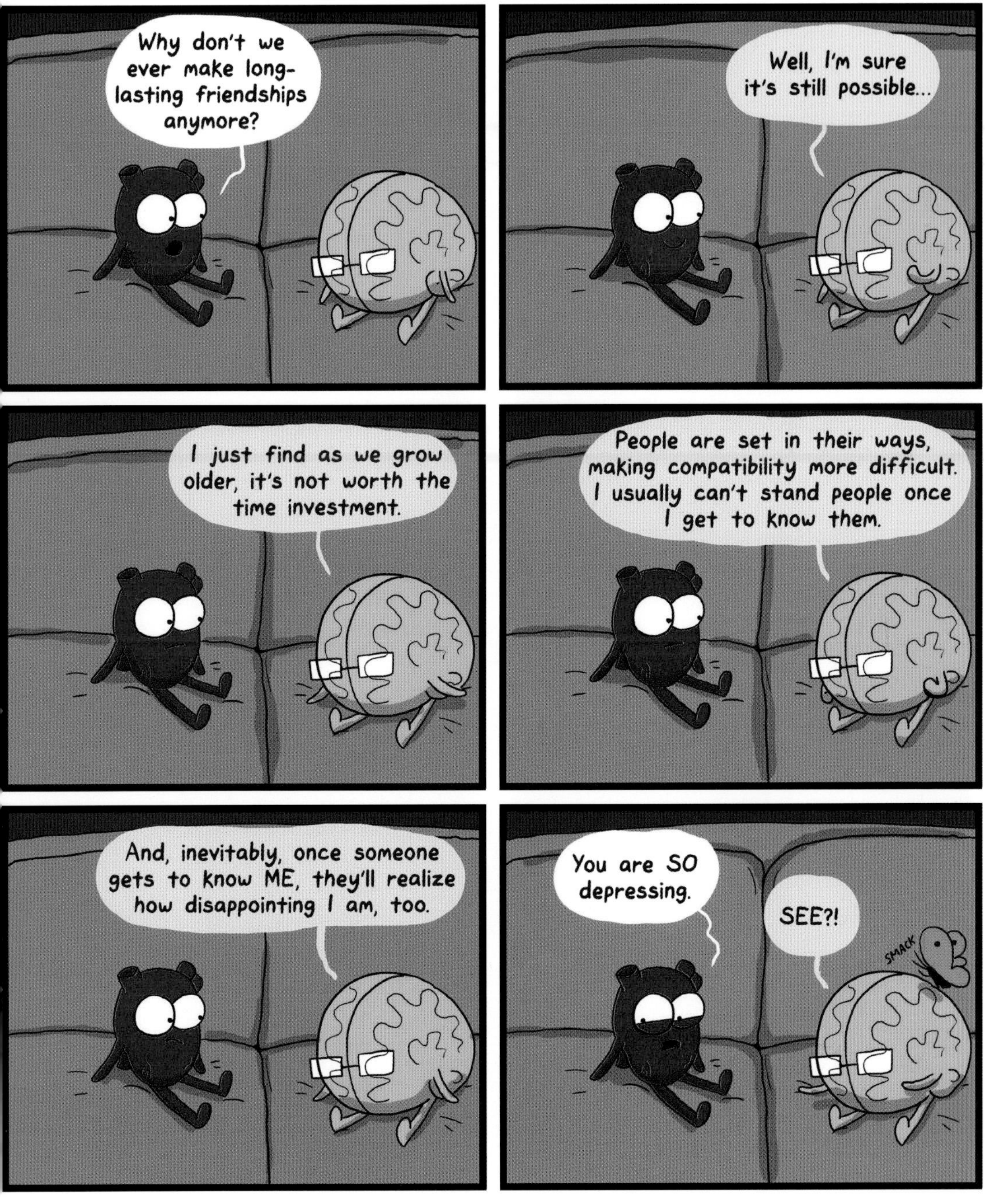
Why don't we ever make long-lasting friendships anymore?
Well, I'm sure it's still possible...
I just find as we grow older, it's not worth the time investment.
People are set in their ways, making compatibility more difficult. I usually can't stand people once I get to know them.
And, inevitably, once someone gets to know ME, they'll realize how disappointing I am, too.
You are SO depressing.
SEE?!
SMACK

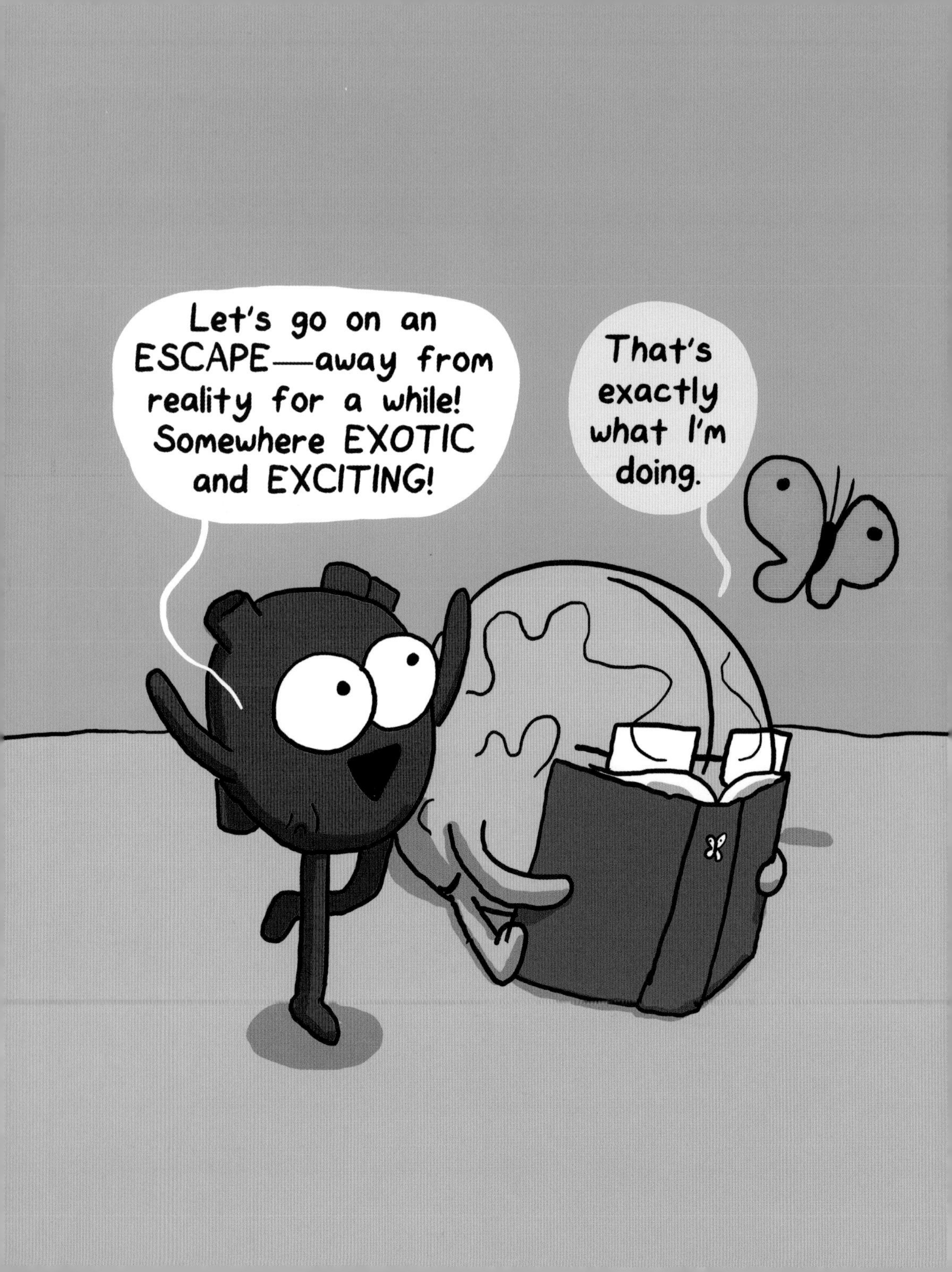
Let's go on an ESCAPE—away from reality for a while! Somewhere EXOTIC and EXCITING!
That's exactly what I'm doing.

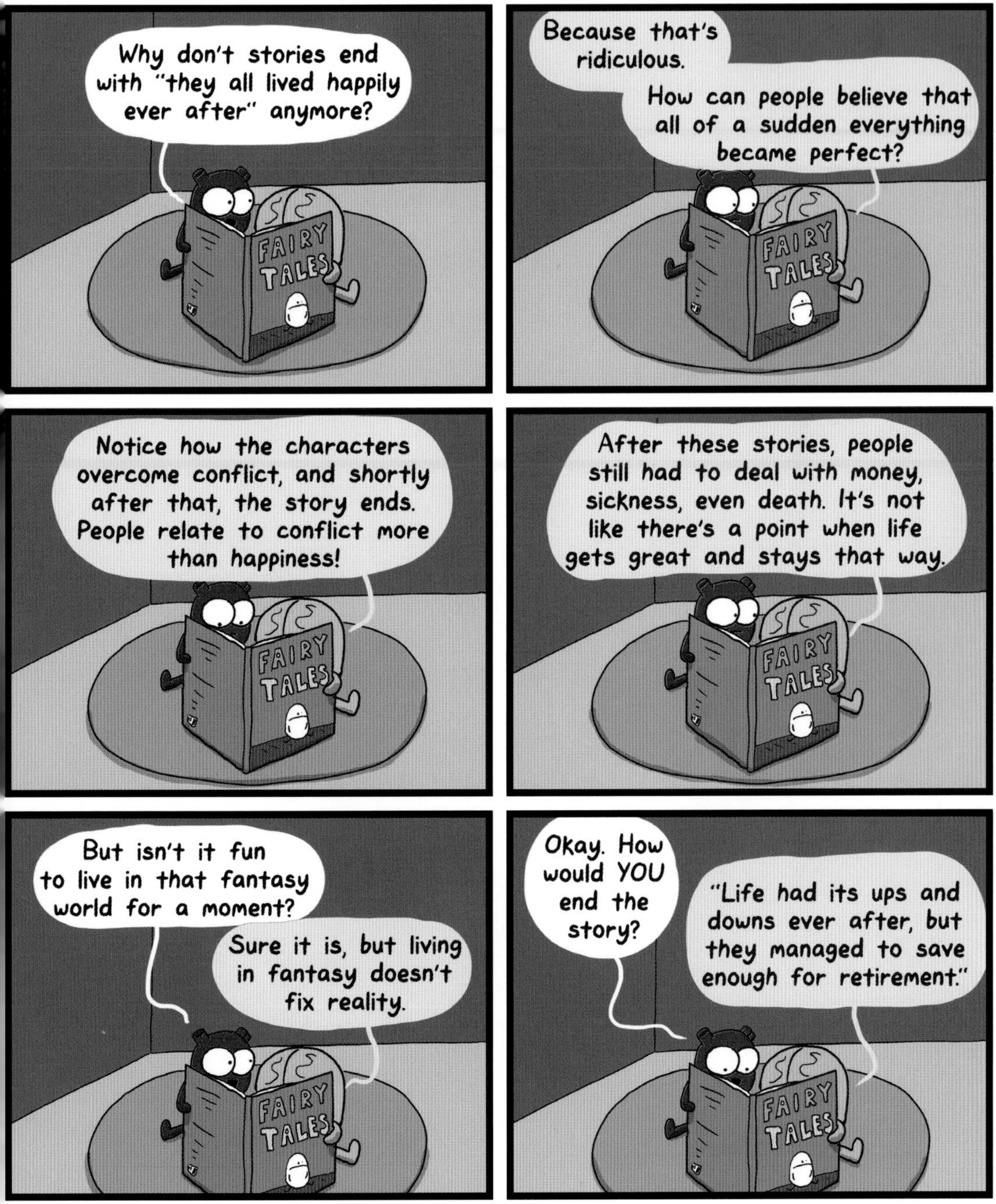
Why don't stories end with "they all lived happily ever after" anymore?
FAIRY TALES
Because that's ridiculous.
How can people believe that all of a sudden everything became perfect?
FAIRY TALES
Notice how the characters overcome conflict, and shortly after that, the story ends. People relate to conflict more than happiness!
FAIRY TALES
After these stories, people still had to deal with money, sickness, even death. It's not like there's a point when life gets great and stays that way.
FAIRY TALES
But isn't it fun to live in that fantasy world for a moment?
Sure it is, but living in fantasy doesn't fix reality.
FAIRY TALES
Okay. How would YOU end the story?
"Life had its ups and downs ever after, but they managed to save enough for retirement."
FAIRY TALES

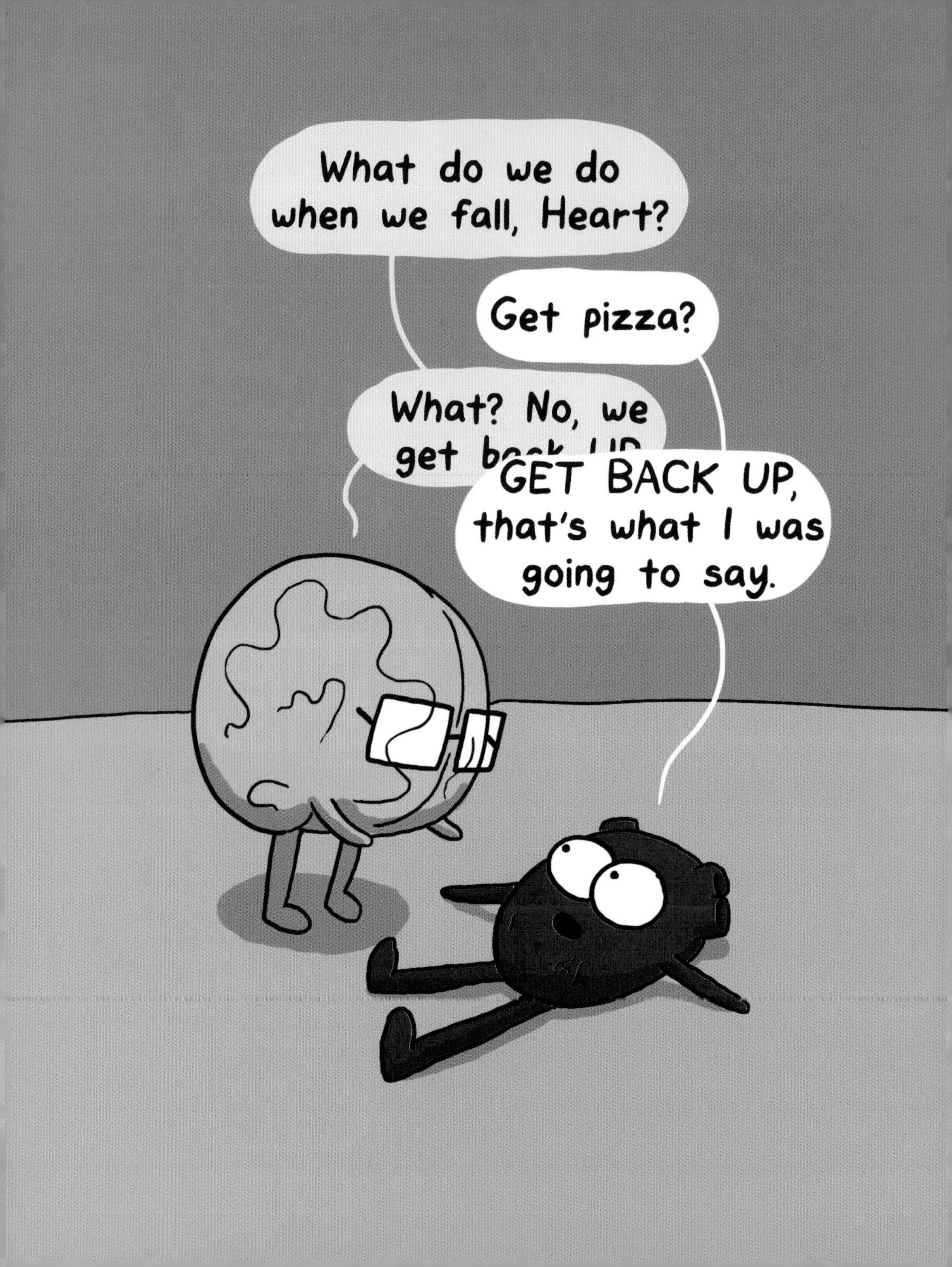
What do we do when we fall, Heart?
Get pizza?
What? No, we get b
GET BACK UP, that's what I was going to say.

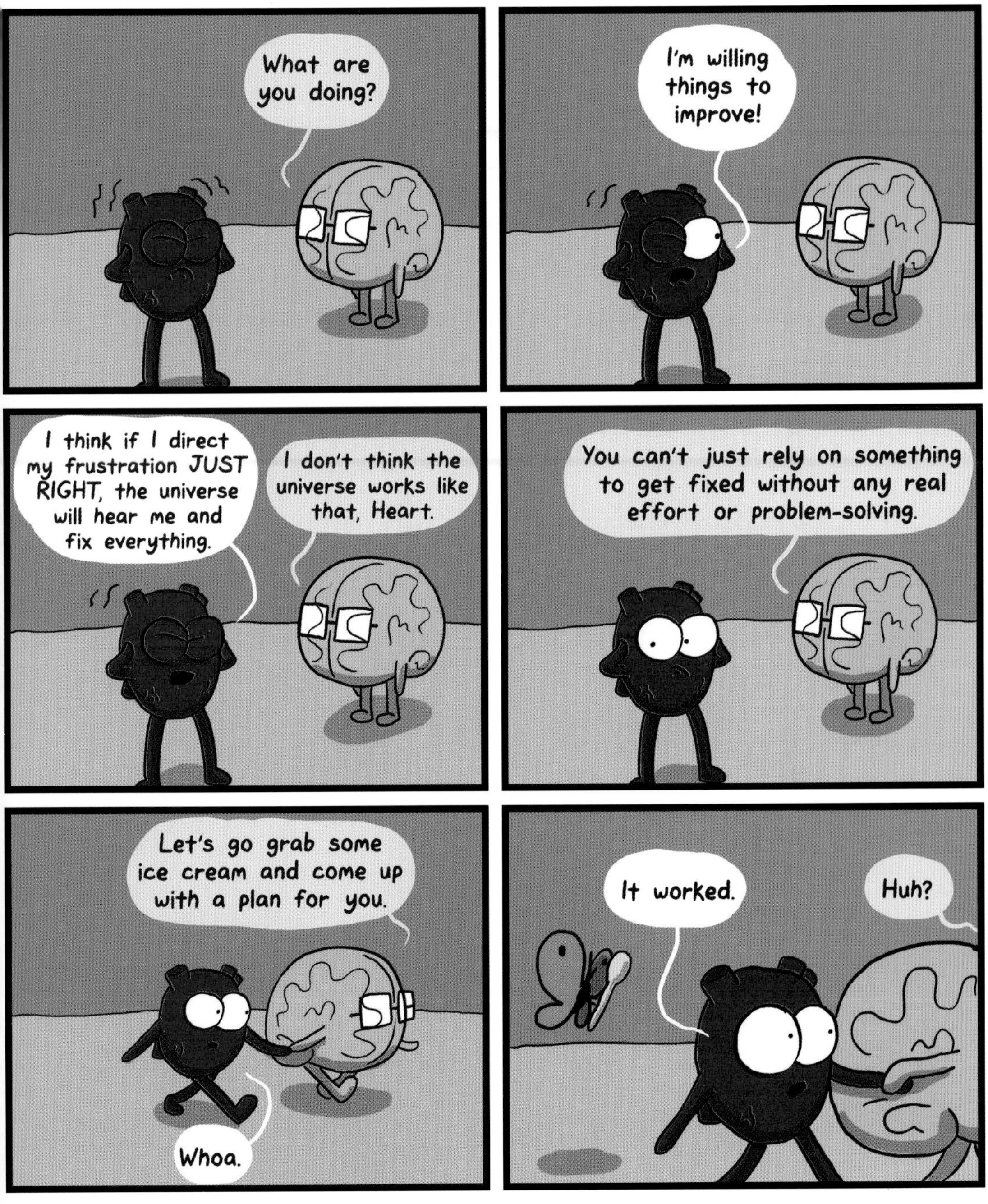
What are you doing?
I'm willing things to improve!
I think if I direct my frustration JUST RIGHT, the universe will hear me and fix everything.
I don't think the universe works like that, Heart.
You can't just rely on something to get fixed without any real effort or problem-solving.
Let's go grab some ice cream and come up with a plan for you.
Whoa.
It worked.
Huh?

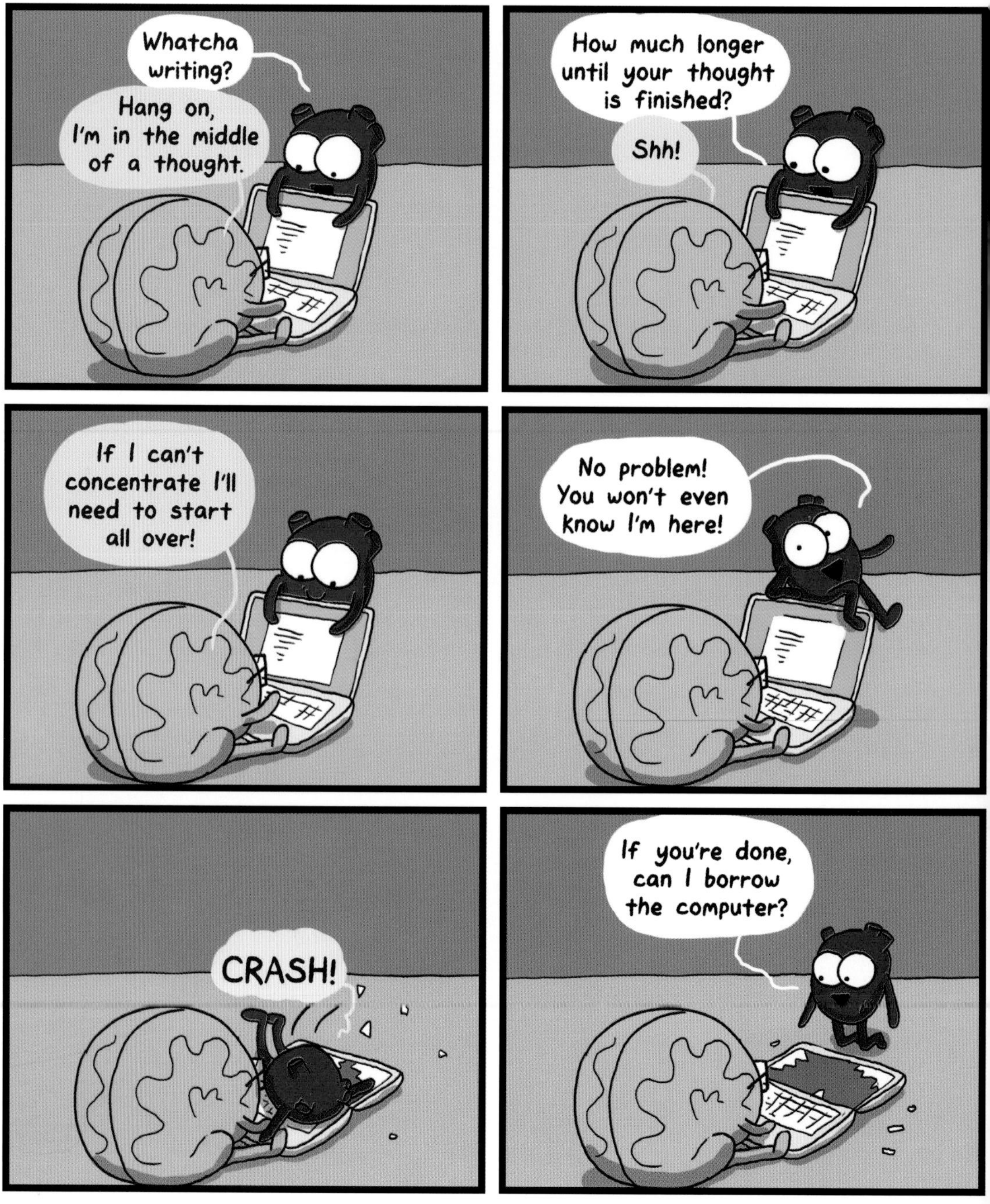
Whatcha writing?
Hang on, I'm in the middle of a thought.
How much longer until your thought is finished?
Shh!
If I can't concentrate I'll need to start all over!
No problem! You won't even know I'm here!
CRASH!
If you're done, can I borrow the computer?

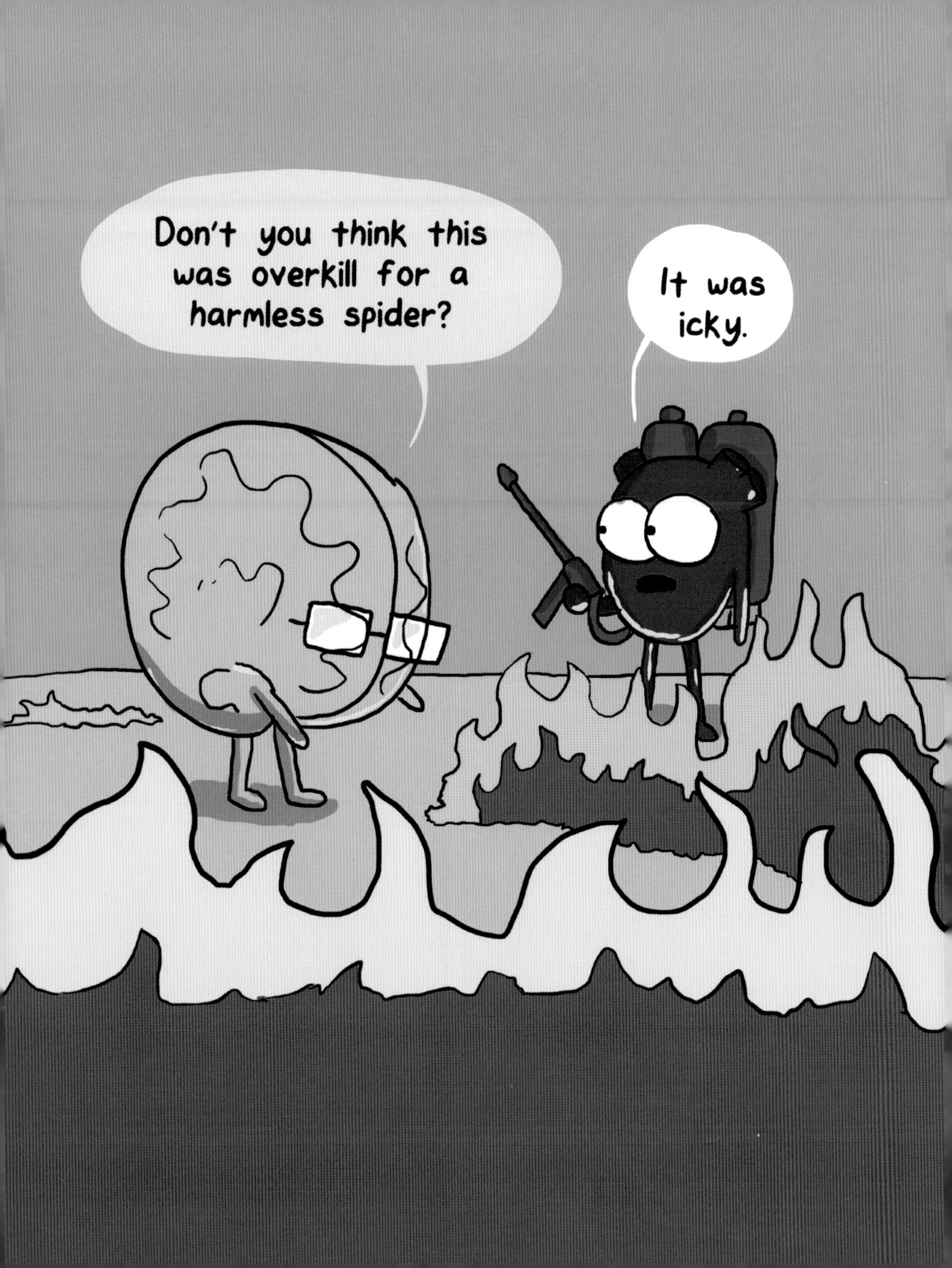
Don't you think this was overkill for a harmless spider?
It was icky.

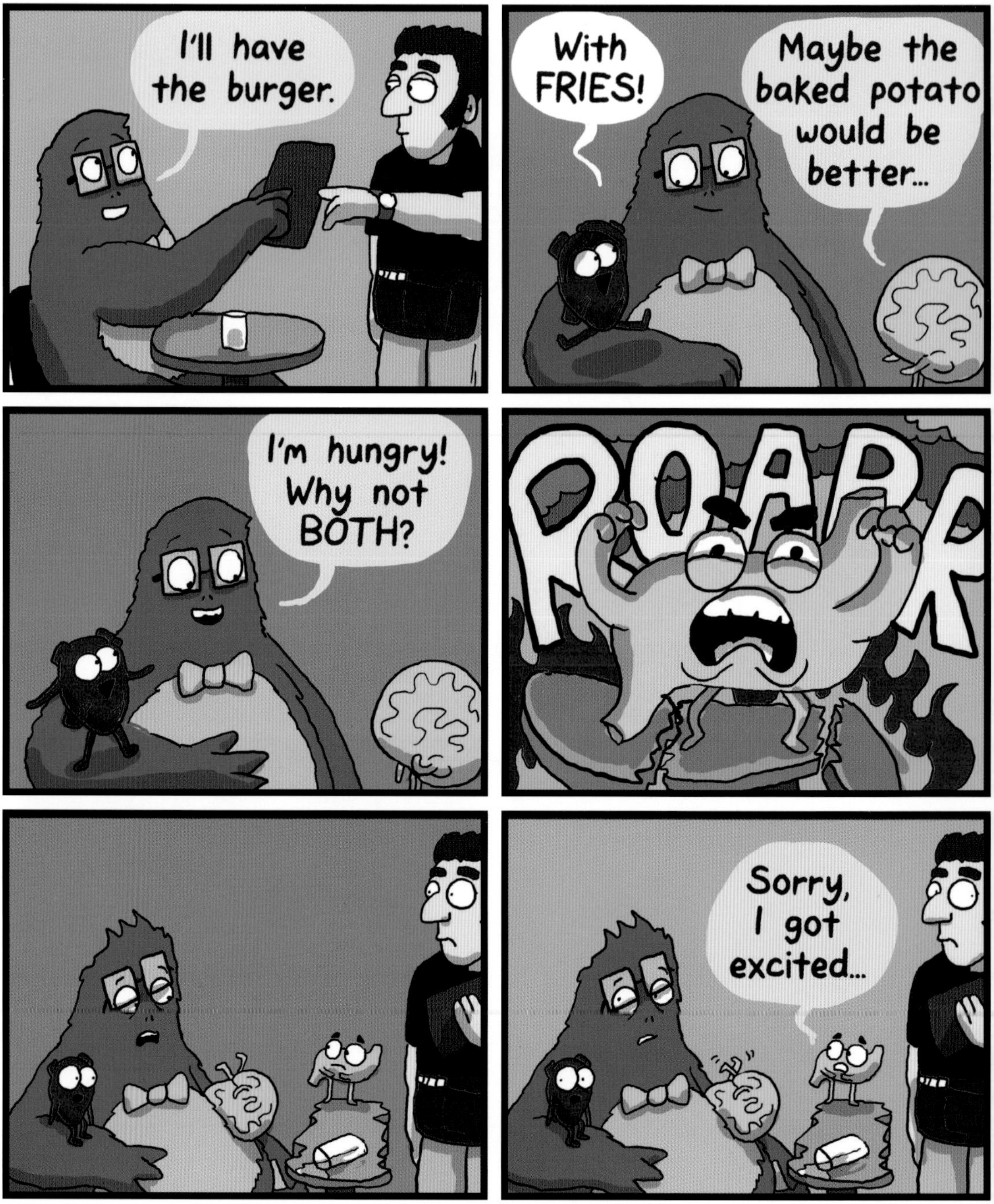
I'll have the burger.
With FRIES!
Maybe the baked potato would be better...
I'm hungry! Why not BOTH?
ROARR
Sorry, I got excited...

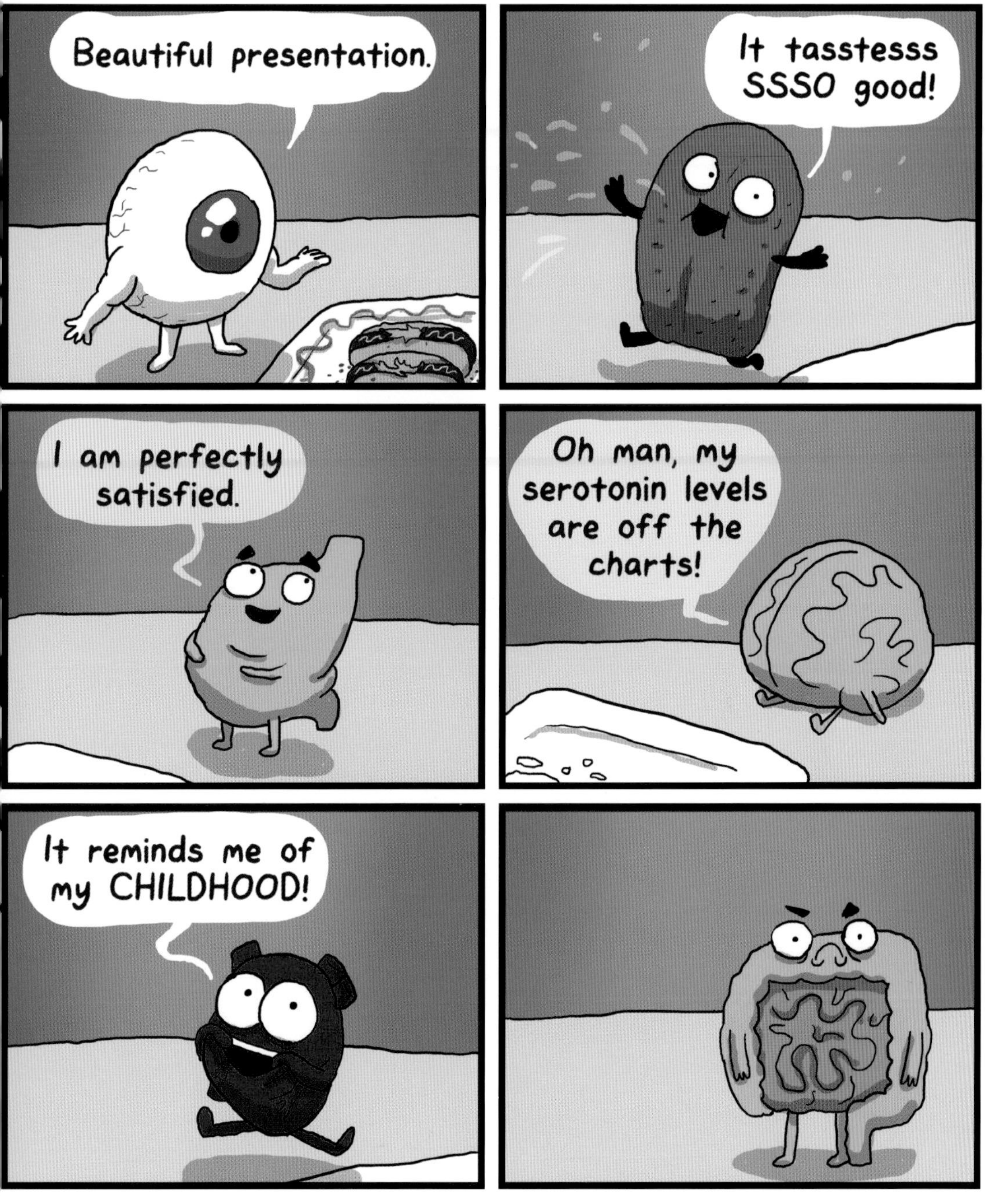
Beautiful presentation.
It tasstesss SSSO good!
I am perfectly satisfied.
Oh man, my serotonin levels are off the charts!
It reminds me of my CHILDHOOD!

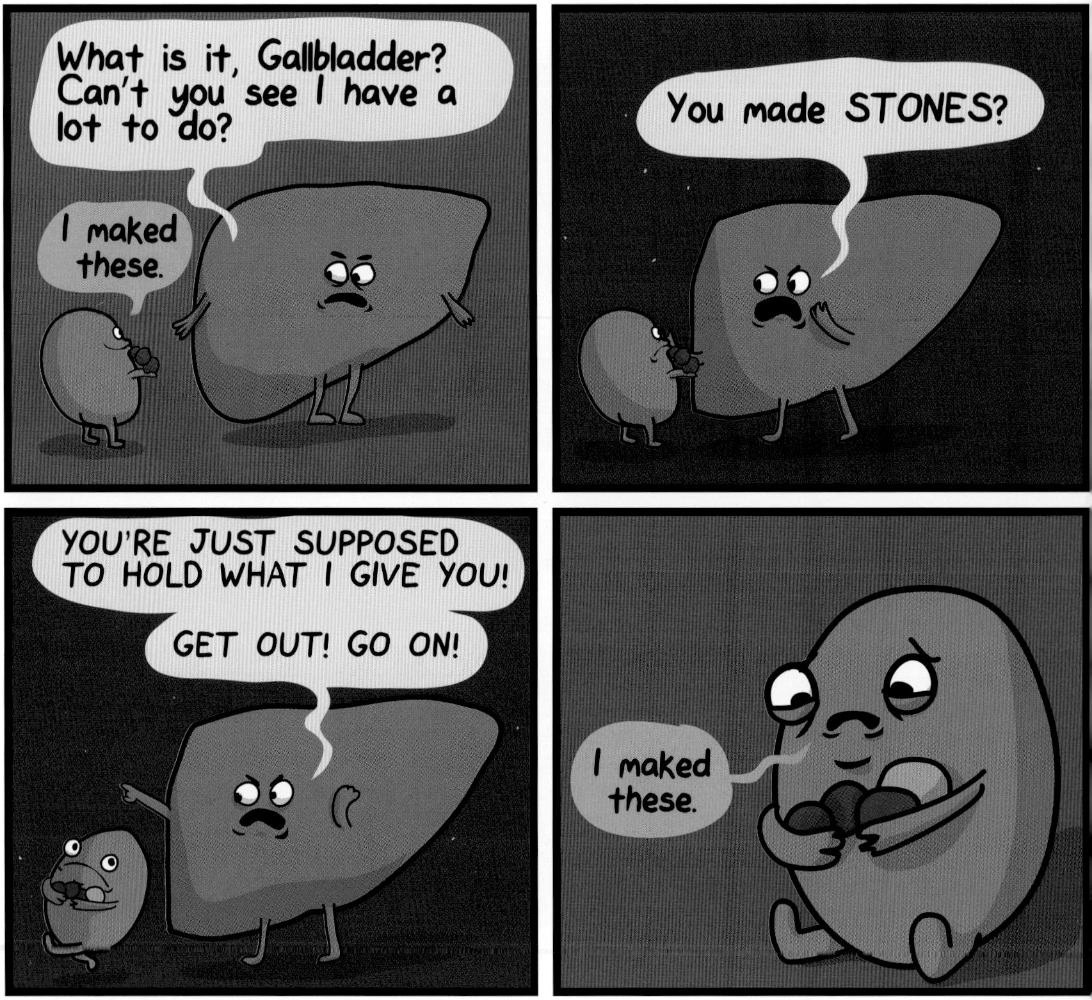
What is it, Gallbladder? Can't you see I have a lot to do?
I maked these.
You made STONES?
YOU'RE JUST SUPPOSED TO HOLD WHAT I GIVE YOU!
GET OUT! GO ON!
I maked these.

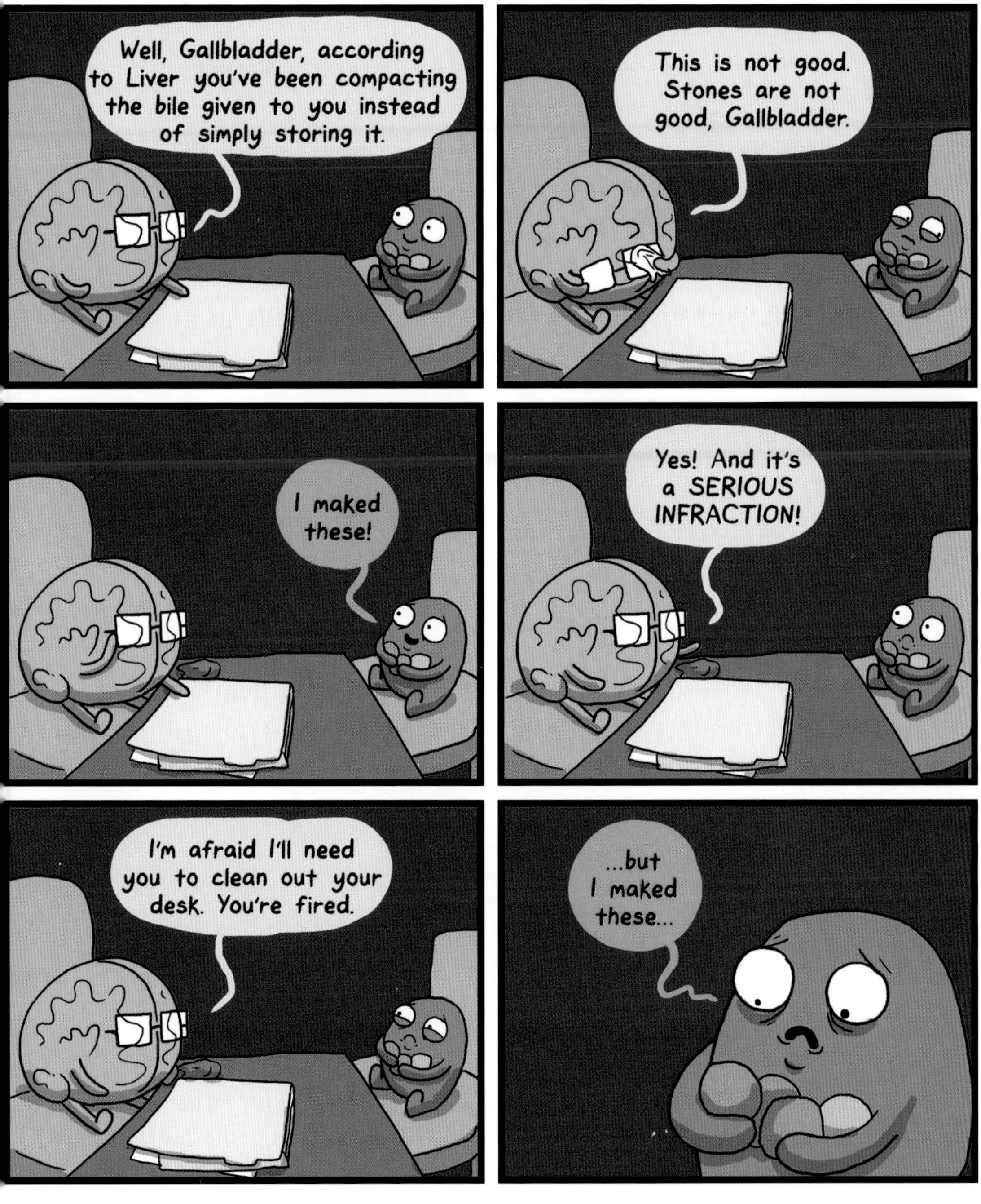
Well, Gallbladder, according to Liver you've been compacting the bile given to you instead of simply storing it.
This is not good. Stones are not good, Gallbladder.
I maked these!
Yes! And it's a SERIOUS INFRACTION!
I'm afraid I'll need you to clean out your desk. You're fired.
...but I maked these...

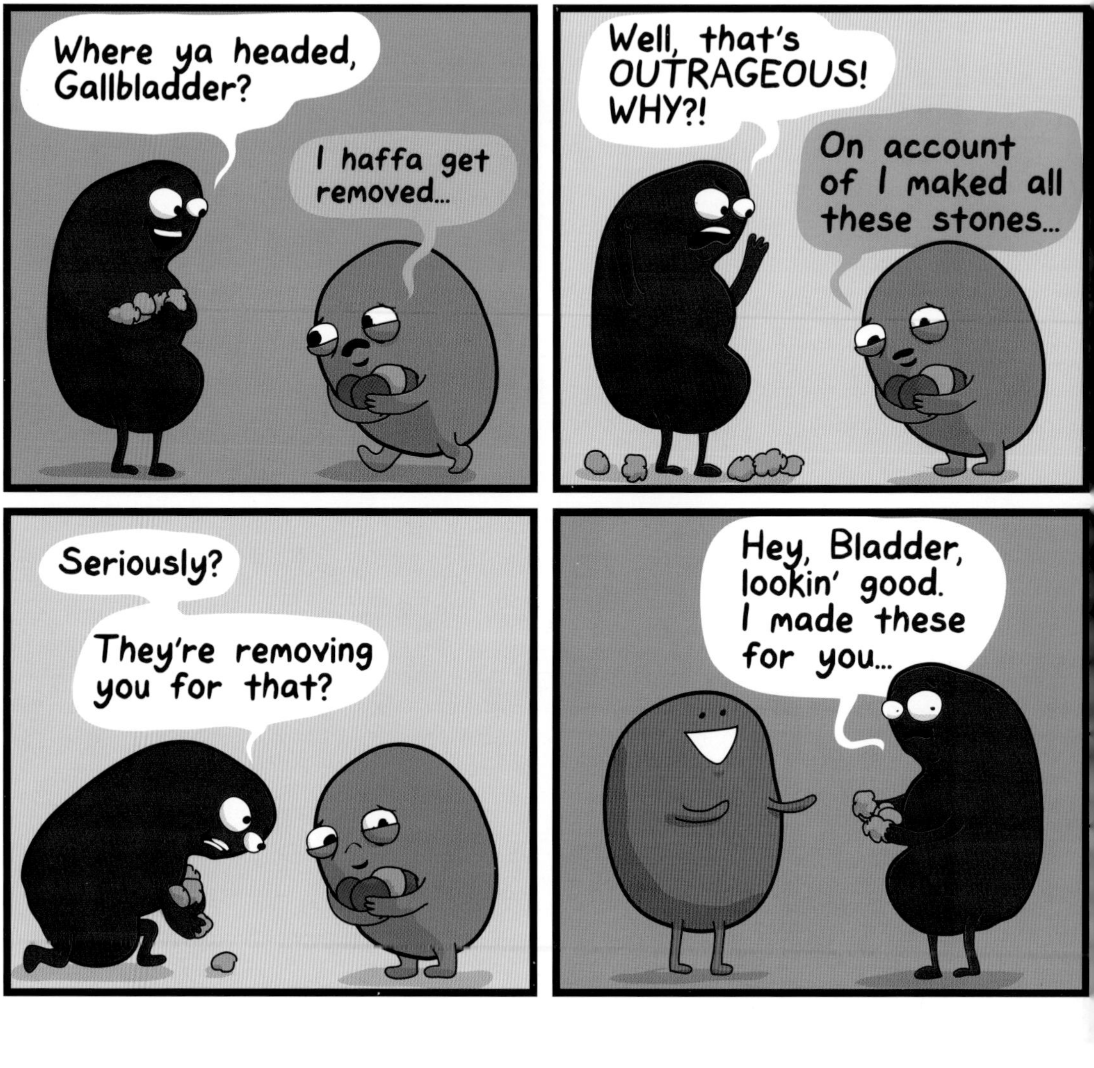
Where ya headed, Gallbladder?
I haffa get removed...
Well, that's OUTRAGEOUS! WHY?!
On account of I maked all these stones...
Seriously?
They're removing you for that?
Hey, Bladder, lookin' good. I made these for you...

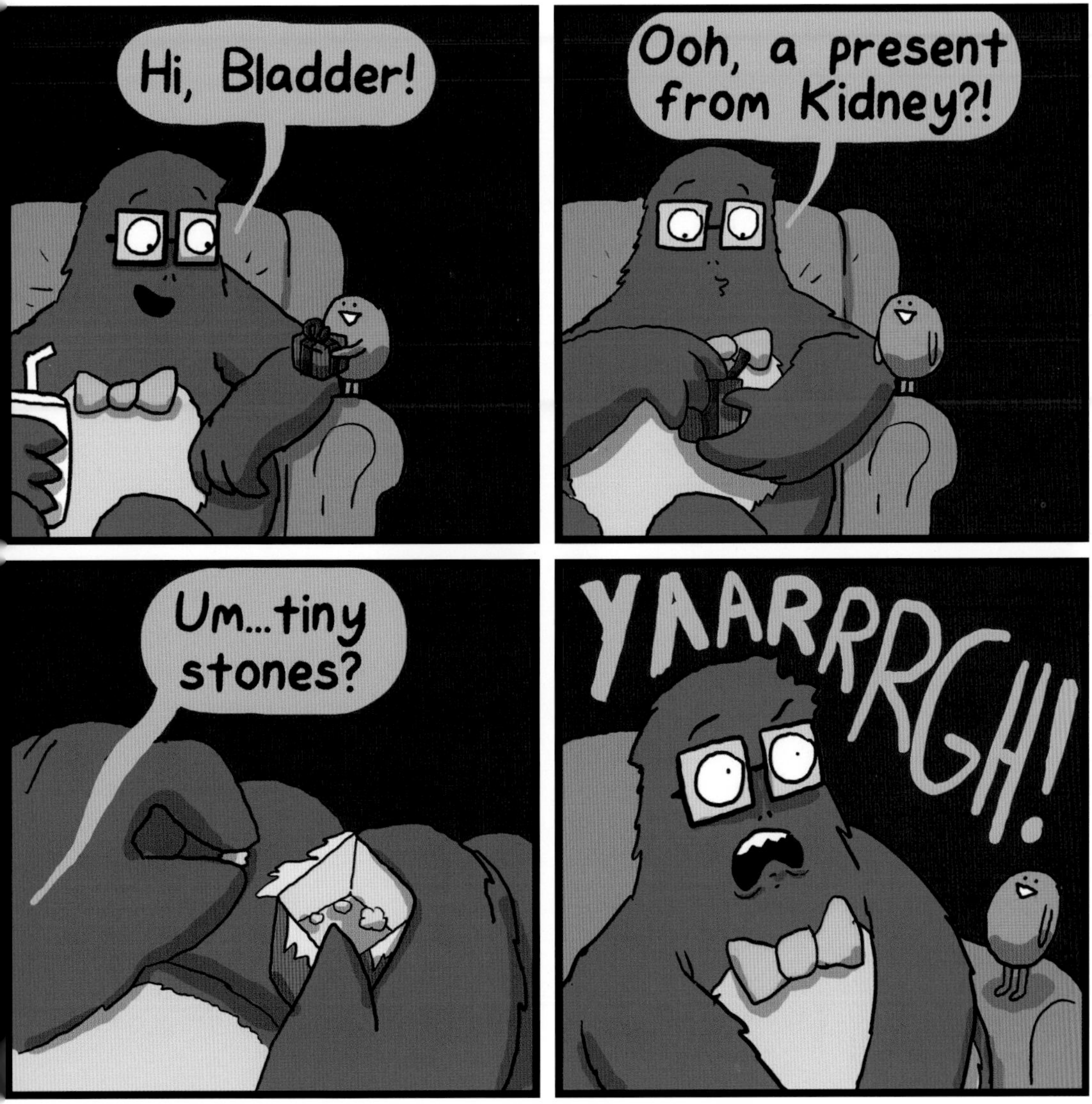
Hi, Bladder!
Ooh, a present from Kidney?!
Um...tiny stones?
YAARRRGH!

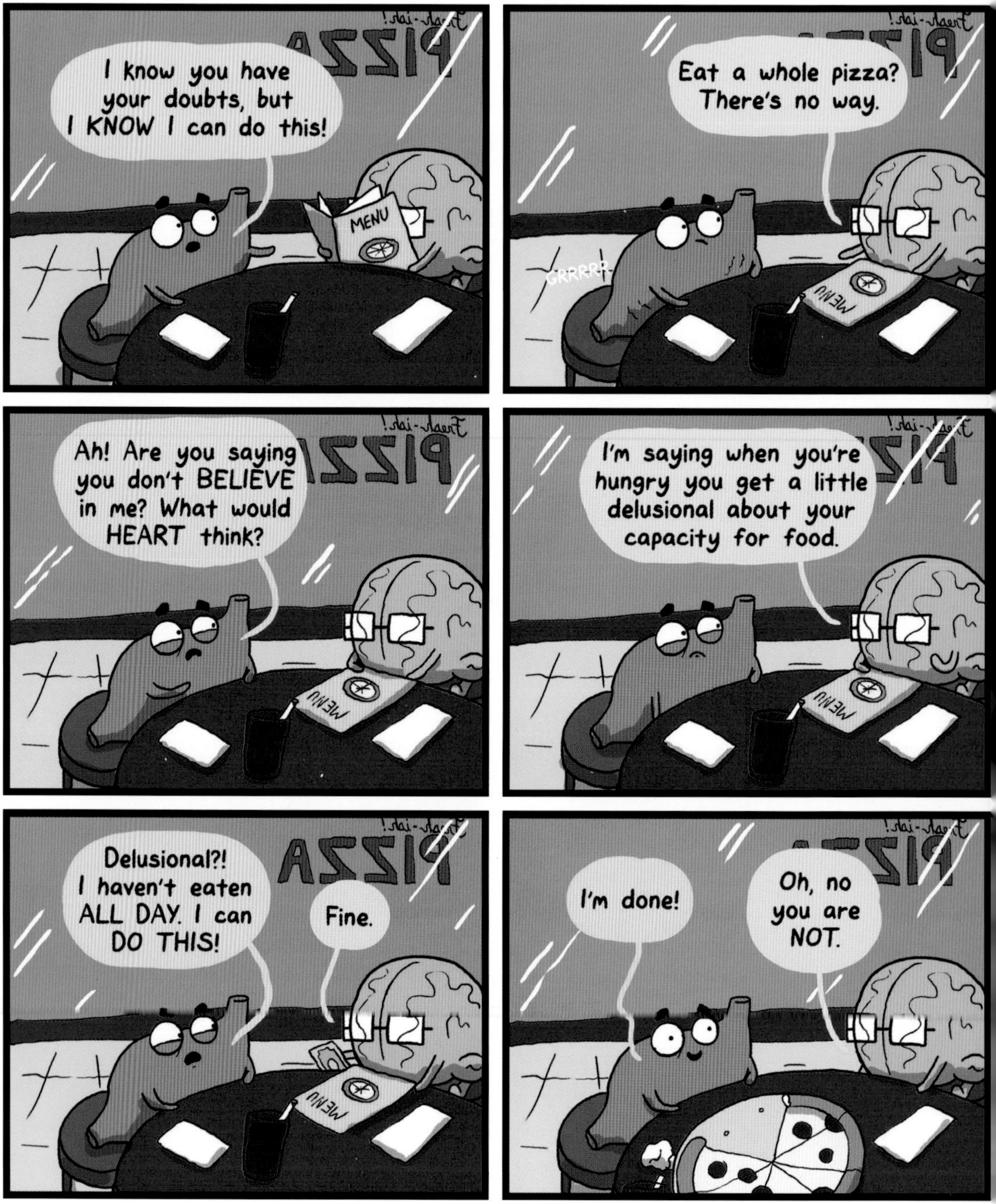
I know you have your doubts, but I KNOW I can do this!
MENU
Eat a whole pizza? There's no way.
GRRRRR
Ah! Are you saying you don't BELIEVE in me? What would HEART think?
I'm saying when you're hungry you get a little delusional about your capacity for food.
Delusional?! I haven't eaten ALL DAY. I can DO THIS!
Fine.
I'm done!
Oh, no you are NOT.

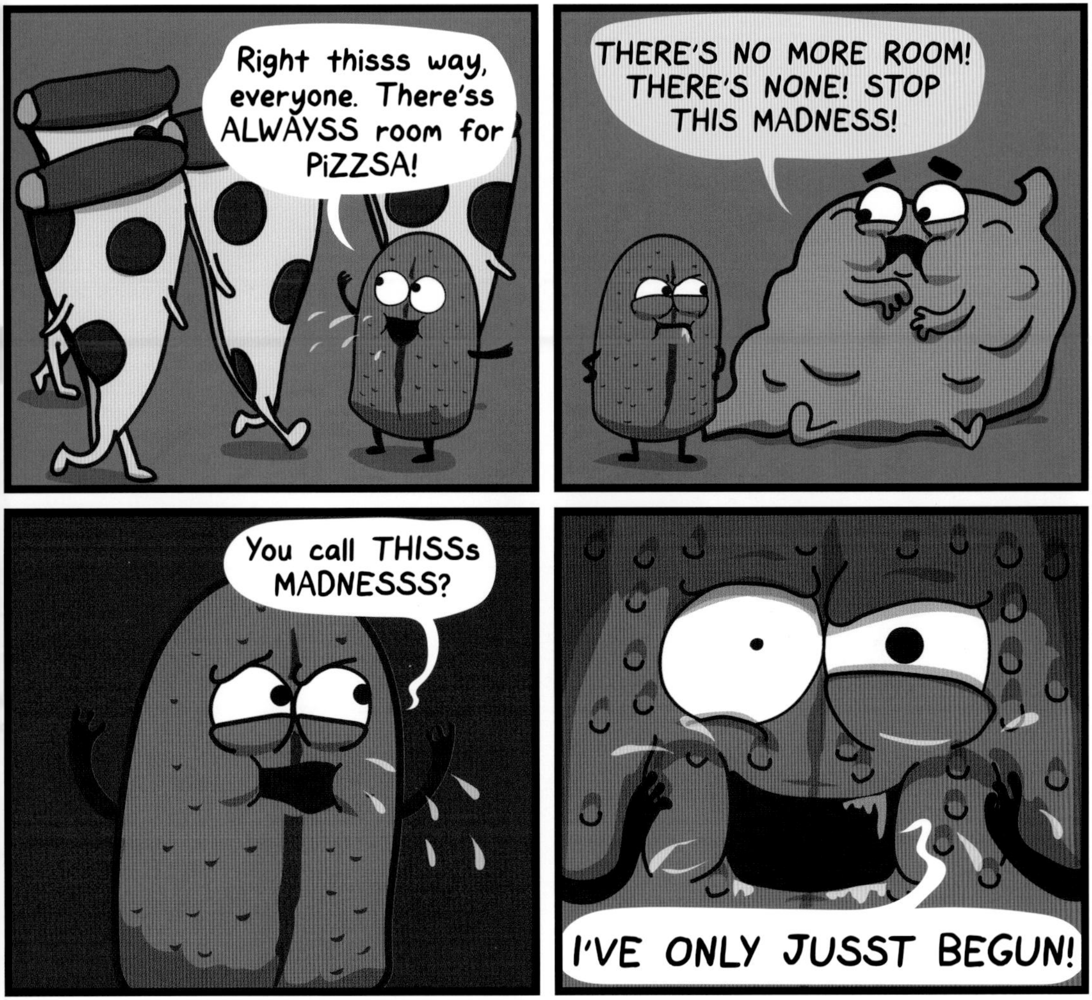
Right thisss way, everyone. There'ss ALWAYSS room for PiZZSA!
THERE'S NO MORE ROOM! THERE'S NONE! STOP THIS MADNESS!
You call THISSs MADNESSS?
I'VE ONLY JUSST BEGUN!

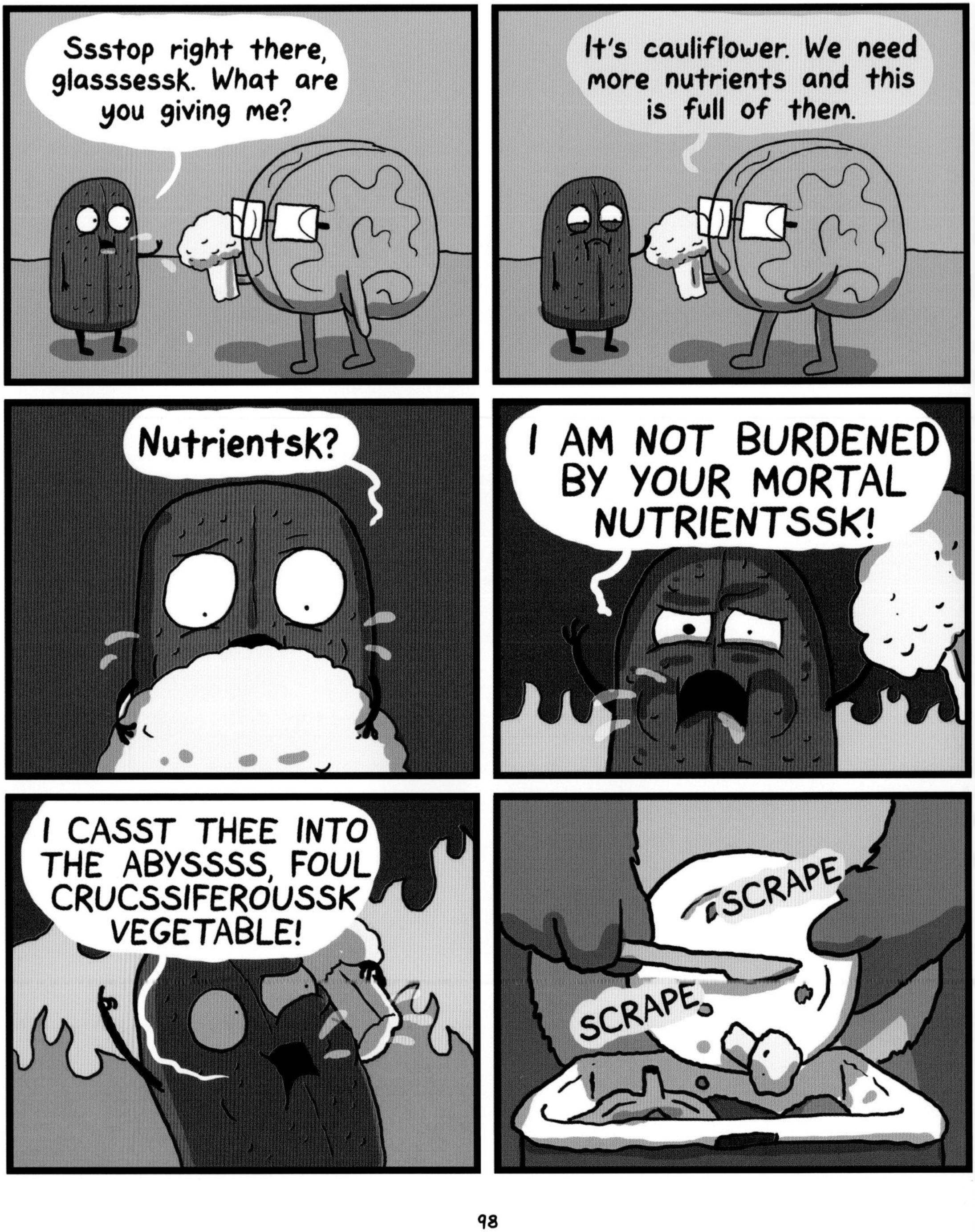
Ssstop right there, glasssessk. What are you giving me?
It's cauliflower. We need more nutrients and this is full of them.
Nutrientsk?
I AM NOT BURDENED BY YOUR MORTAL NUTRIENTSSK!
I CASST THEE INTO THE ABYSSSS, FOUL CRUCSSIFEROUSSK VEGETABLE!
SCRAPE
SCRAPE

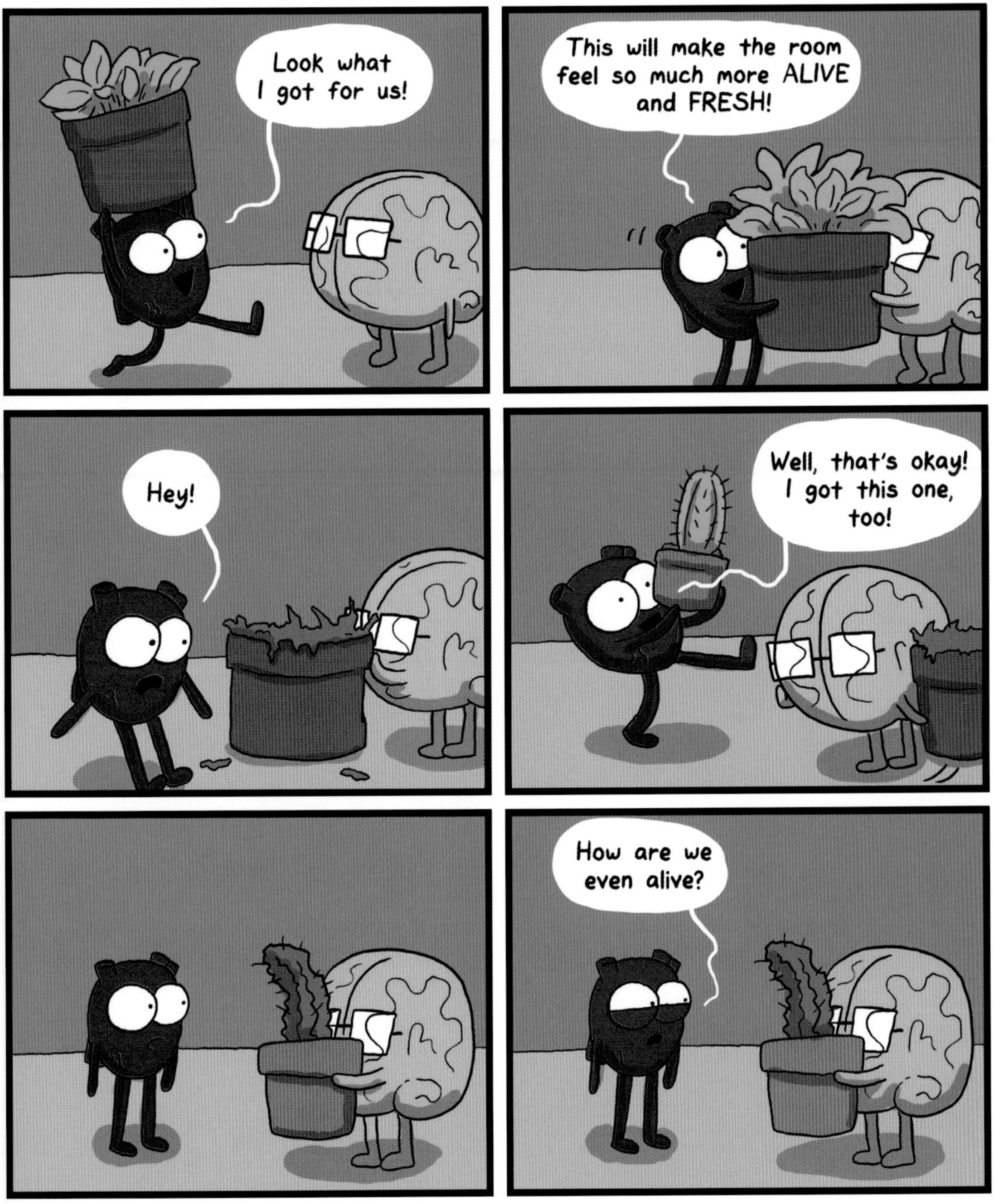
Look what I got for us!
This will make the room feel so much more ALIVE and FRESH!
Hey!
Well, that's okay! I got this one, too!
How are we even alive?

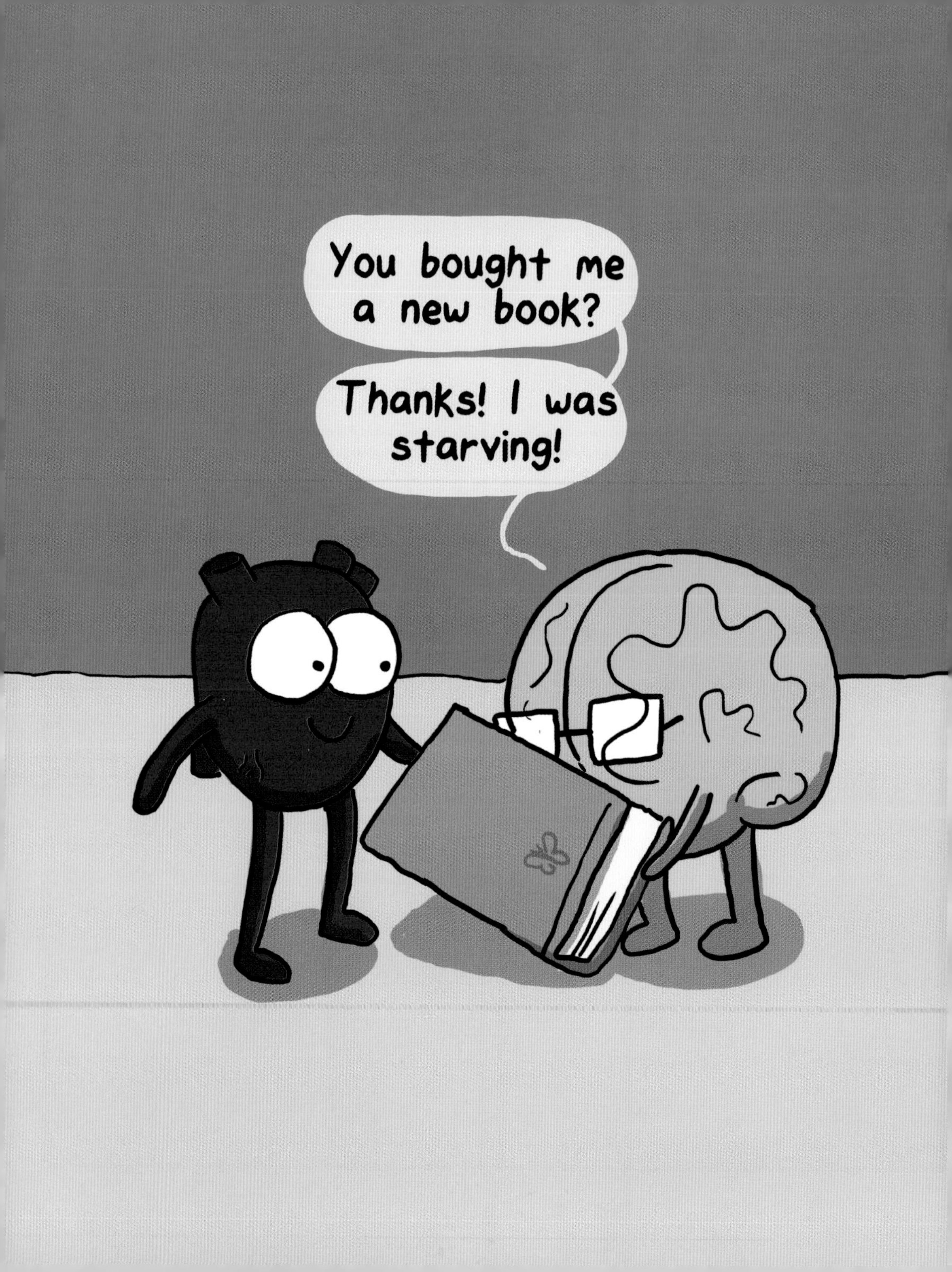
You bought me a new book?
Thanks! I was starving!

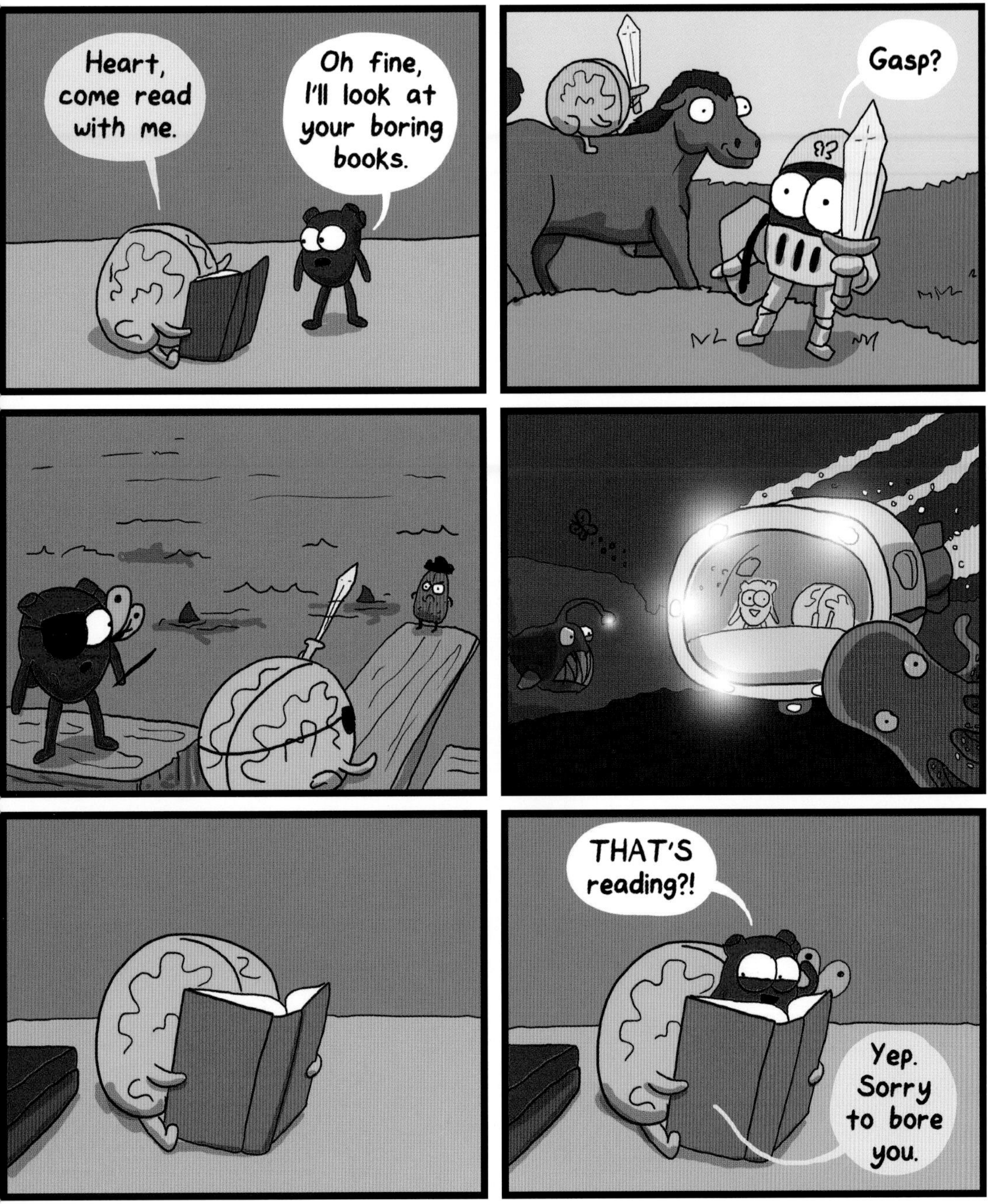
Heart, come read with me.
Oh fine, I'll look at your boring books.
Gasp?
THAT'S reading?!
Yep. Sorry to bore you.

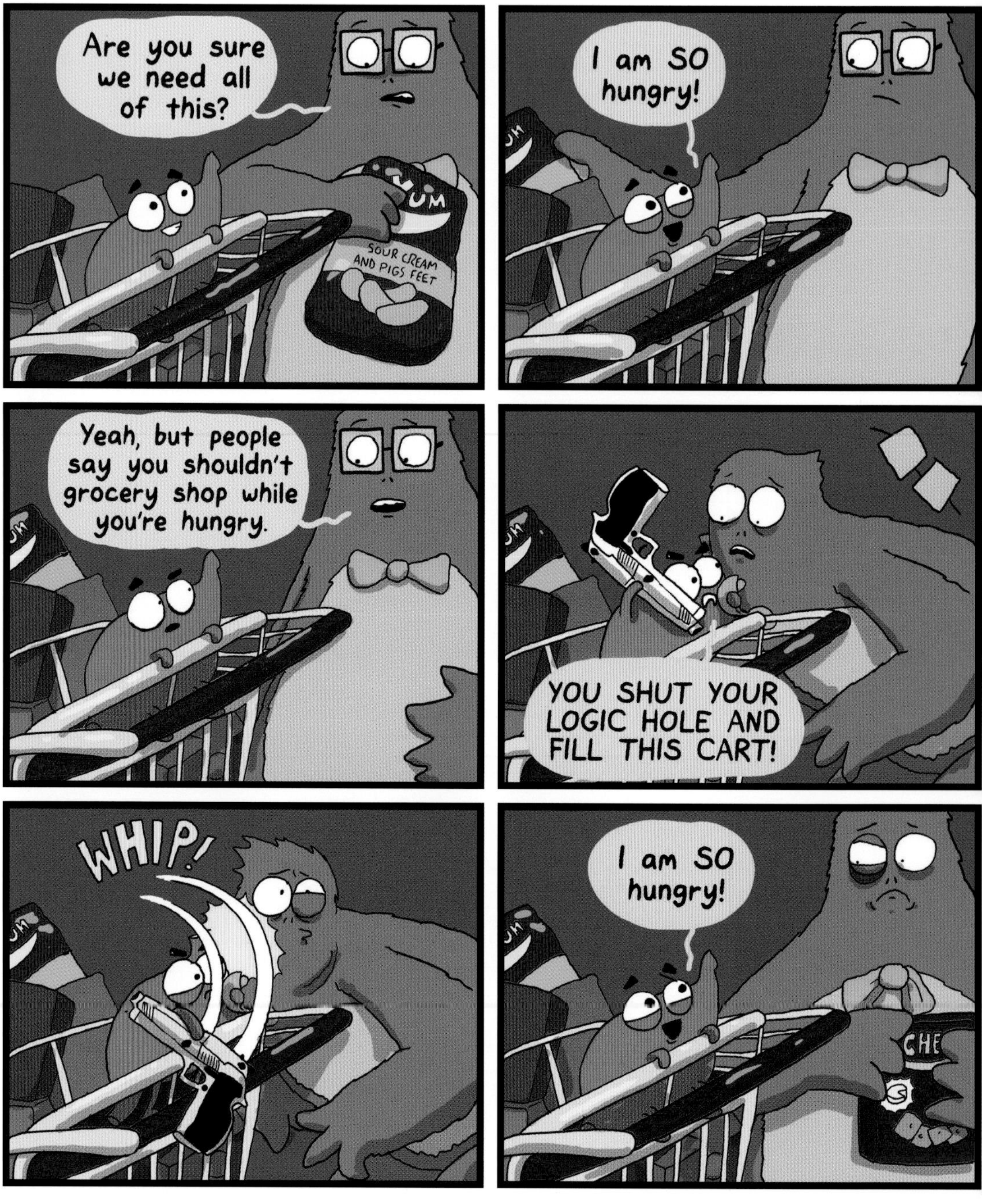
Are you sure we need all of this?
YUM
SOUR CREAM AND PIGS FEET
I am SO hungry!
Yeah, but people say you shouldn't grocery shop while you're hungry.
YOU SHUT YOUR LOGIC HOLE AND FILL THIS CART!
WHIP!
I am SO hungry!
CHE

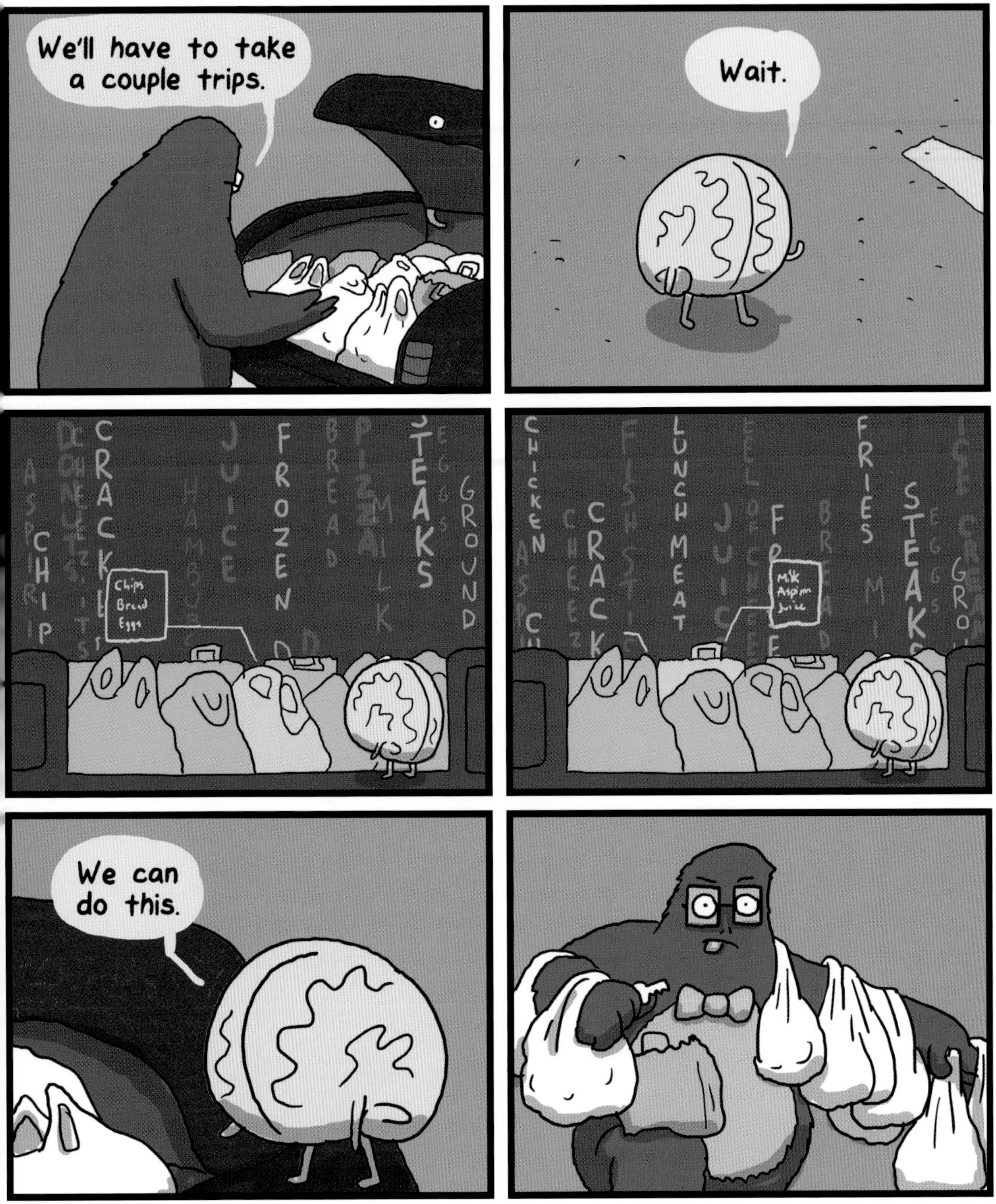
We'll have to take a couple trips.
Wait.
Chips
Bread
Eggs
Milk
Aspirin
Juice
We can do this.

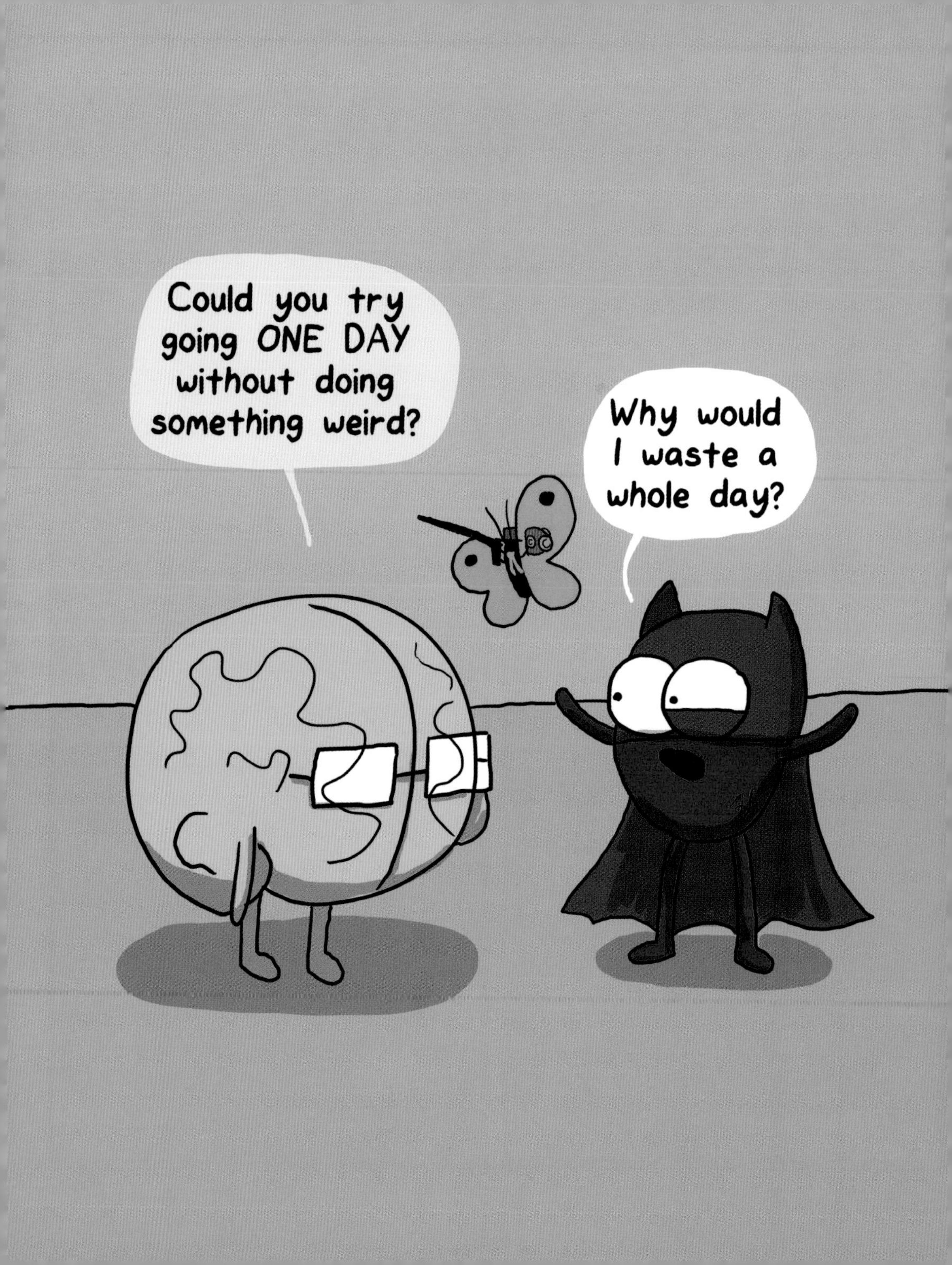
Could you try going ONE DAY without doing something weird?
Why would I waste a whole day?

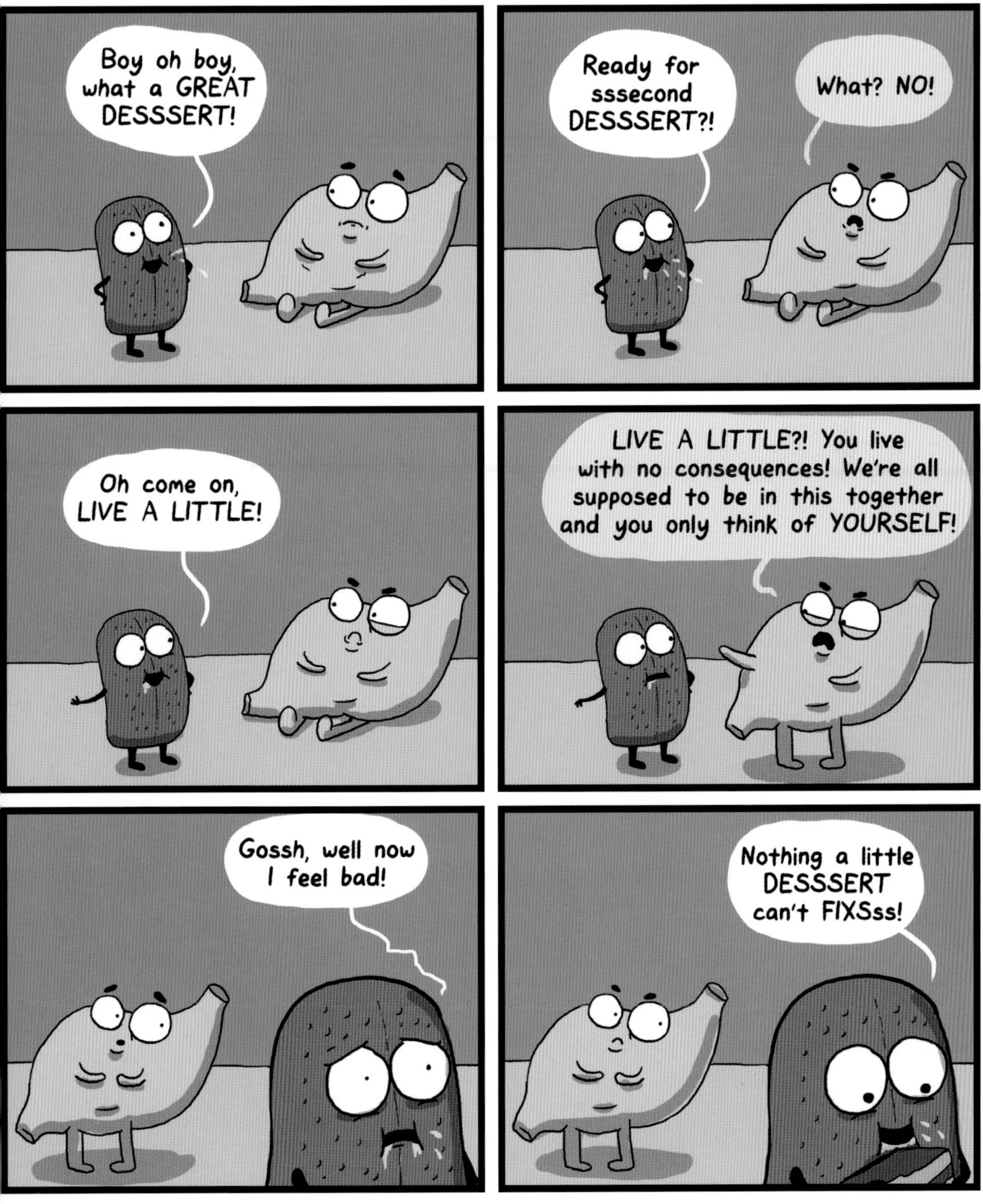
Boy oh boy, what a GREAT DESSSERT!
Ready for sssecond DESSSERT?!
What? NO!
Oh come on, LIVE A LITTLE!
LIVE A LITTLE?! You live with no consequences! We're all supposed to be in this together and you only think of YOURSELF!
Gossh, well now I feel bad!
Nothing a little DESSSERT can't FIXSss!

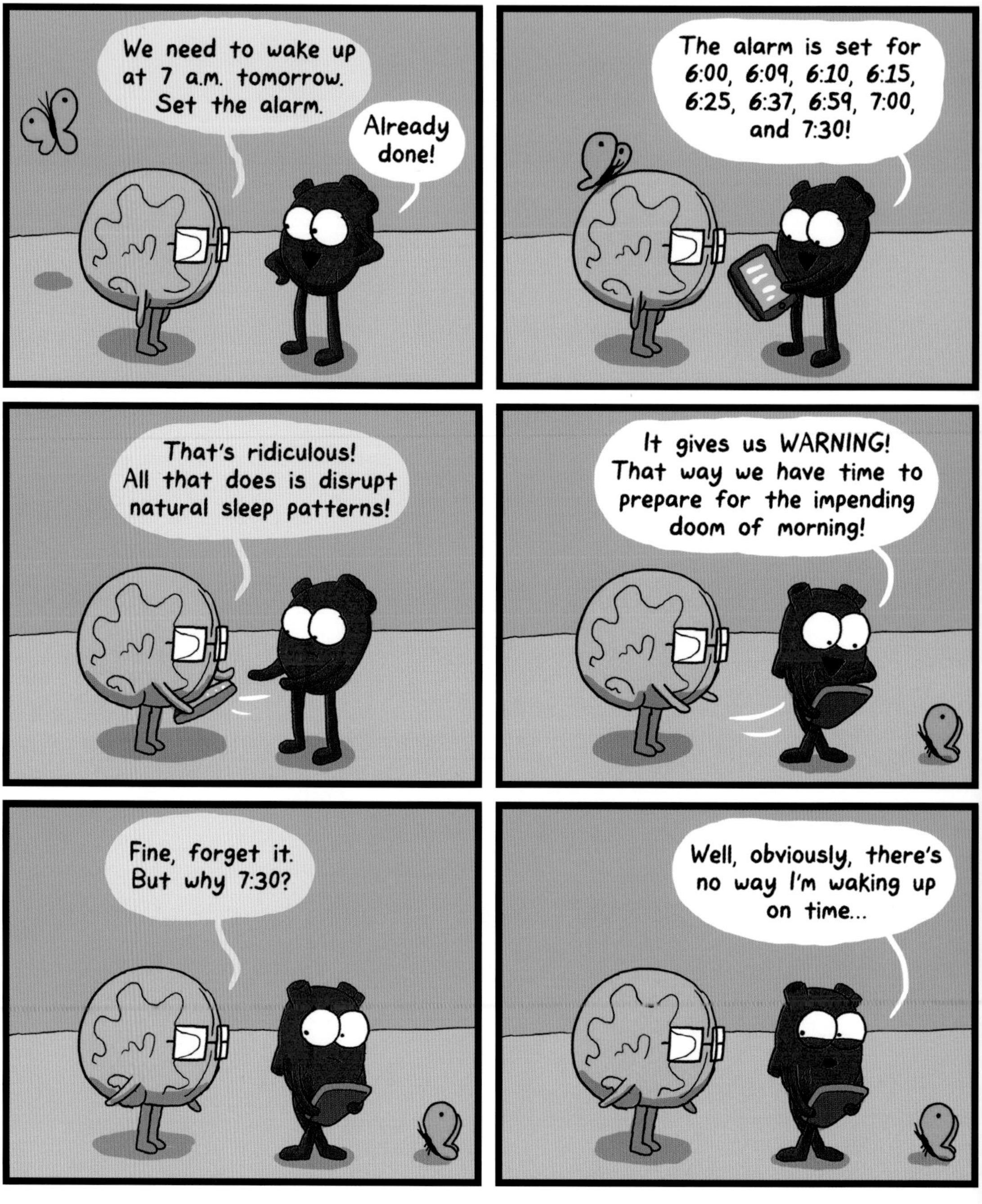
We need to wake up at 7 a.m. tomorrow. Set the alarm.
Already done!
The alarm is set for 6:00, 6:09, 6:10, 6:15, 6:25, 6:37, 6:59, 7:00, and 7:30!
That's ridiculous! All that does is disrupt natural sleep patterns!
It gives us WARNING! That way we have time to prepare for the impending doom of morning!
Fine, forget it. But why 7:30?
Well, obviously, there's no way I'm waking up on time...

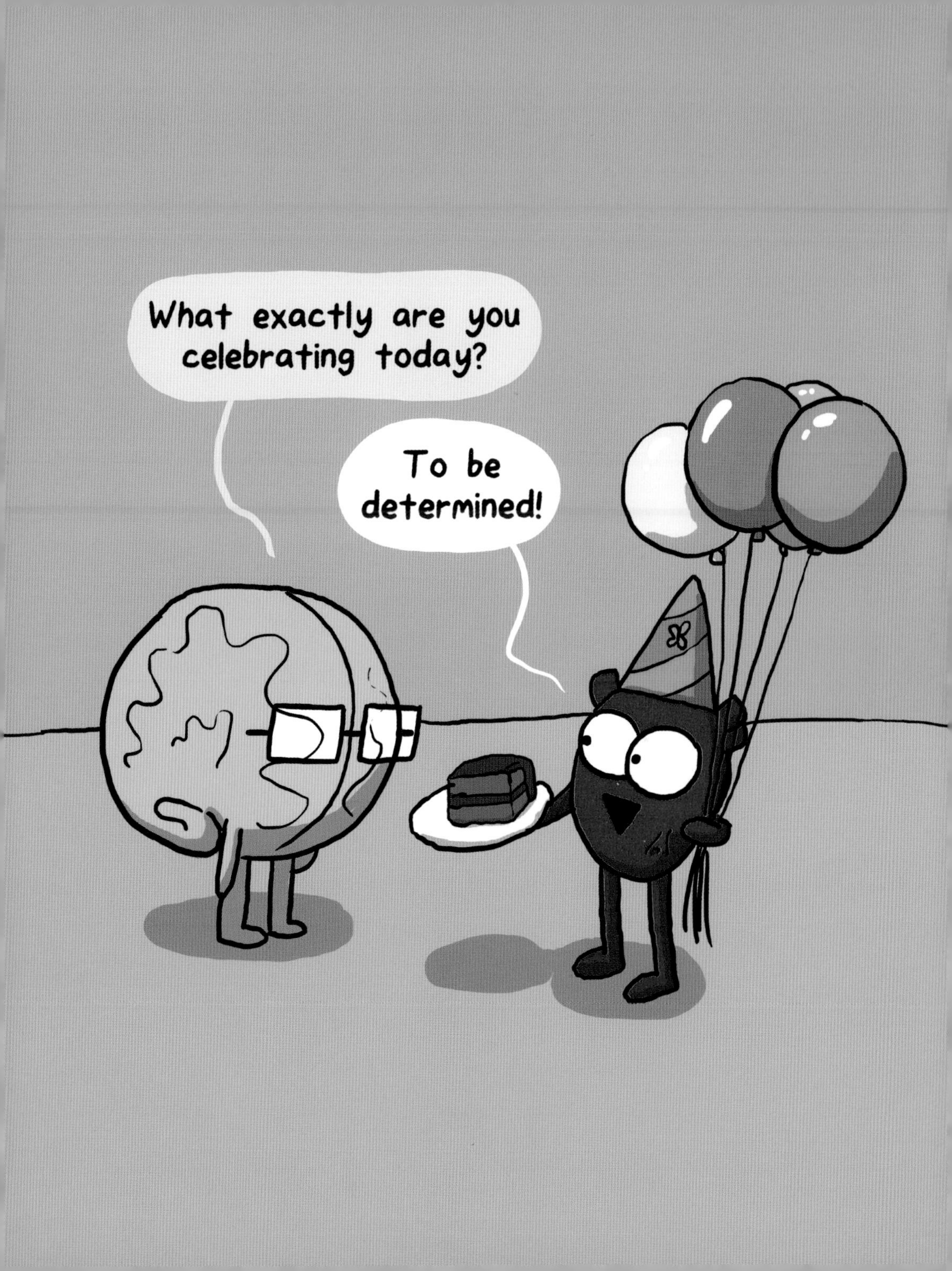
What exactly are you celebrating today?
To be determined!

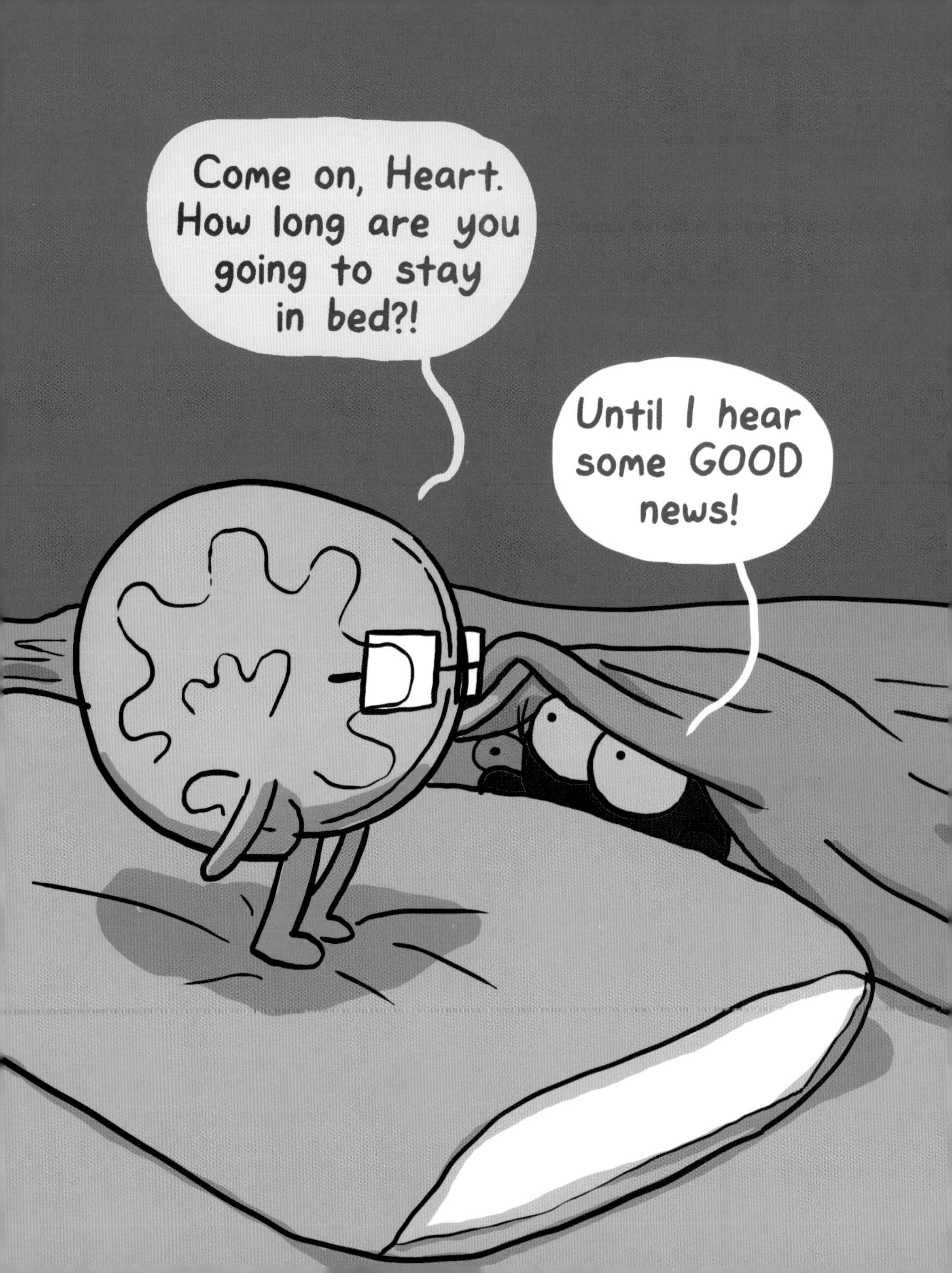
Come on, Heart. How long are you going to stay in bed?!
Until I hear some GOOD news!

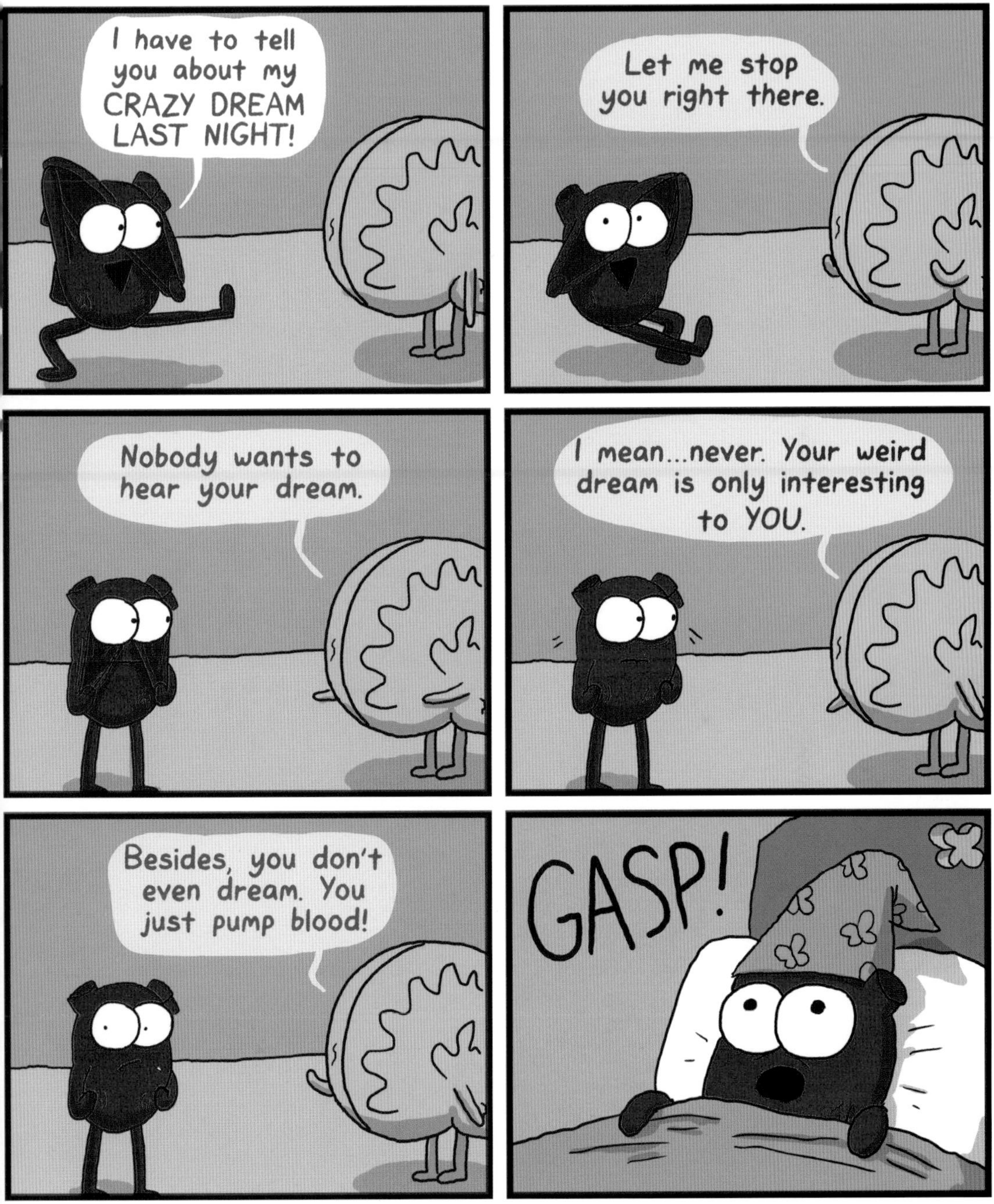
I have to tell you about my CRAZY DREAM LAST NIGHT!
Let me stop you right there.
Nobody wants to hear your dream.
I mean...never. Your weird dream is only interesting to YOU.
Besides, you don't even dream. You just pump blood!
GASP!

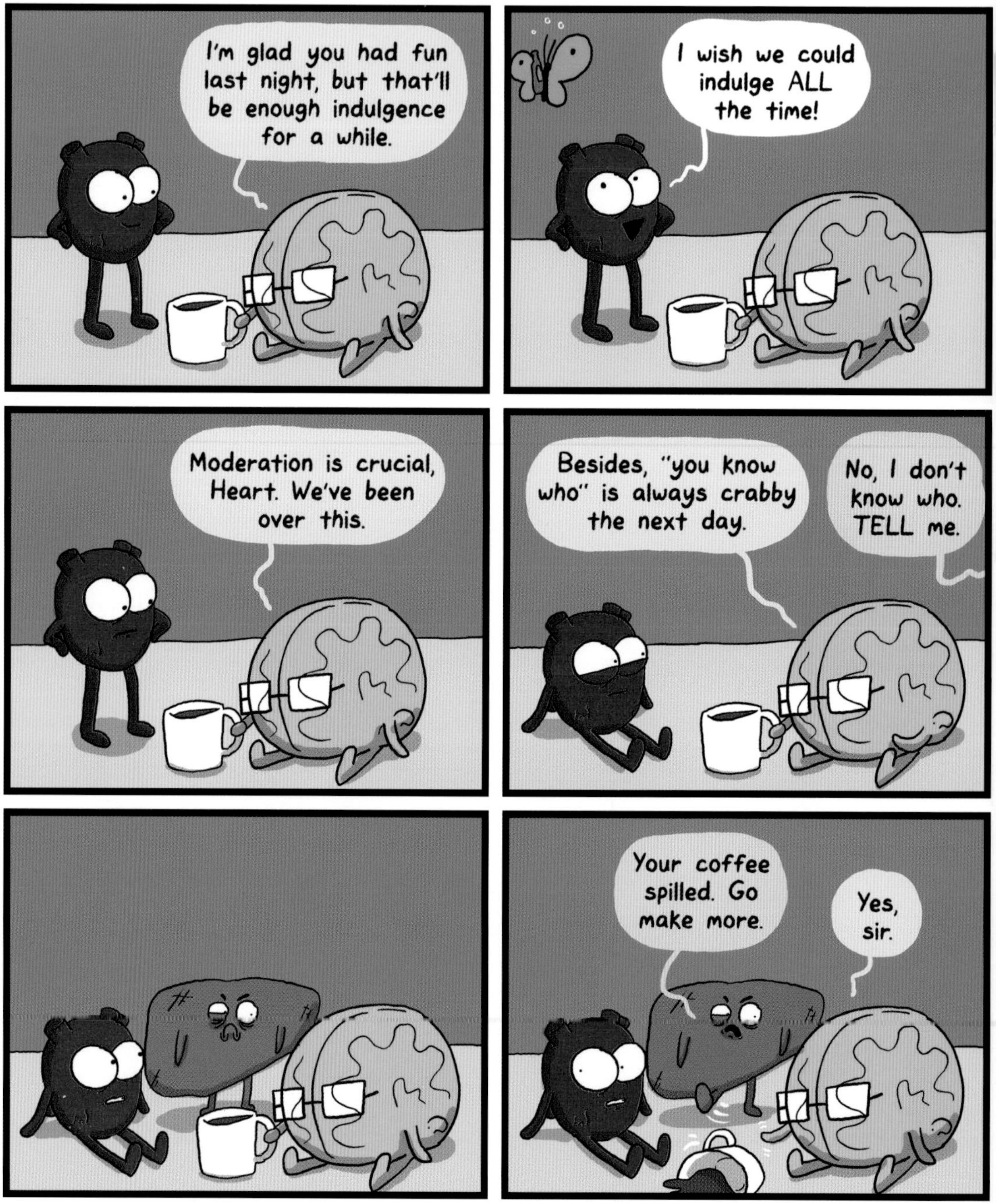
I'm glad you had fun last night, but that'll be enough indulgence for a while.
I wish we could indulge ALL the time!
Moderation is crucial, Heart. We've been over this.
Besides, "you know who" is always crabby the next day.
No, I don't know who. TELL me.
Your coffee spilled. Go make more.
Yes, sir.

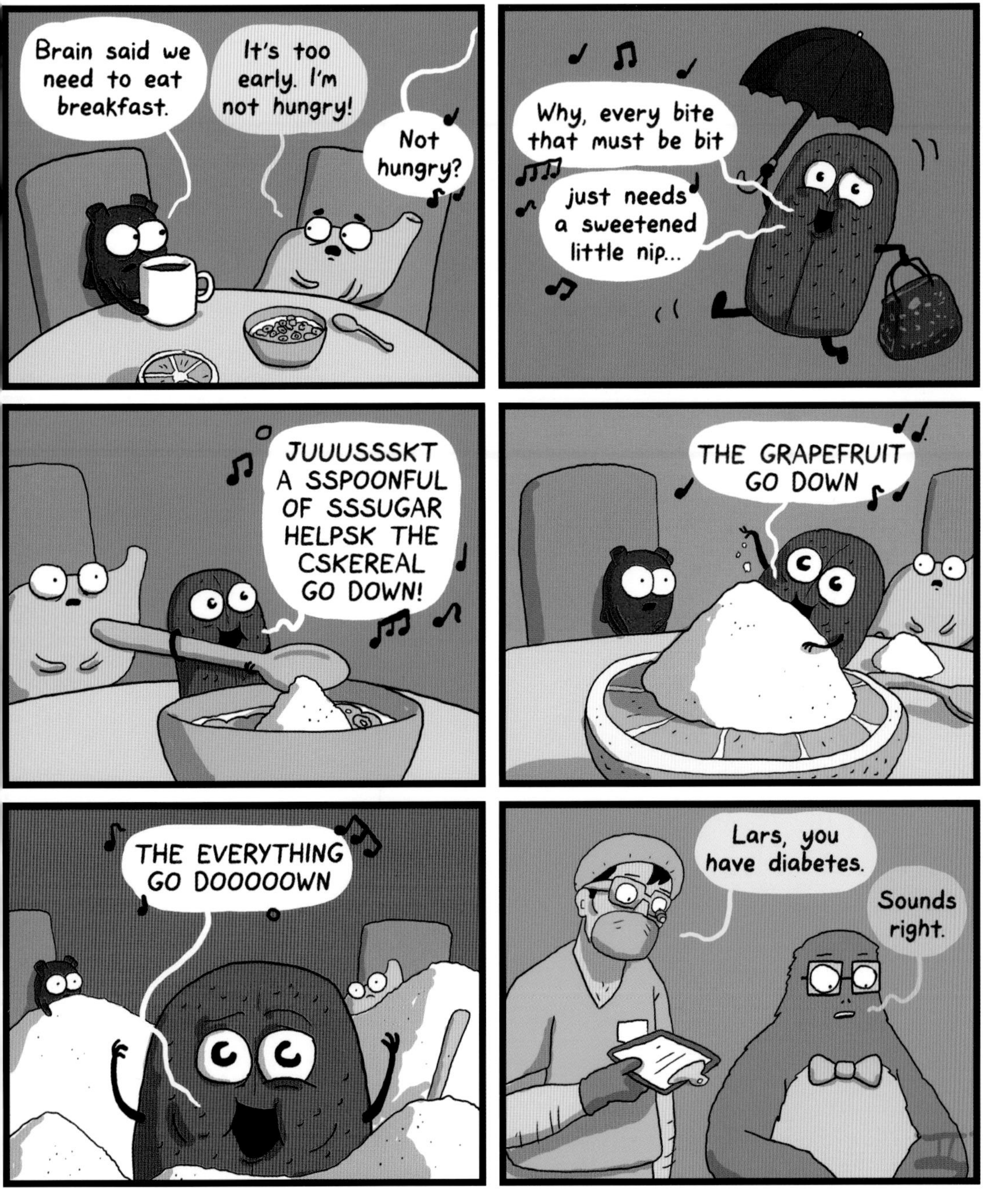
Brain said we need to eat breakfast.
It's too early. I'm not hungry!
Not hungry?
Why, every bite that must be bit
just needs a sweetened little nip...
JUUUSSSKT A SSPOONFUL OF SSSUGAR HELPSK THE CSKEREAL GO DOWN!
THE GRAPEFRUIT GO DOWN
THE EVERYTHING GO DOOOOOWN
Lars, you have diabetes.
Sounds right.

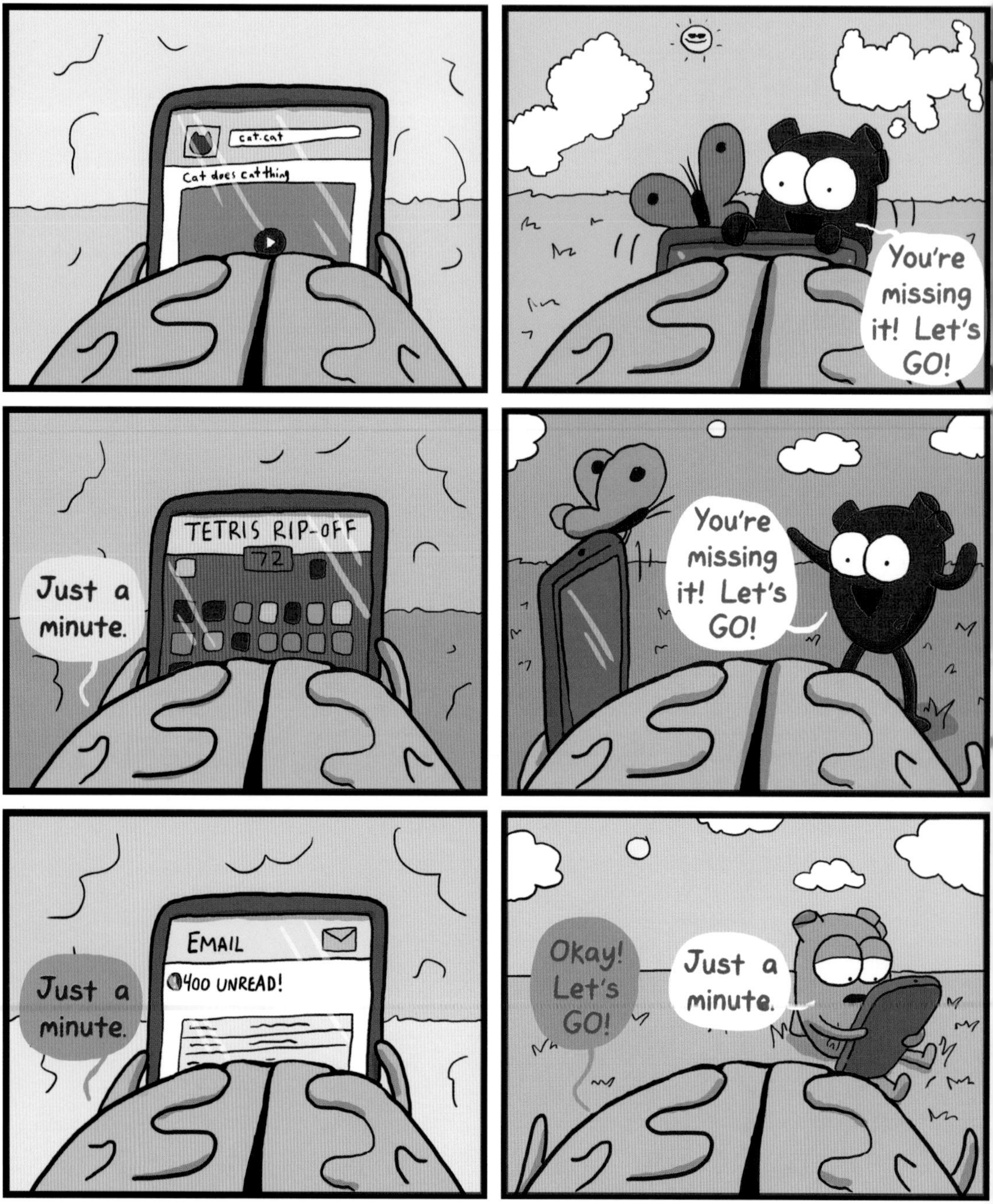
cat.cat
Cat does cat thing
You're missing it! Let's GO!
TETRIS RIP-OFF
72
Just a minute.
You're missing it! Let's GO!
EMAIL
400 UNREAD!
Just a minute.
Okay! Let's GO!
Just a minute.

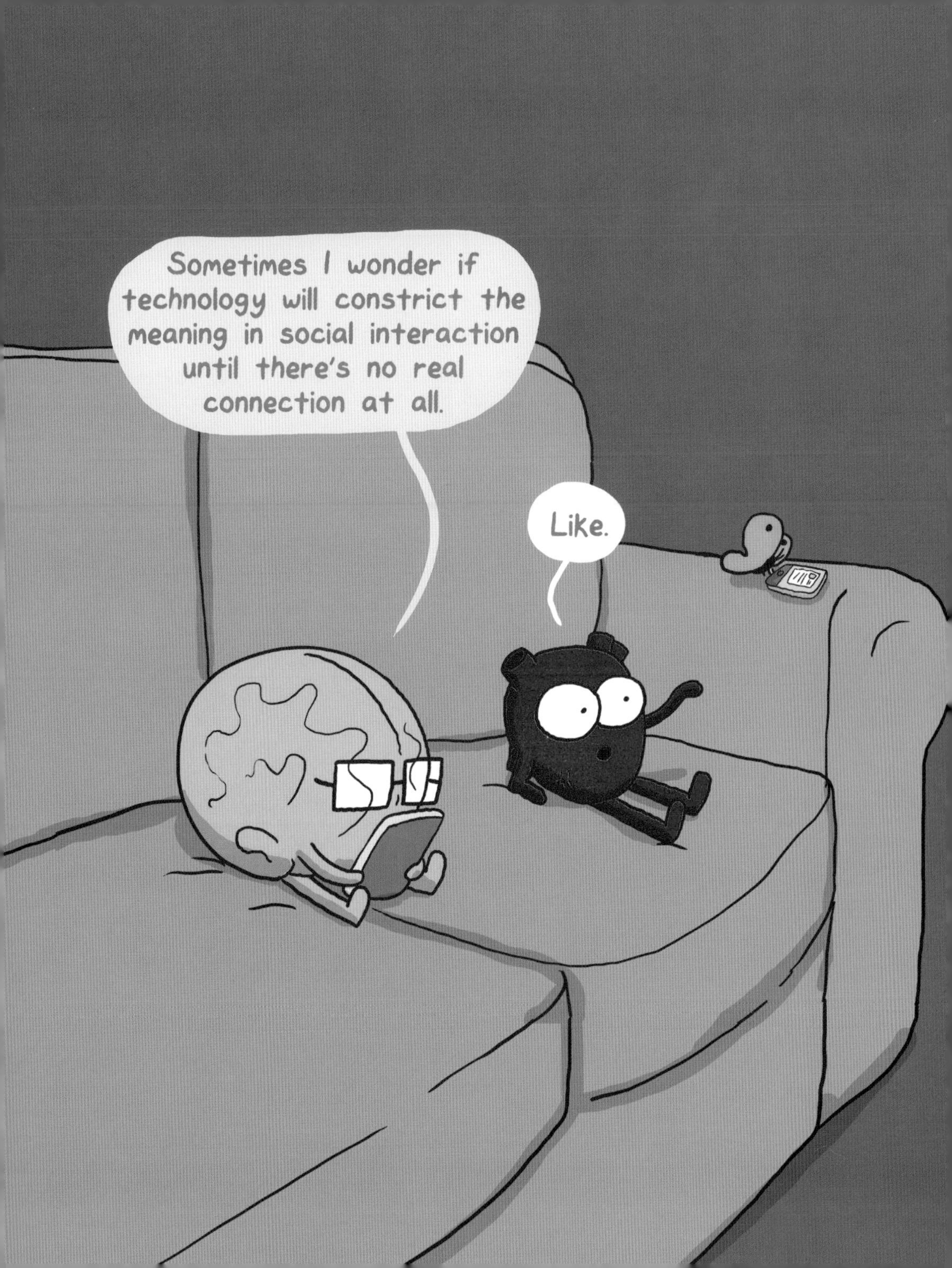
Sometimes I wonder if technology will constrict the meaning in social interaction until there's no real connection at all.
Like.

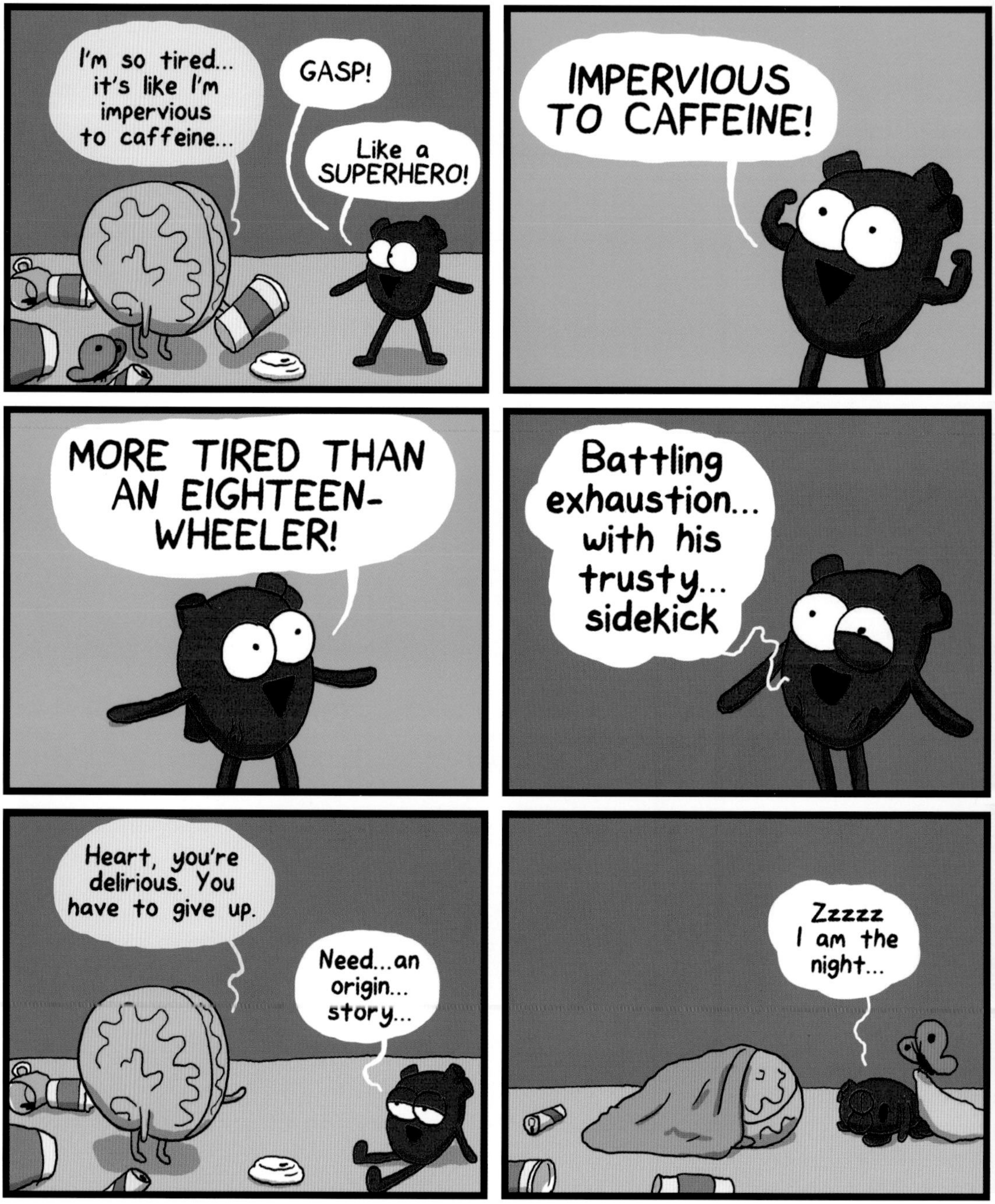
I'm so tired... it's like I'm impervious to caffeine...
GASP!
Like a SUPERHERO!
IMPERVIOUS TO CAFFEINE!
MORE TIRED THAN AN EIGHTEEN-WHEELER!
Battling exhaustion... with his trusty... sidekick
Heart, you're delirious. You have to give up.
Need...an origin... story...
Zzzzz I am the night...

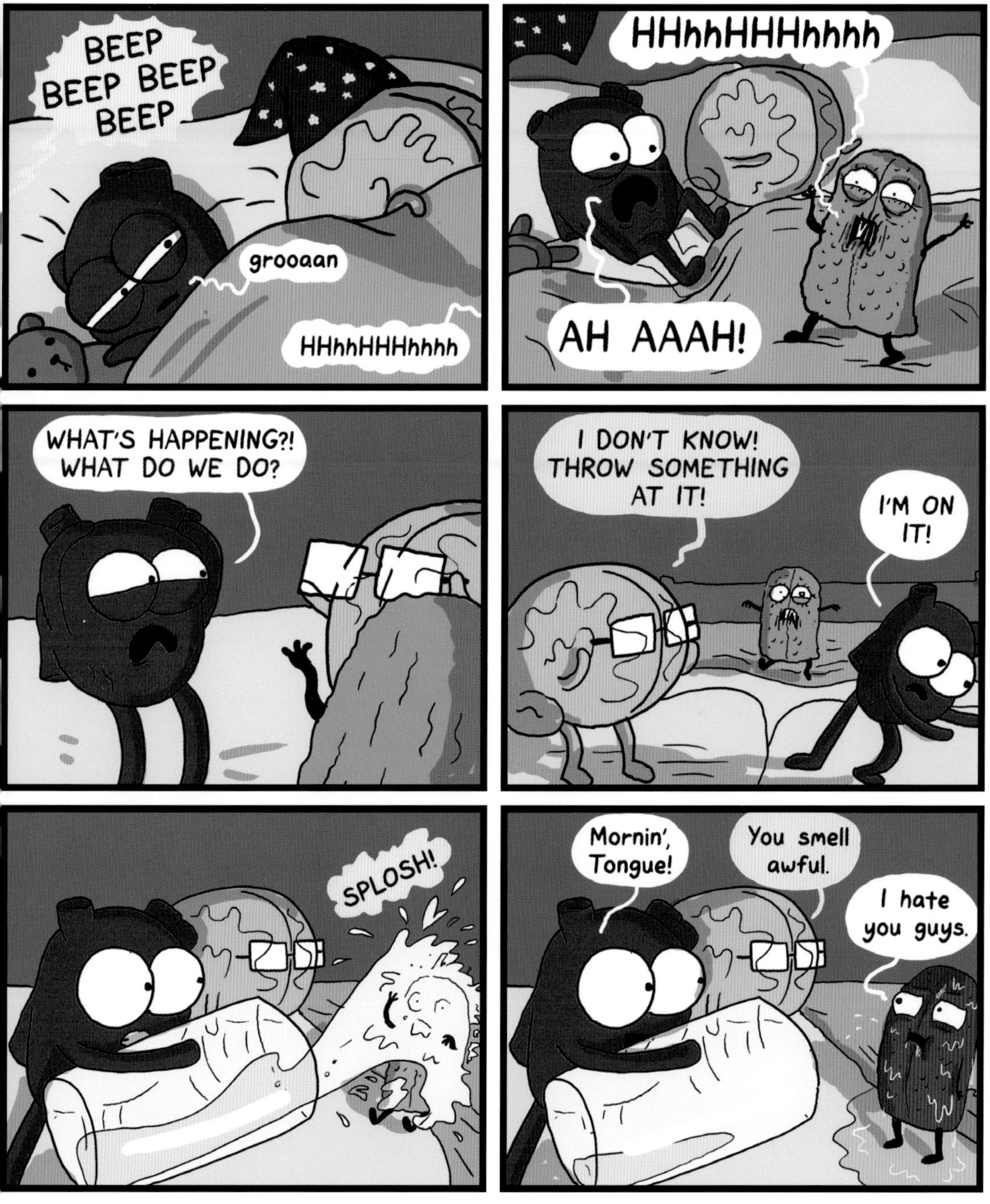
BEEP BEEP BEEP BEEP
grooaan
HHhhHHHhhhh
HHhhHHHhhhh
AH AAAH!
WHAT'S HAPPENING?! WHAT DO WE DO?
I DON'T KNOW! THROW SOMETHING AT IT!
I'M ON IT!
SPLOSH!
Mornin', Tongue!
You smell awful.
I hate you guys.

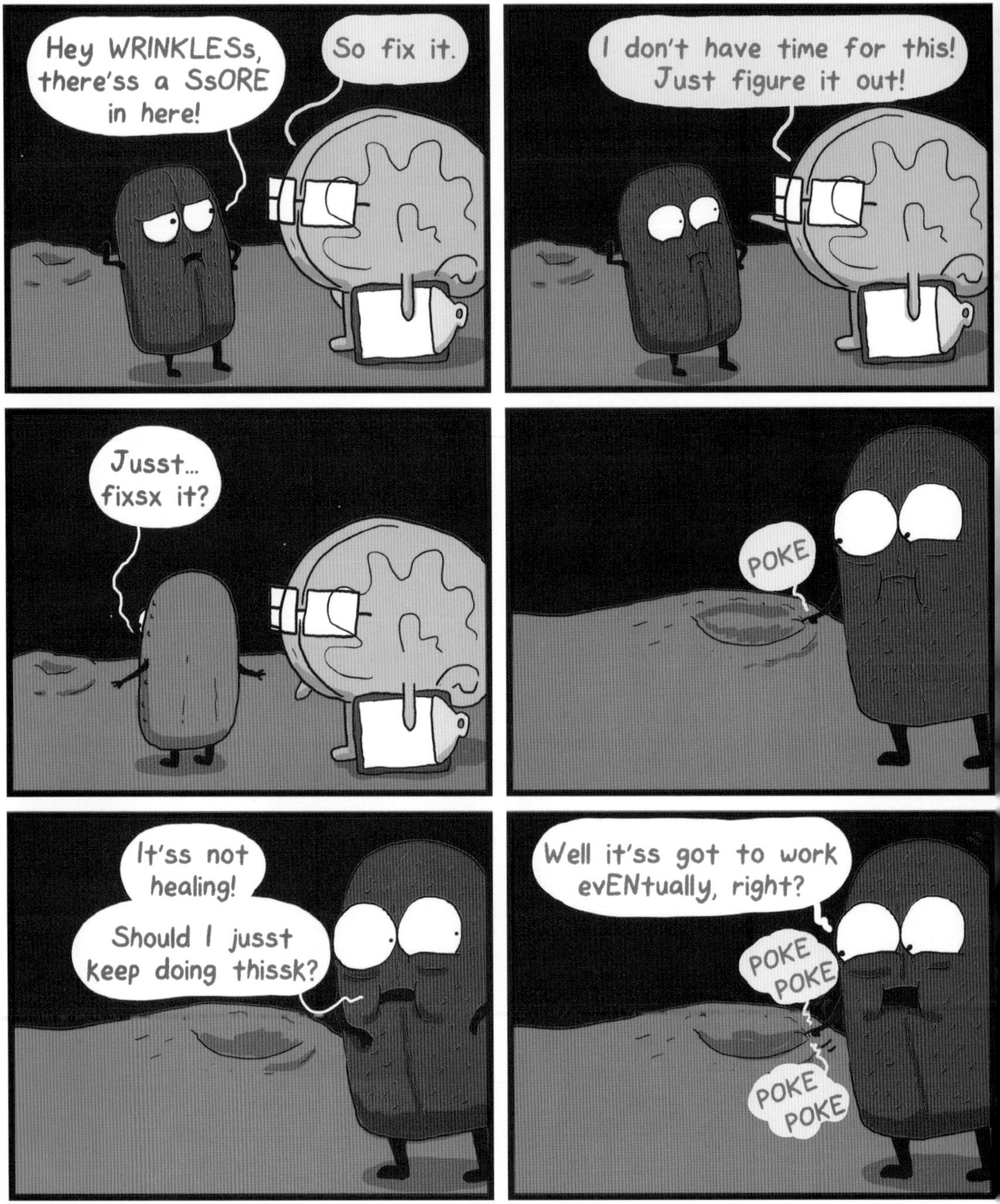
Hey WRINKLESs, there'ss a SsORE in here!
So fix it.
I don't have time for this! Just figure it out!
Jusst... fixsx it?
POKE
It'ss not healing!
Should I jusst keep doing thissk?
Well it'ss got to work evENtually, right?
POKE POKE
POKE POKE

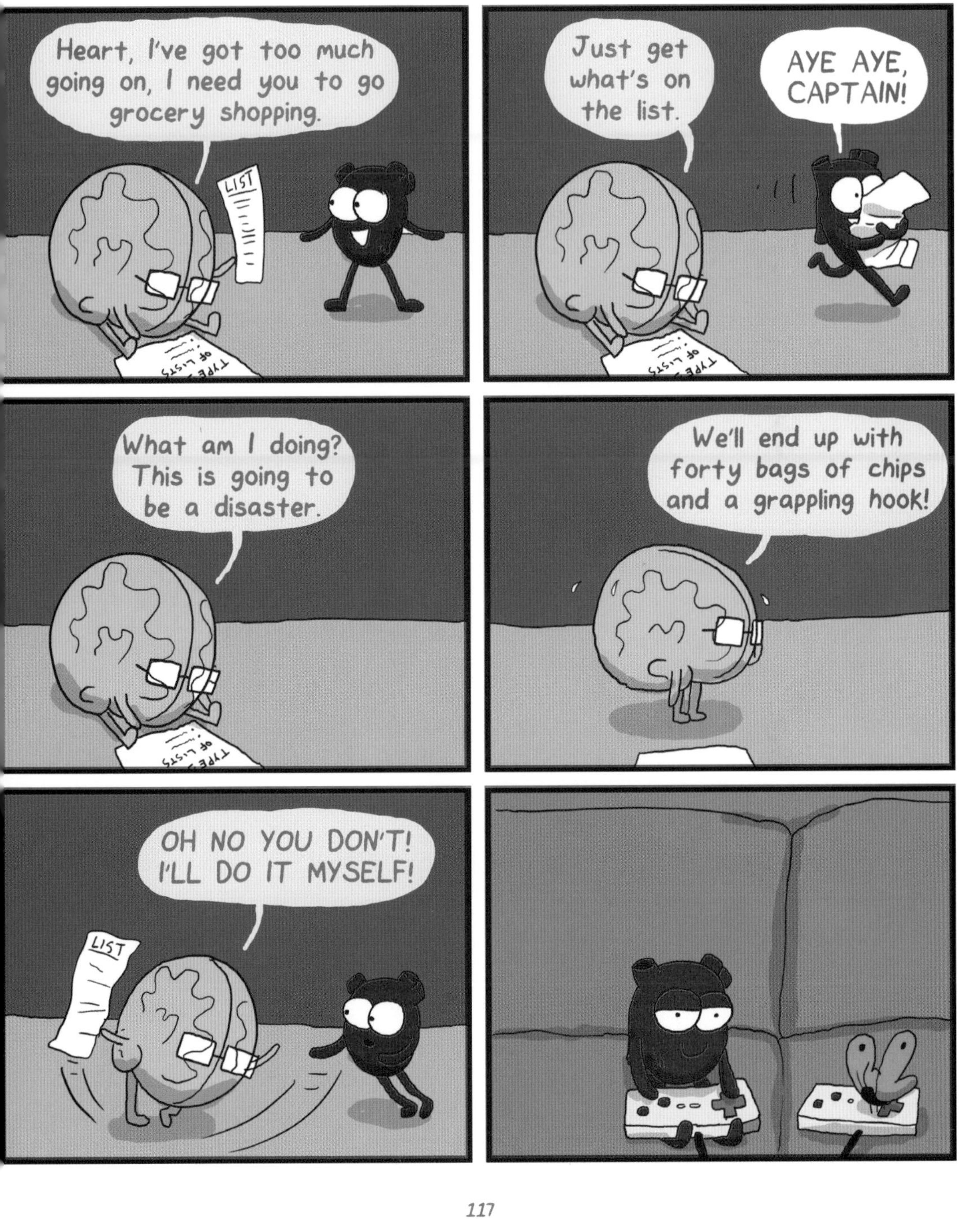
Heart, I've got too much going on, I need you to go grocery shopping.
LIST
Just get what's on the list.
AYE AYE, CAPTAIN!
What am I doing? This is going to be a disaster.
We'll end up with forty bags of chips and a grappling hook!
LIST
OH NO YOU DON'T! I'LL DO IT MYSELF!

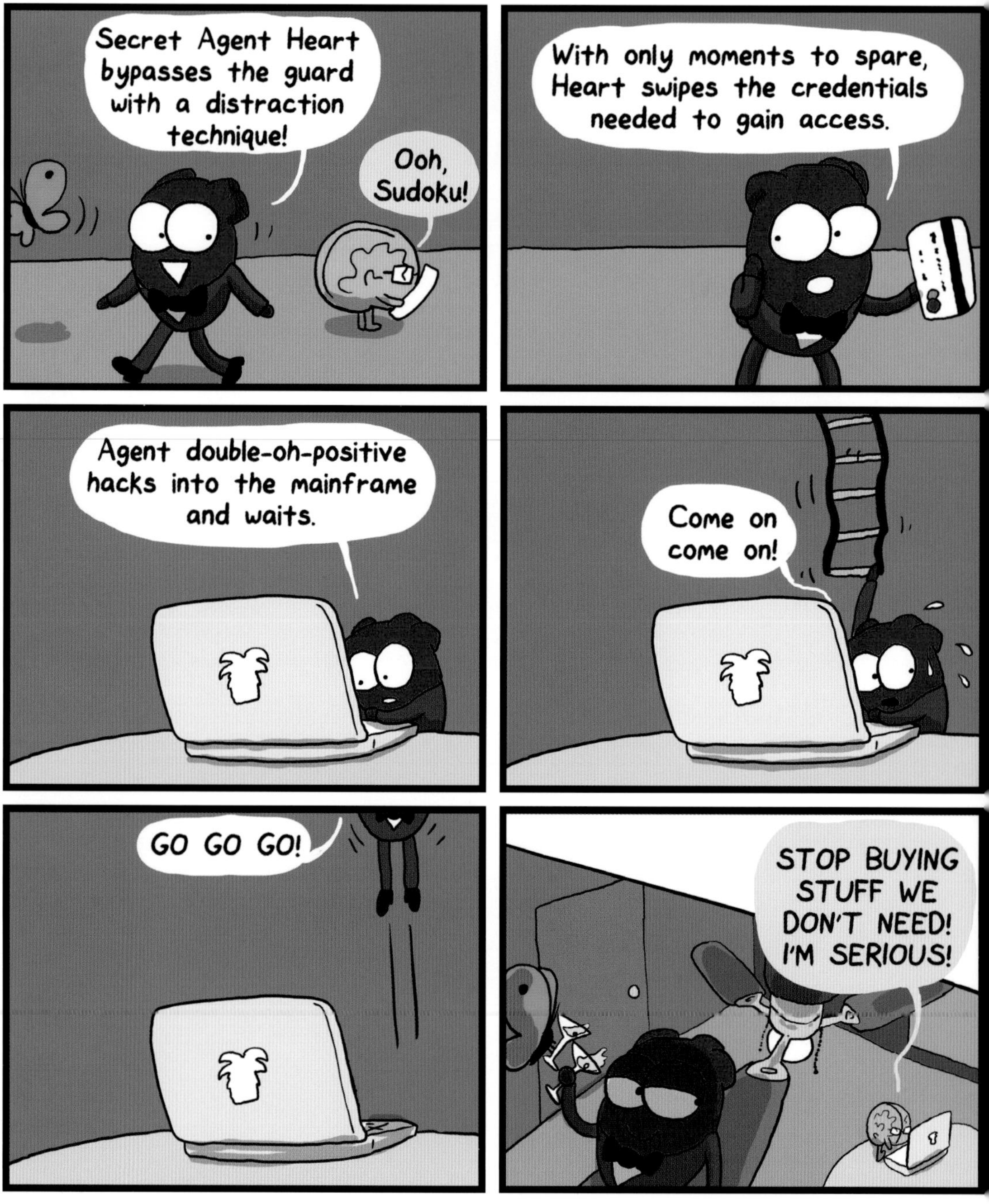
Secret Agent Heart bypasses the guard with a distraction technique!
Ooh, Sudoku!
With only moments to spare, Heart swipes the credentials needed to gain access.
Agent double-oh-positive hacks into the mainframe and waits.
Come on come on!
GO GO GO!
STOP BUYING STUFF WE DON'T NEED! I'M SERIOUS!

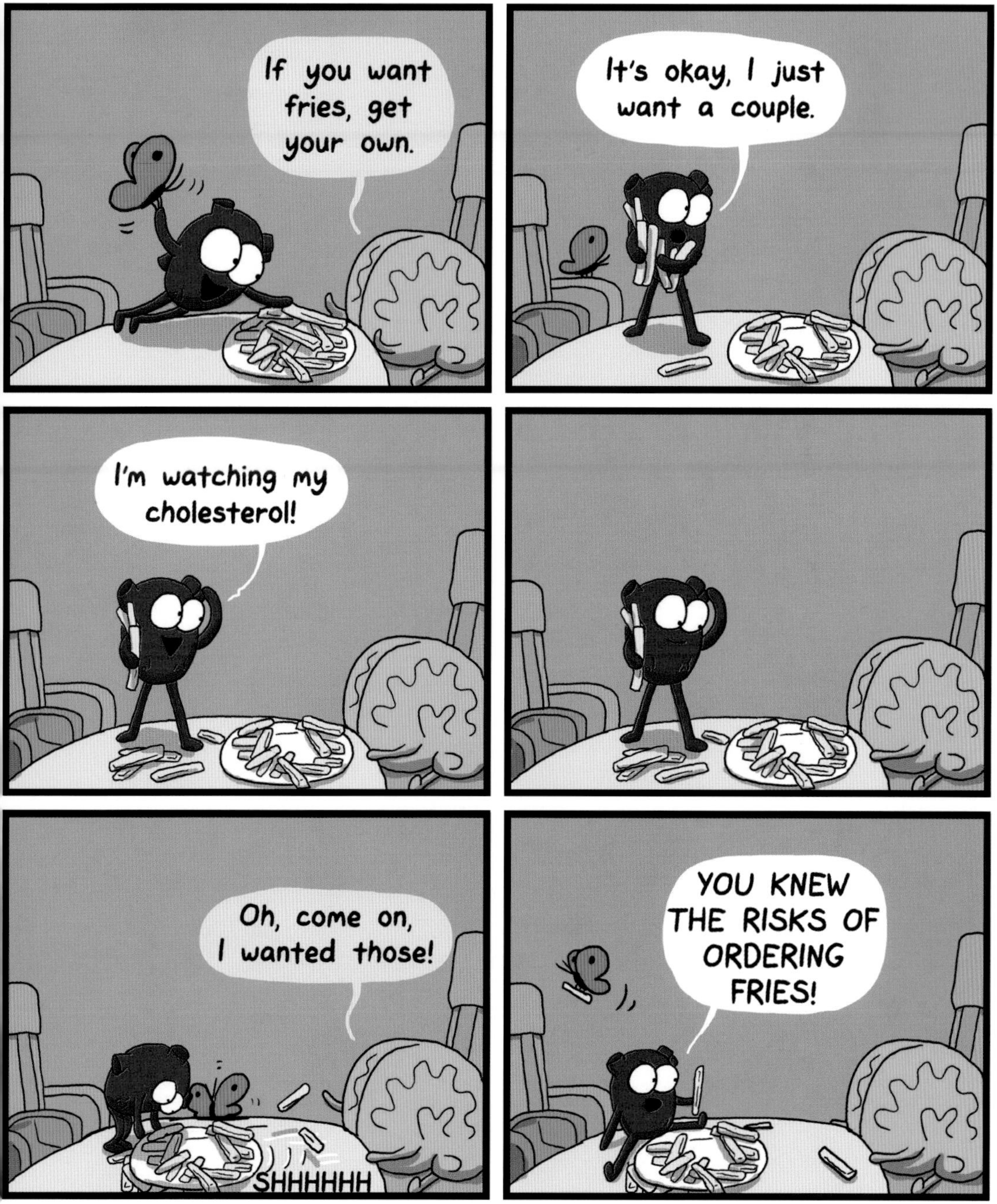
If you want fries, get your own.
It's okay, I just want a couple.
I'm watching my cholesterol!
Oh, come on, I wanted those!
SHHHHHH
YOU KNEW THE RISKS OF ORDERING FRIES!

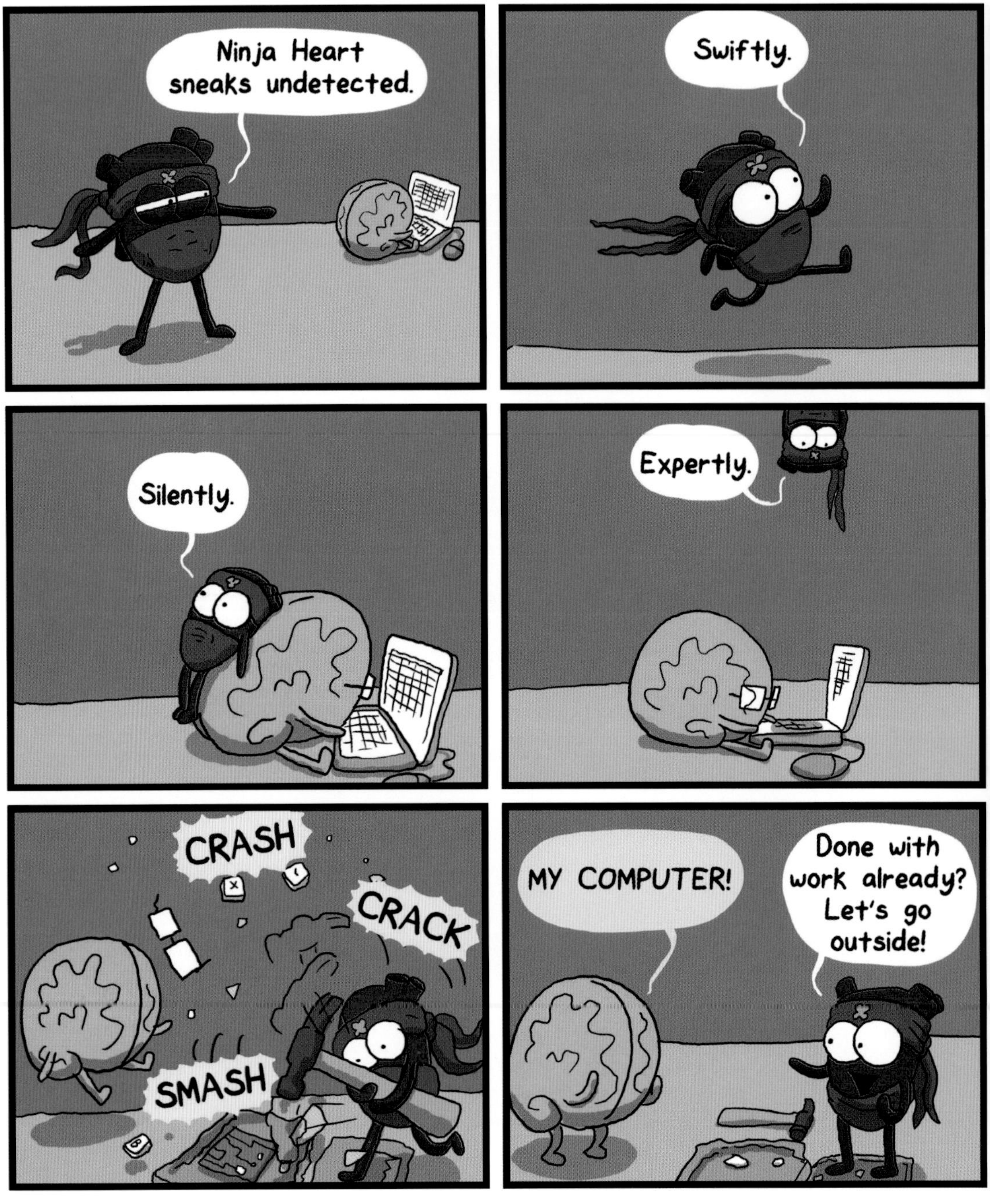
Ninja Heart sneaks undetected.
Swiftly.
Silently.
Expertly.
CRASH
CRACK
SMASH
MY COMPUTER!
Done with work already? Let's go outside!

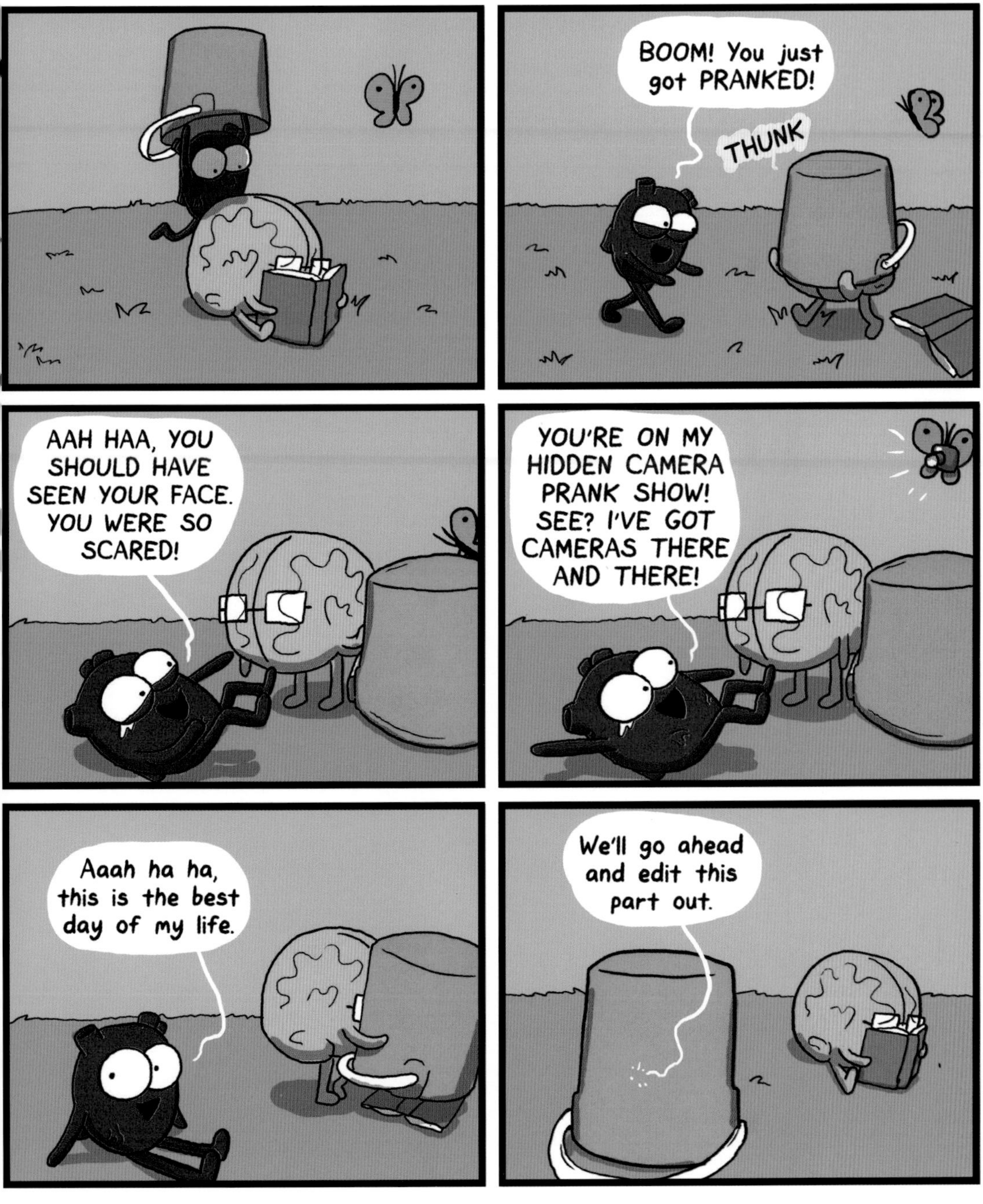
BOOM! You just got PRANKED!
THUNK
AAH HAA, YOU SHOULD HAVE SEEN YOUR FACE. YOU WERE SO SCARED!
YOU'RE ON MY HIDDEN CAMERA PRANK SHOW! SEE? I'VE GOT CAMERAS THERE AND THERE!
Aaah ha ha, this is the best day of my life.
We'll go ahead and edit this part out.

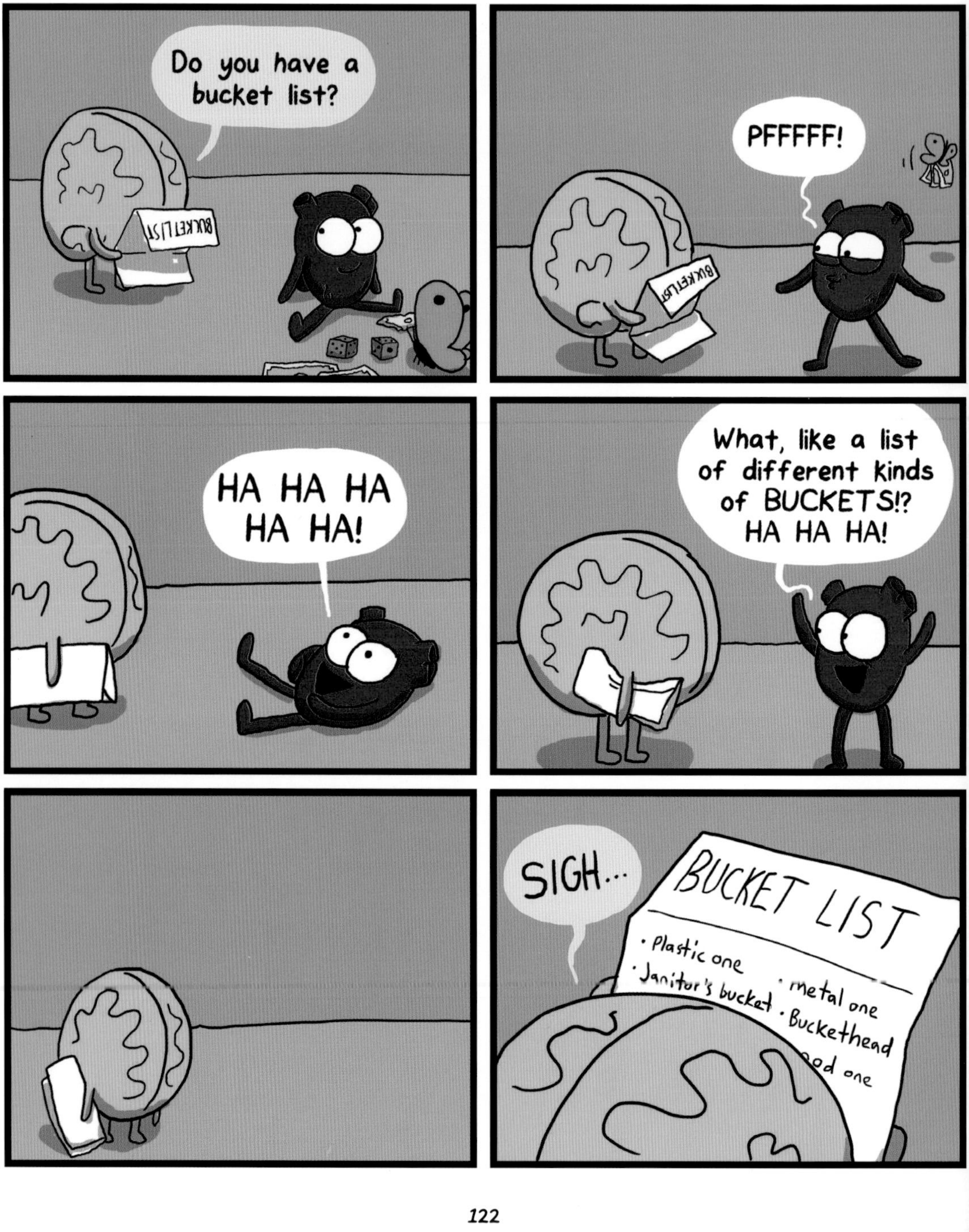
Do you have a bucket list?
BUCKET LIST
PFFFFF!
HA HA HA HA HA!
What, like a list of different kinds of BUCKETS!? HA HA HA!
SIGH...
BUCKET LIST
· Plastic one
· metal one
· Janitor's bucket
· Buckethead

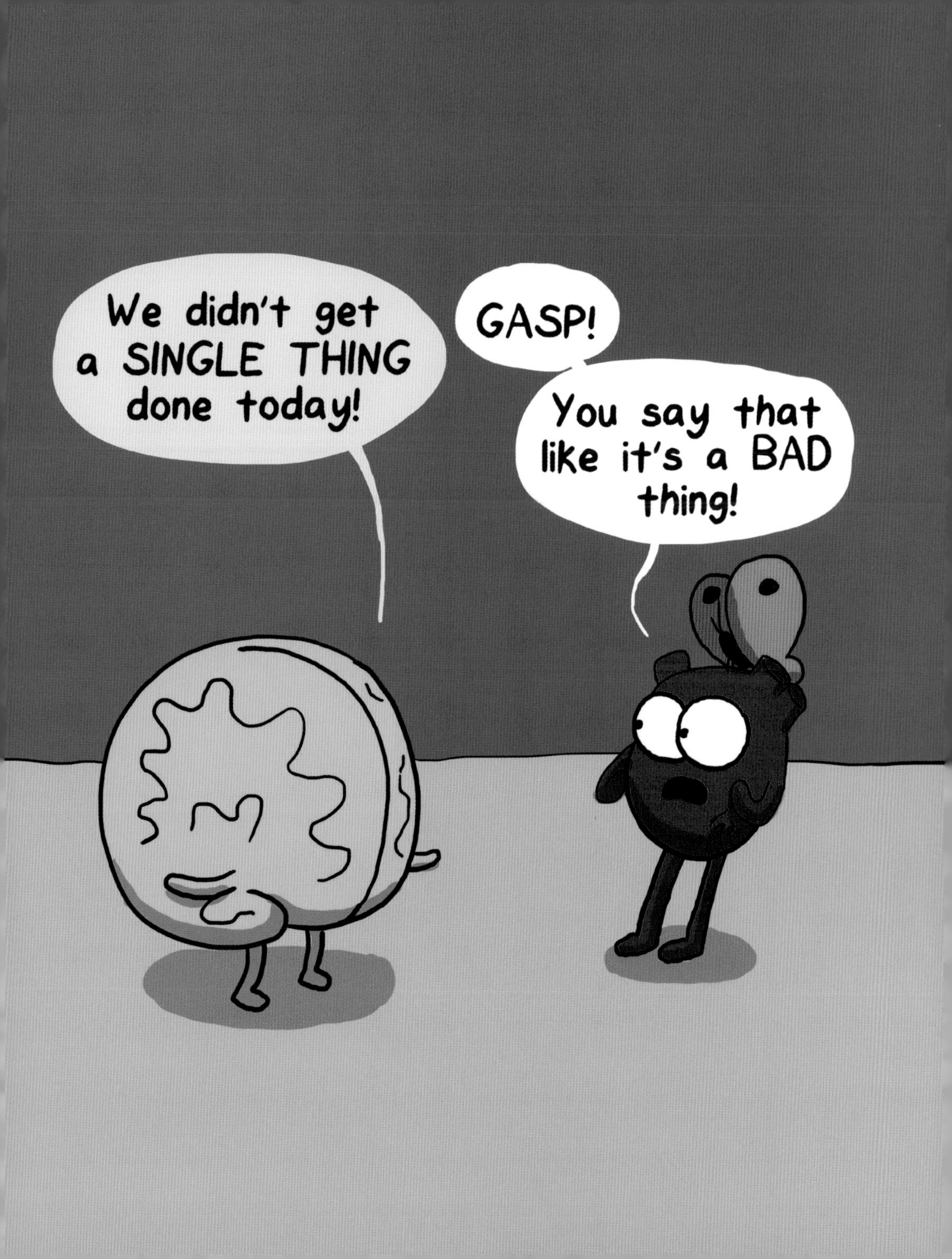
We didn't get a SINGLE THING done today!
GASP!
You say that like it's a BAD thing!

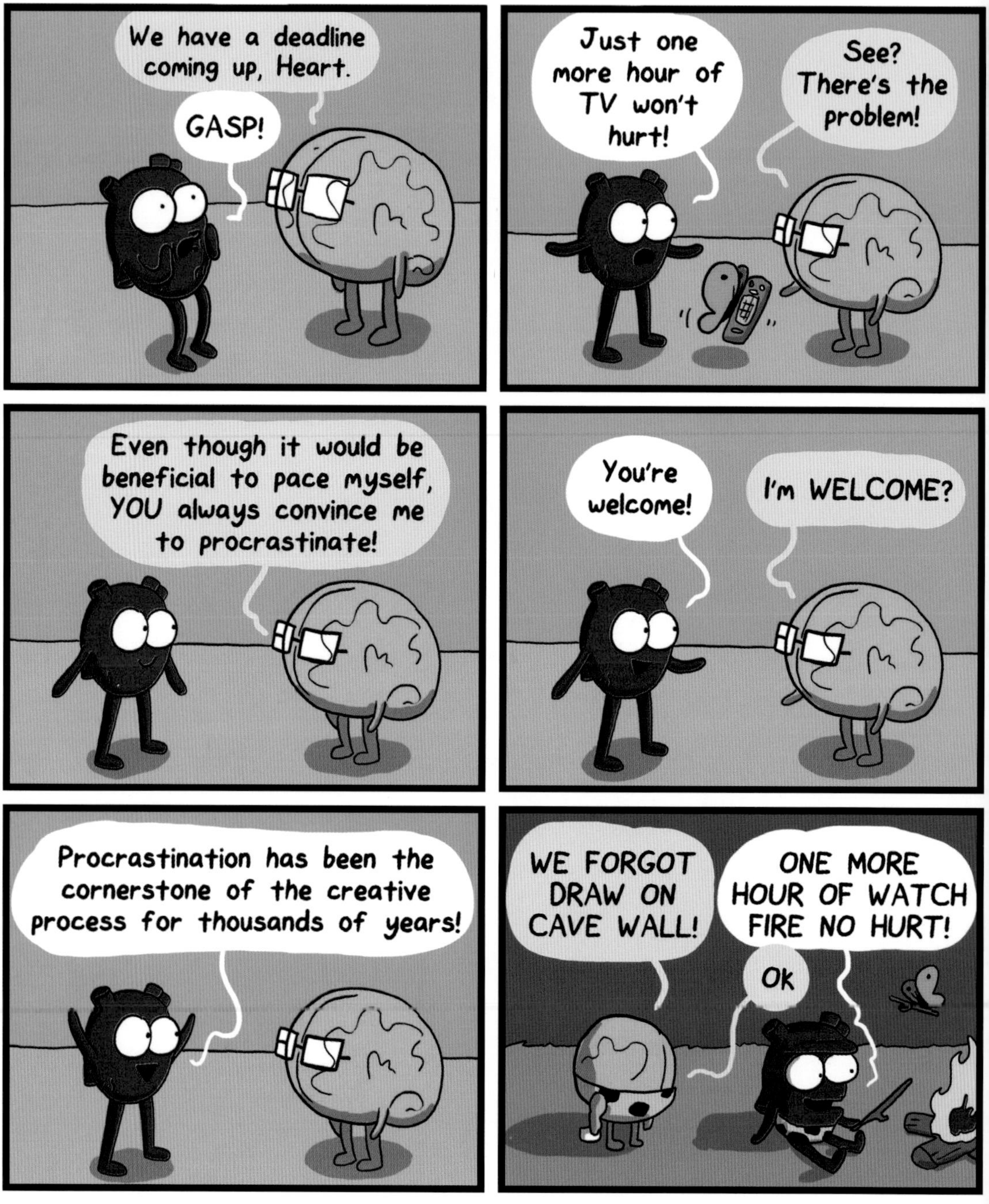

We have a deadline coming up, Heart.
GASP!
Just one more hour of TV won't hurt!
See? There's the problem!
Even though it would be beneficial to pace myself, YOU always convince me to procrastinate!
You're welcome!
I'm WELCOME?
Procrastination has been the cornerstone of the creative process for thousands of years!
WE FORGOT DRAW ON CAVE WALL!
ONE MORE HOUR OF WATCH FIRE NO HURT!
Ok

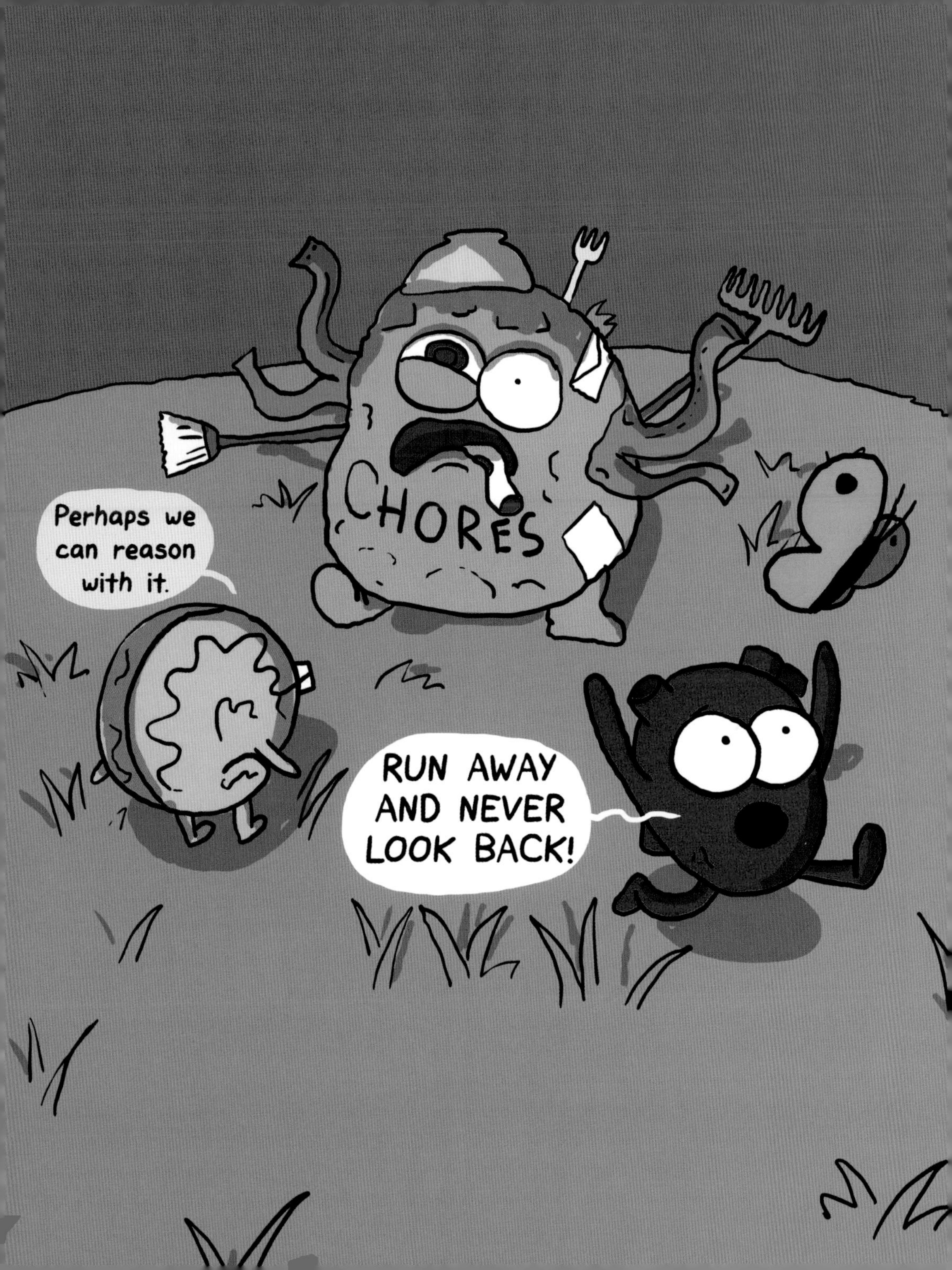
CHORES
Perhaps we can reason with it.
RUN AWAY AND NEVER LOOK BACK!

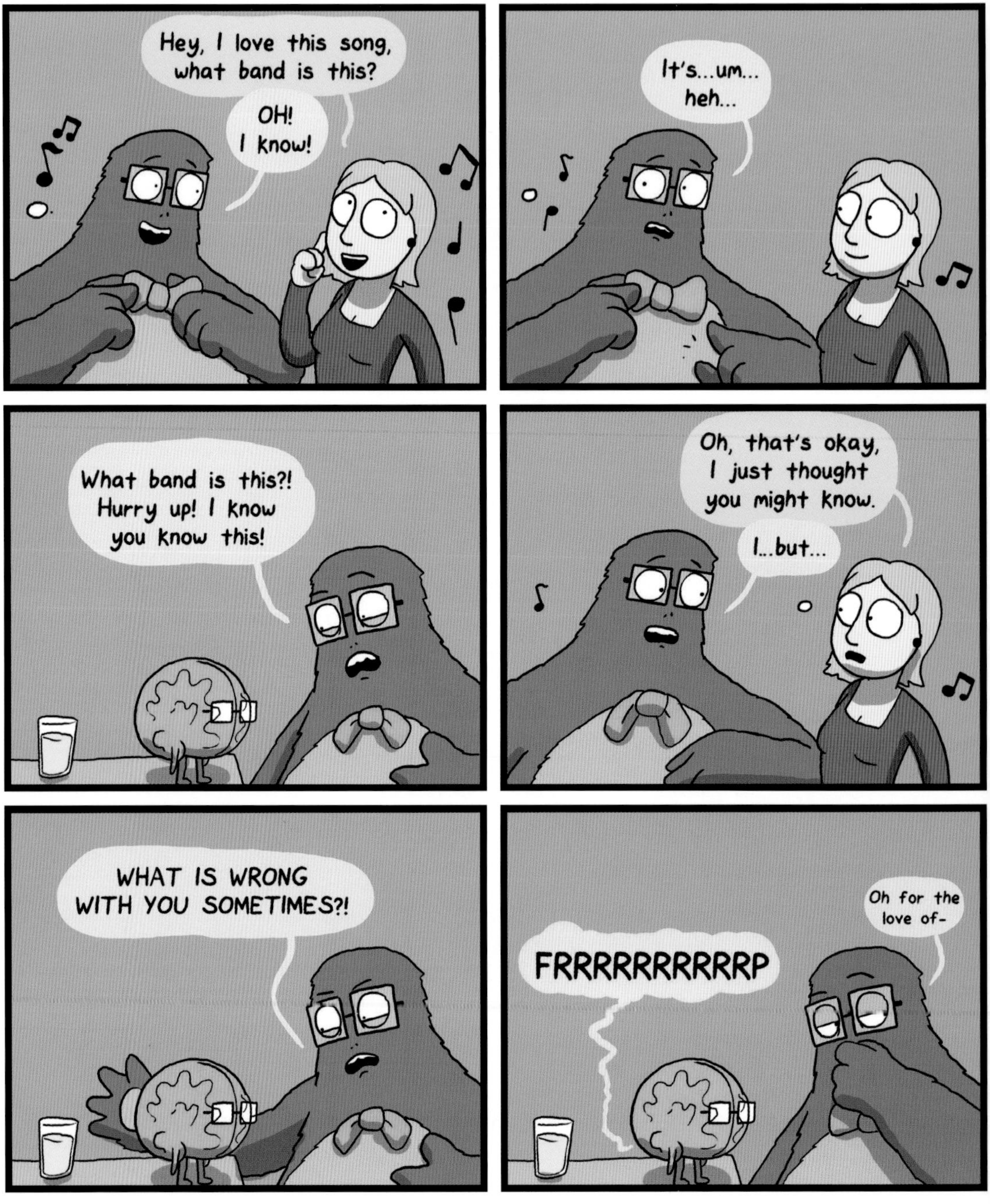
Hey, I love this song, what band is this?
OH! I know!
It's...um... heh...
What band is this?! Hurry up! I know you know this!
Oh, that's okay, I just thought you might know.
I...but...
WHAT IS WRONG WITH YOU SOMETIMES?!
FRRRRRRRRRRP
Oh for the love of-

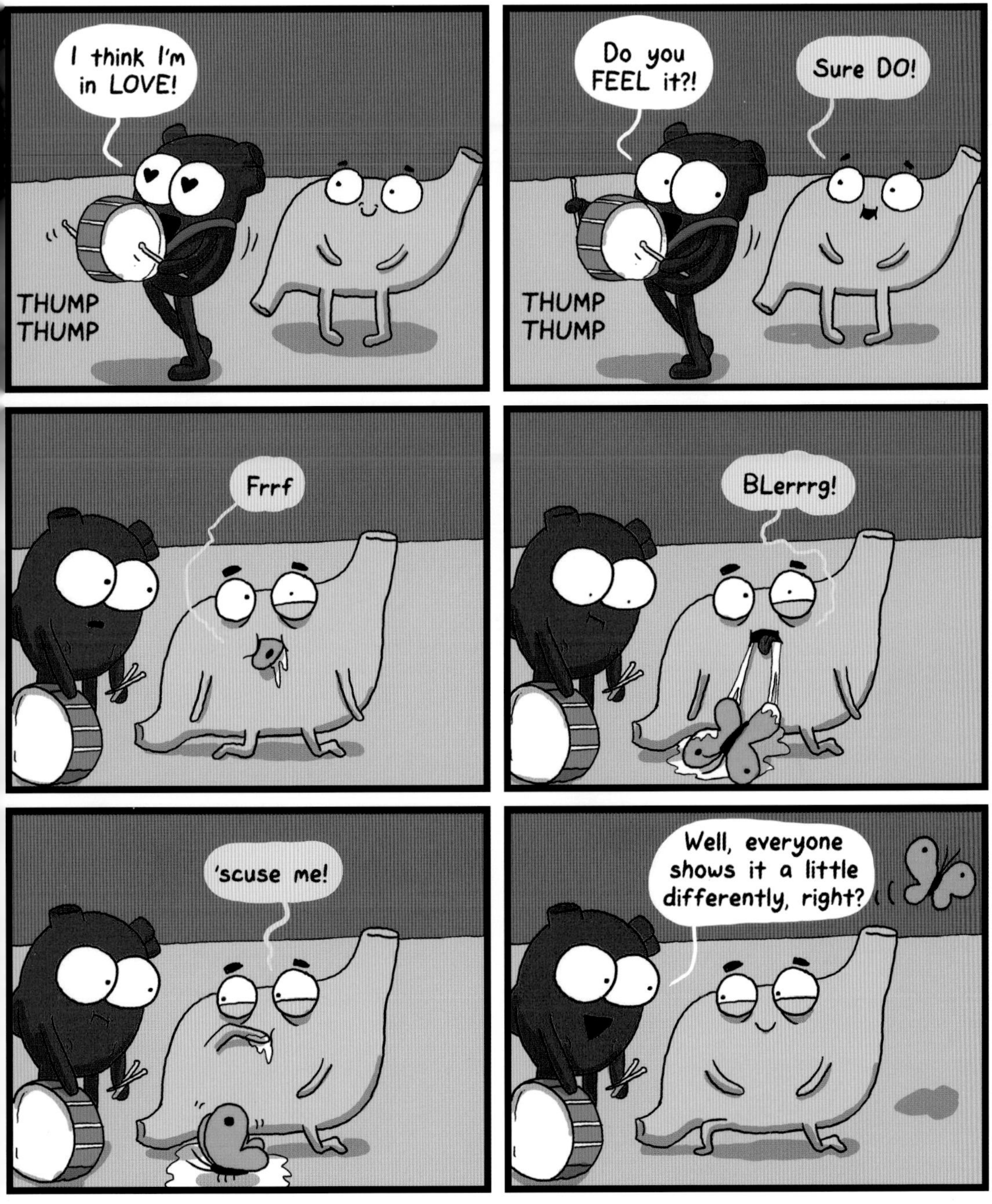
I think I'm in LOVE!
THUMP THUMP
Do you FEEL it?!
Sure DO!
THUMP THUMP
Frrf
BLerrrg!
'scuse me!
Well, everyone shows it a little differently, right?

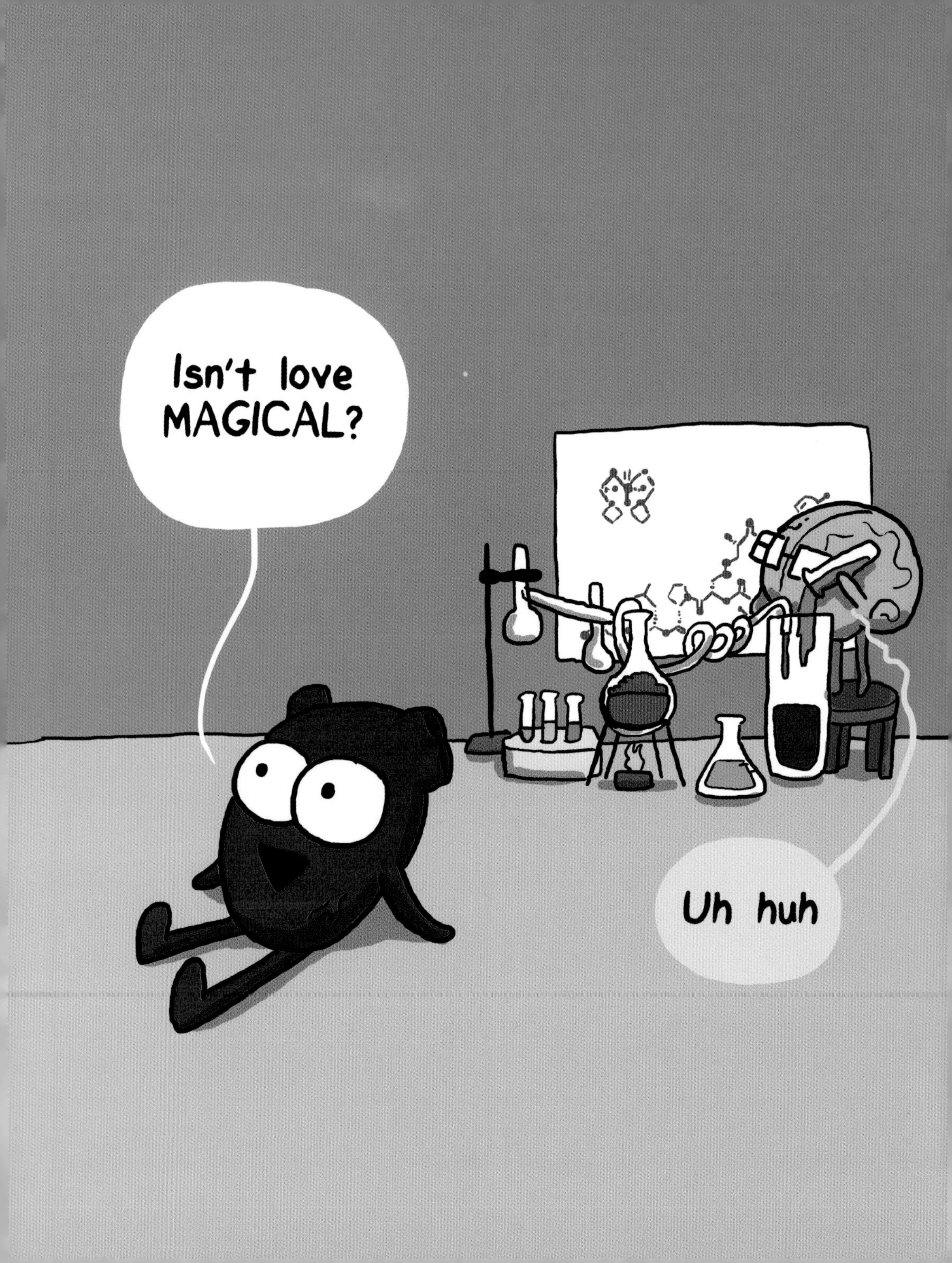
Isn't love MAGICAL?
Uh huh

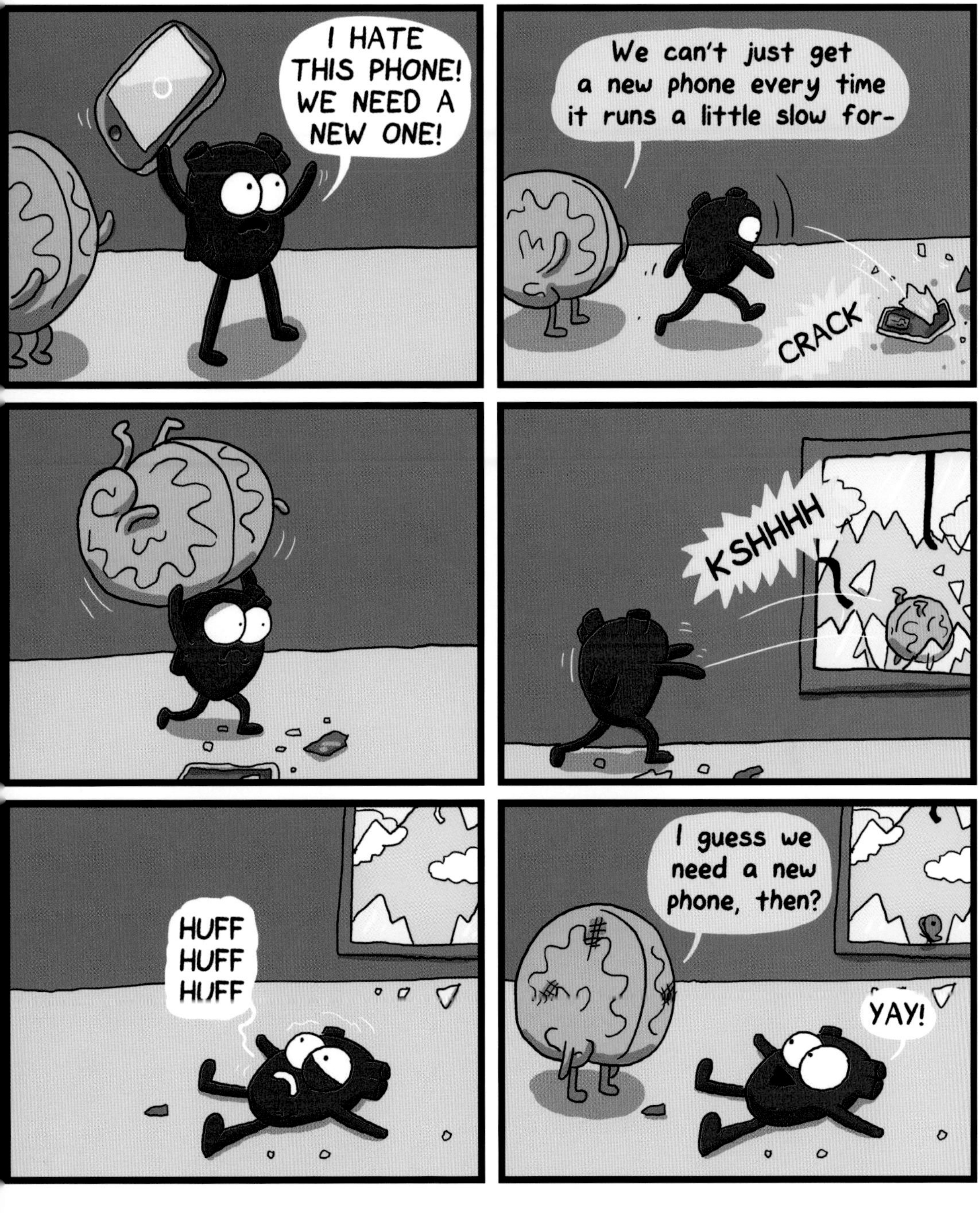
I HATE THIS PHONE! WE NEED A NEW ONE!
We can't just get a new phone every time it runs a little slow for-
CRACK
KSHHHH
HUFF HUFF HUFF
I guess we need a new phone, then?
YAY!

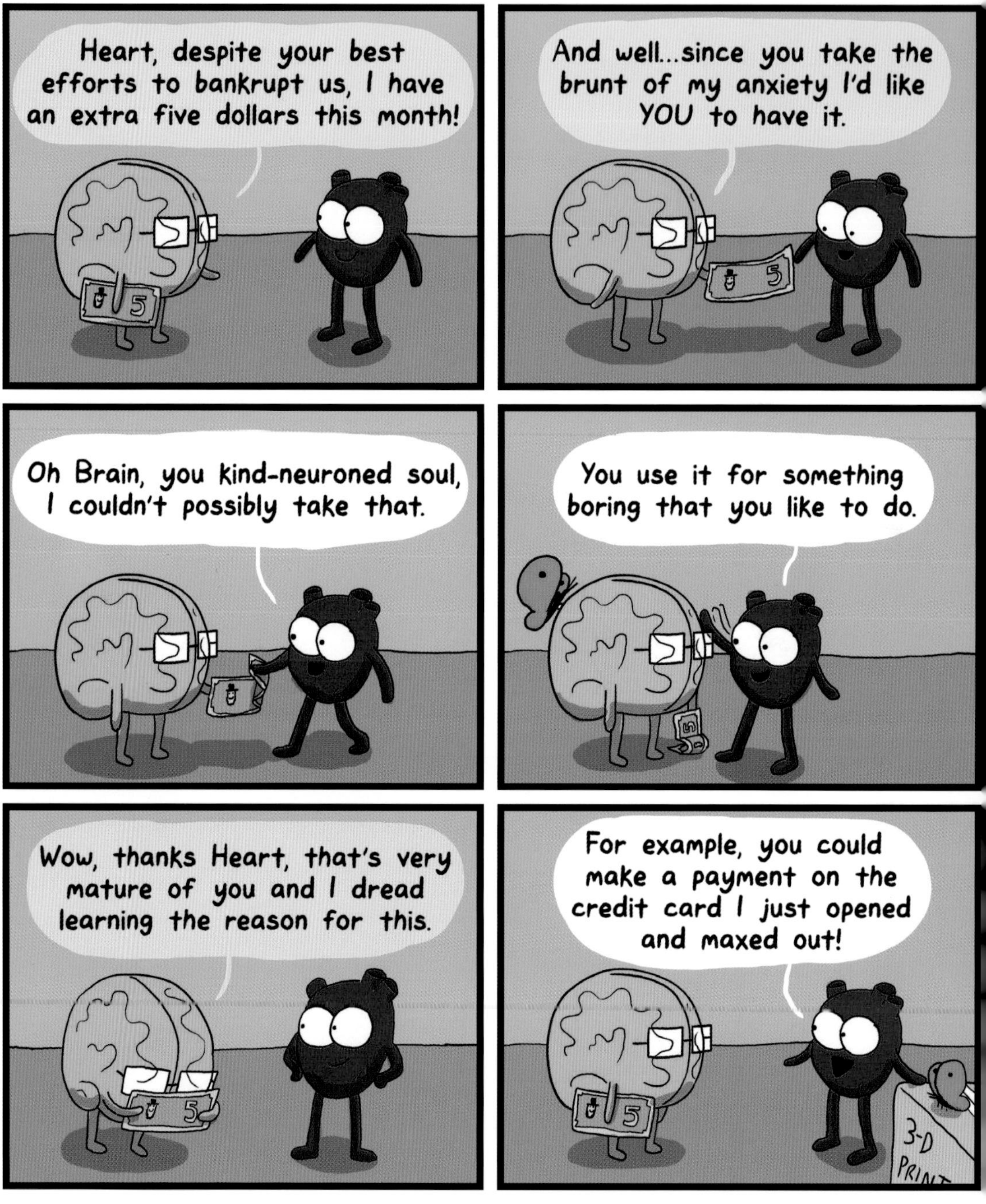
Heart, despite your best efforts to bankrupt us, I have an extra five dollars this month!
And well...since you take the brunt of my anxiety I'd like YOU to have it.
Oh Brain, you kind-neuroned soul, I couldn't possibly take that.
You use it for something boring that you like to do.
Wow, thanks Heart, that's very mature of you and I dread learning the reason for this.
For example, you could make a payment on the credit card I just opened and maxed out!
3-D PRINT

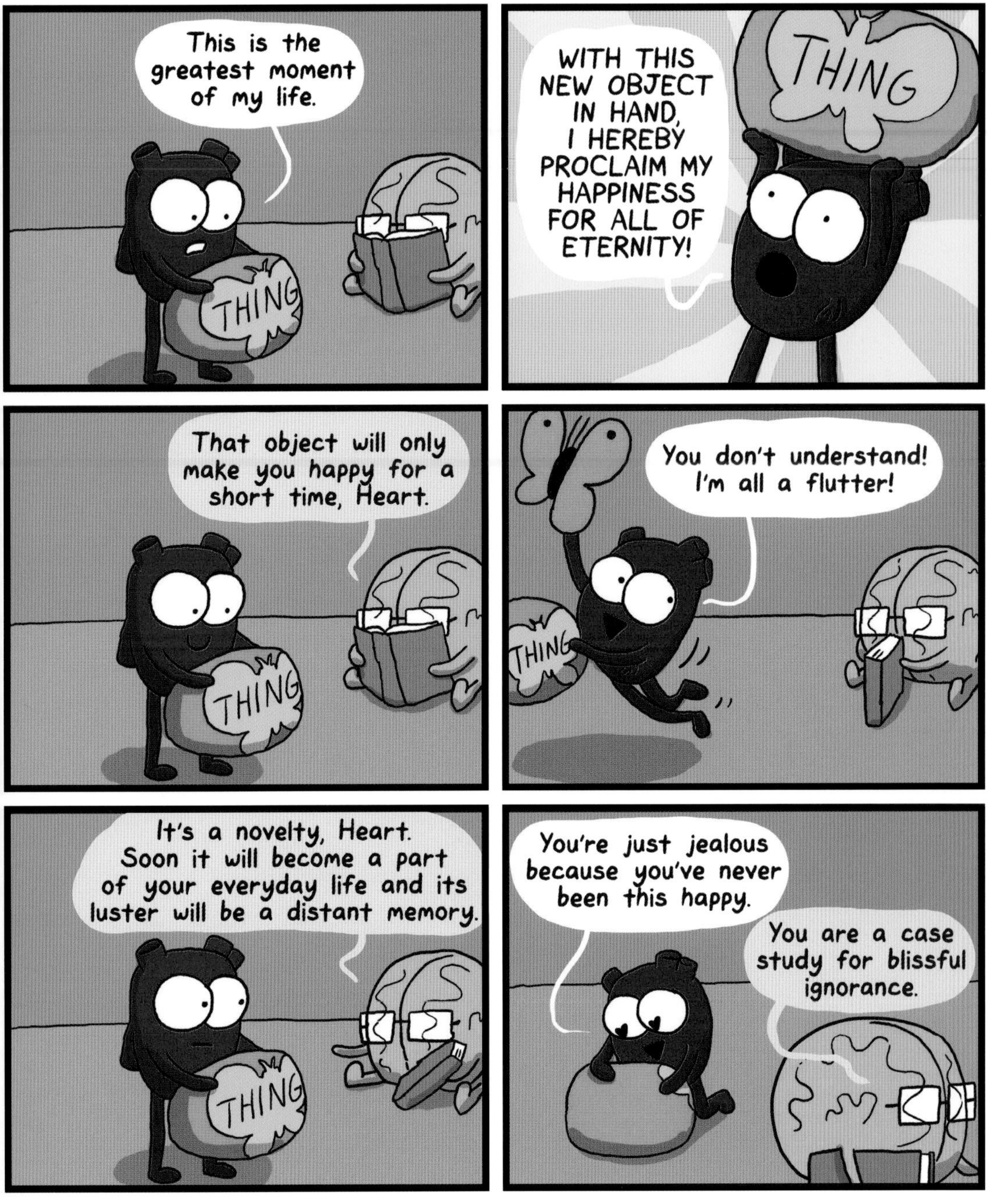
This is the greatest moment of my life.
THING
WITH THIS NEW OBJECT IN HAND, I HEREBY PROCLAIM MY HAPPINESS FOR ALL OF ETERNITY!
THING
That object will only make you happy for a short time, Heart.
THING
You don't understand! I'm all a flutter!
THING
It's a novelty, Heart. Soon it will become a part of your everyday life and its luster will be a distant memory.
THING
You're just jealous because you've never been this happy.
You are a case study for blissful ignorance.

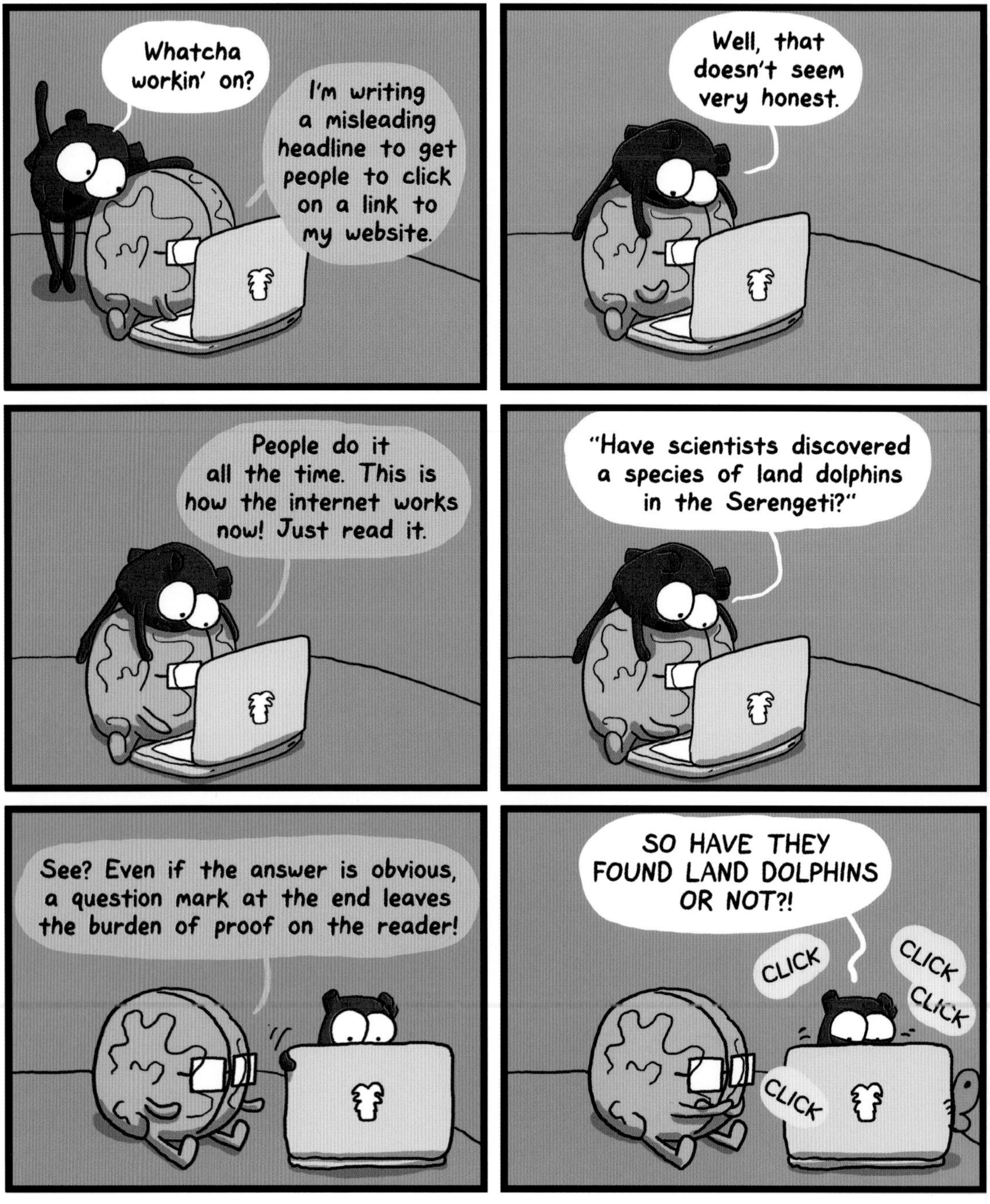
Whatcha workin' on?
I'm writing a misleading headline to get people to click on a link to my website.
Well, that doesn't seem very honest.
People do it all the time. This is how the internet works now! Just read it.
"Have scientists discovered a species of land dolphins in the Serengeti?"
See? Even if the answer is obvious, a question mark at the end leaves the burden of proof on the reader!
SO HAVE THEY FOUND LAND DOLPHINS OR NOT?!
CLICK
CLICK
CLICK
CLICK

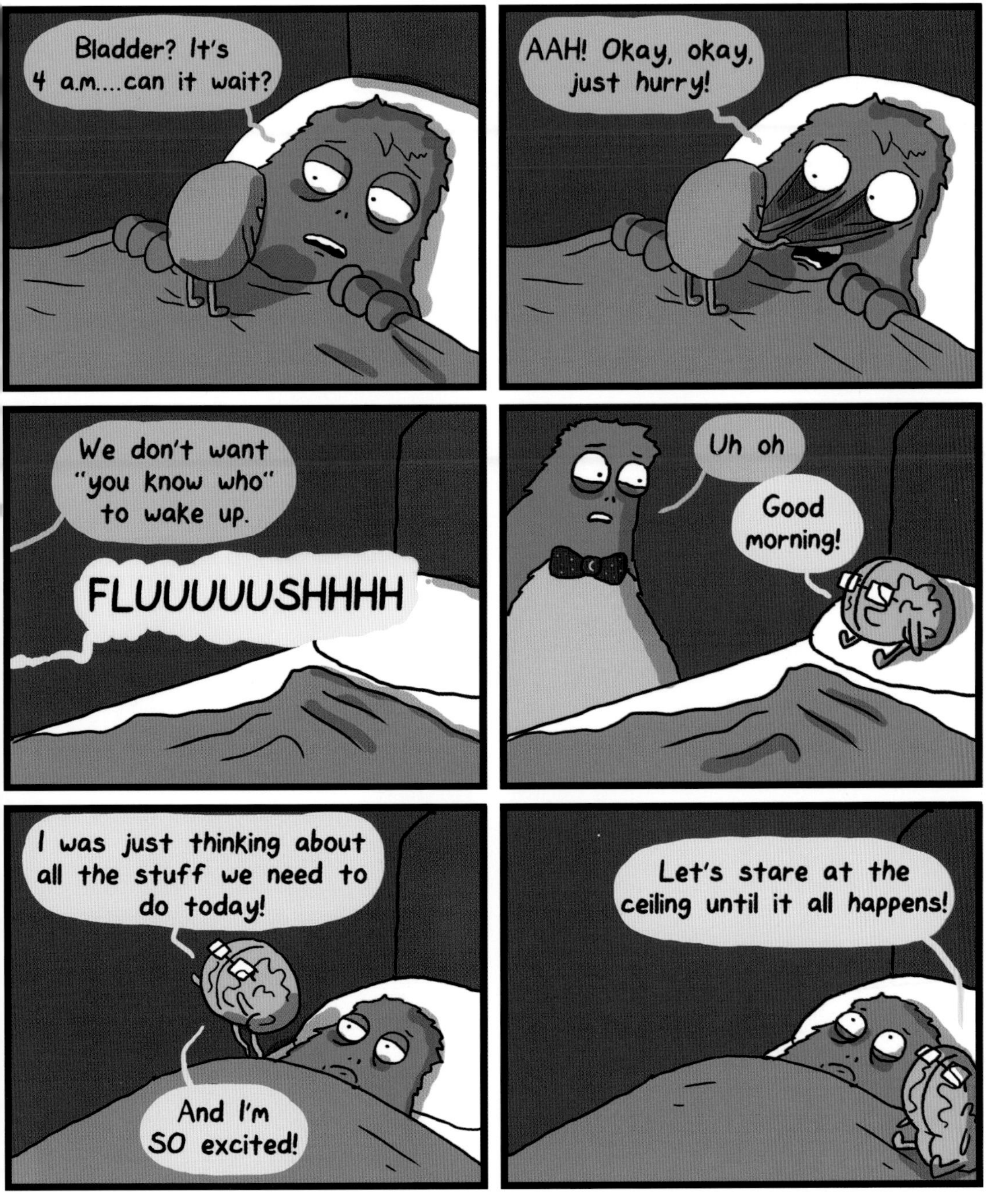
Bladder? It's 4 a.m....can it wait?
AAH! Okay, okay, just hurry!
We don't want "you know who" to wake up.
FLUUUUUSHHHH
Uh oh
Good morning!
I was just thinking about all the stuff we need to do today!
And I'm SO excited!
Let's stare at the ceiling until it all happens!

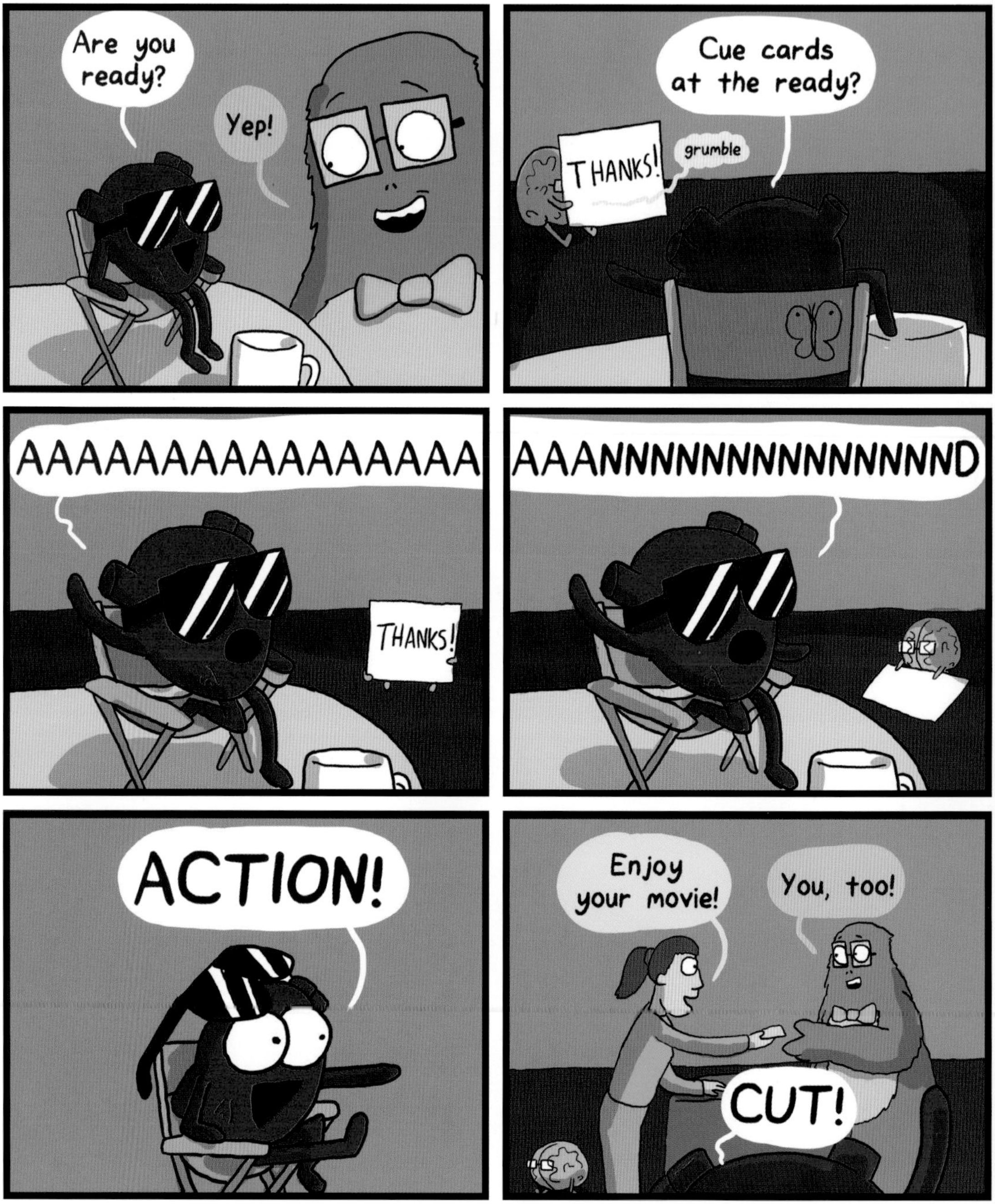
Are you ready?
Yep!
Cue cards at the ready?
THANKS!
grumble
AAAAAAAAAAAAAAAAA
THANKS!
AAANNNNNNNNNNNNNND
ACTION!
Enjoy your movie!
You, too!
CUT!

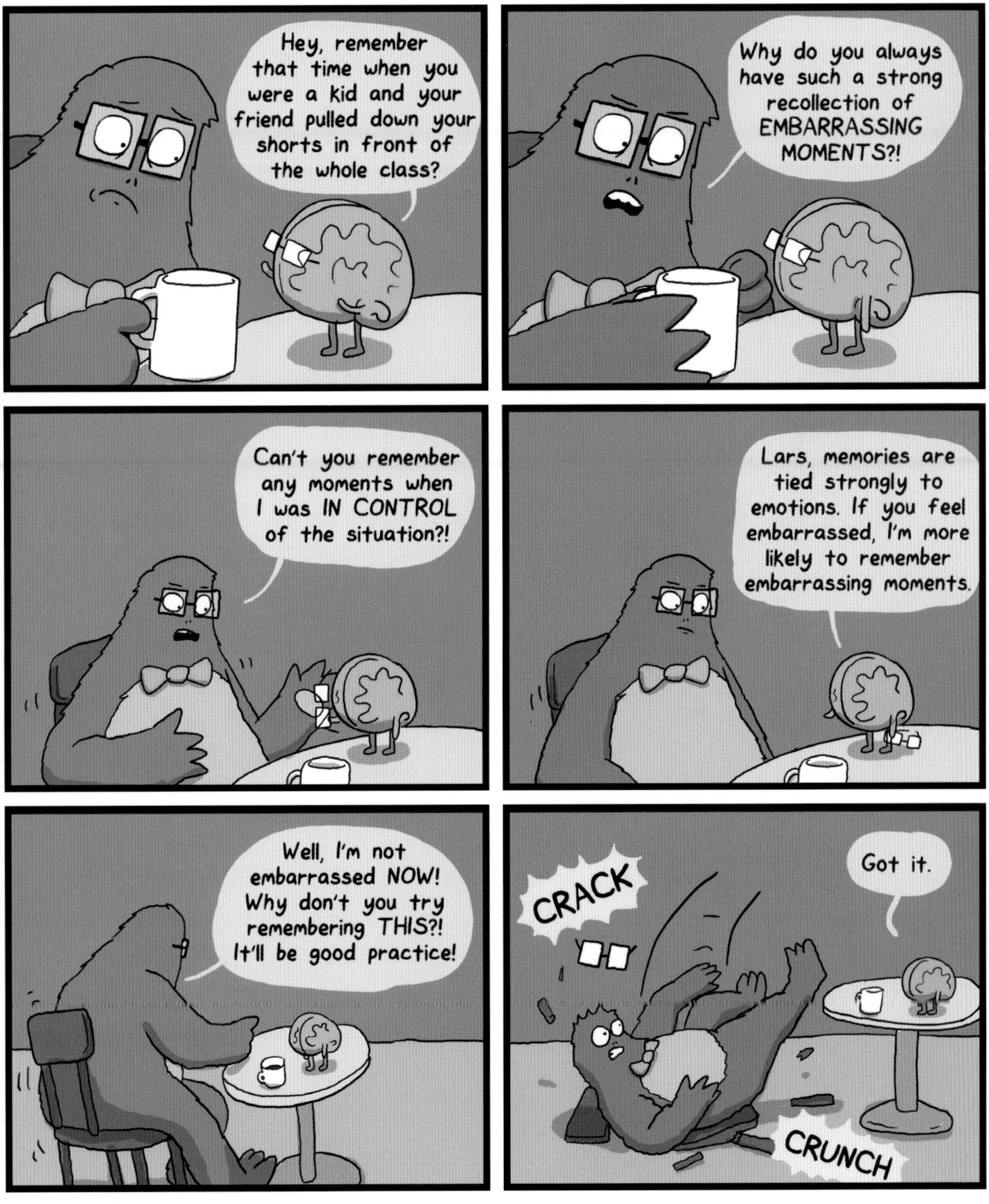
Hey, remember that time when you were a kid and your friend pulled down your shorts in front of the whole class?
Why do you always have such a strong recollection of EMBARRASSING MOMENTS?!
Can't you remember any moments when I was IN CONTROL of the situation?!
Lars, memories are tied strongly to emotions. If you feel embarrassed, I'm more likely to remember embarrassing moments.
Well, I'm not embarrassed NOW! Why don't you try remembering THIS?! It'll be good practice!
CRACK
Got it.
CRUNCH

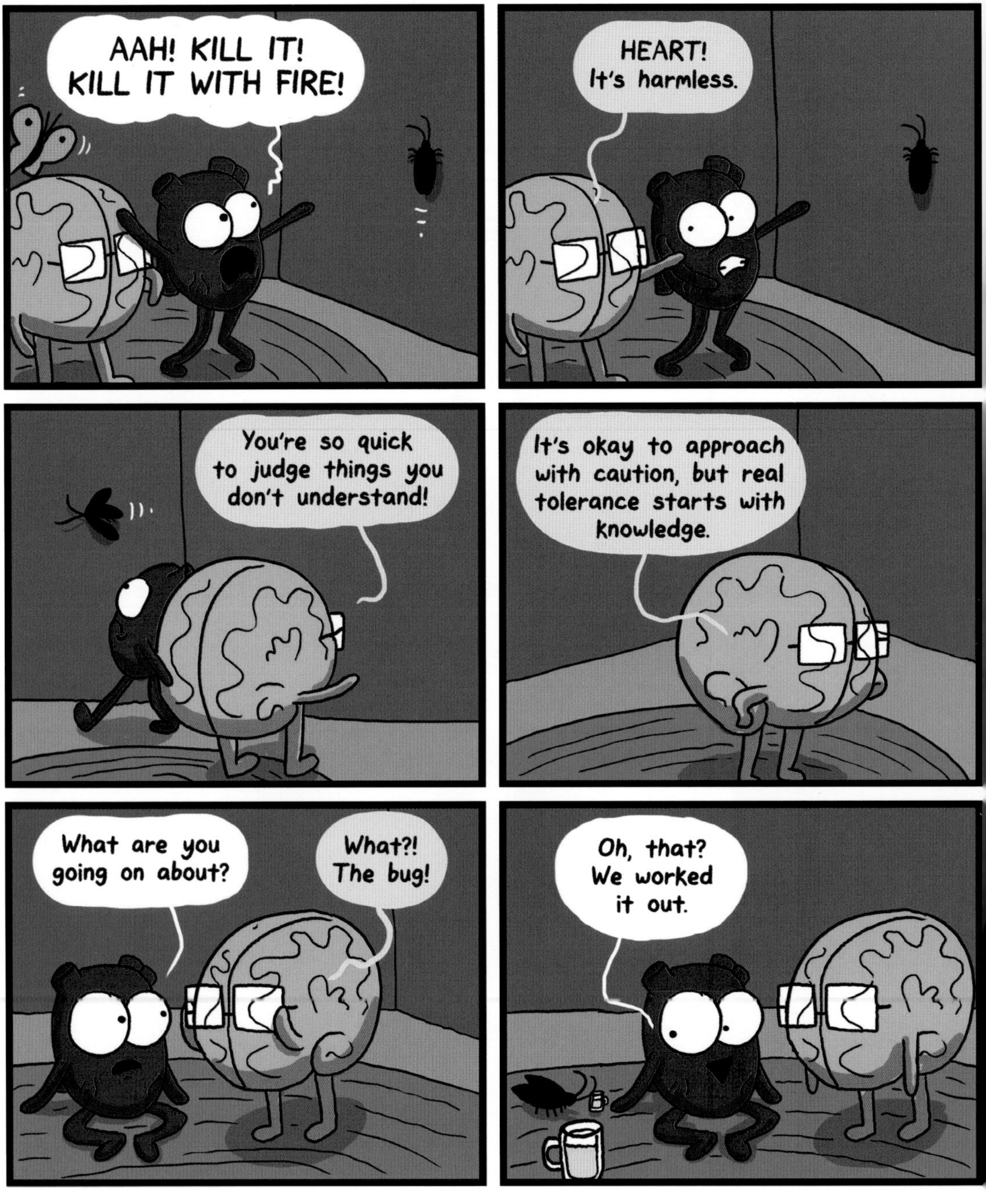
AAH! KILL IT! KILL IT WITH FIRE!
HEART! It's harmless.
You're so quick to judge things you don't understand!
It's okay to approach with caution, but real tolerance starts with knowledge.
What are you going on about?
What?! The bug!
Oh, that? We worked it out.

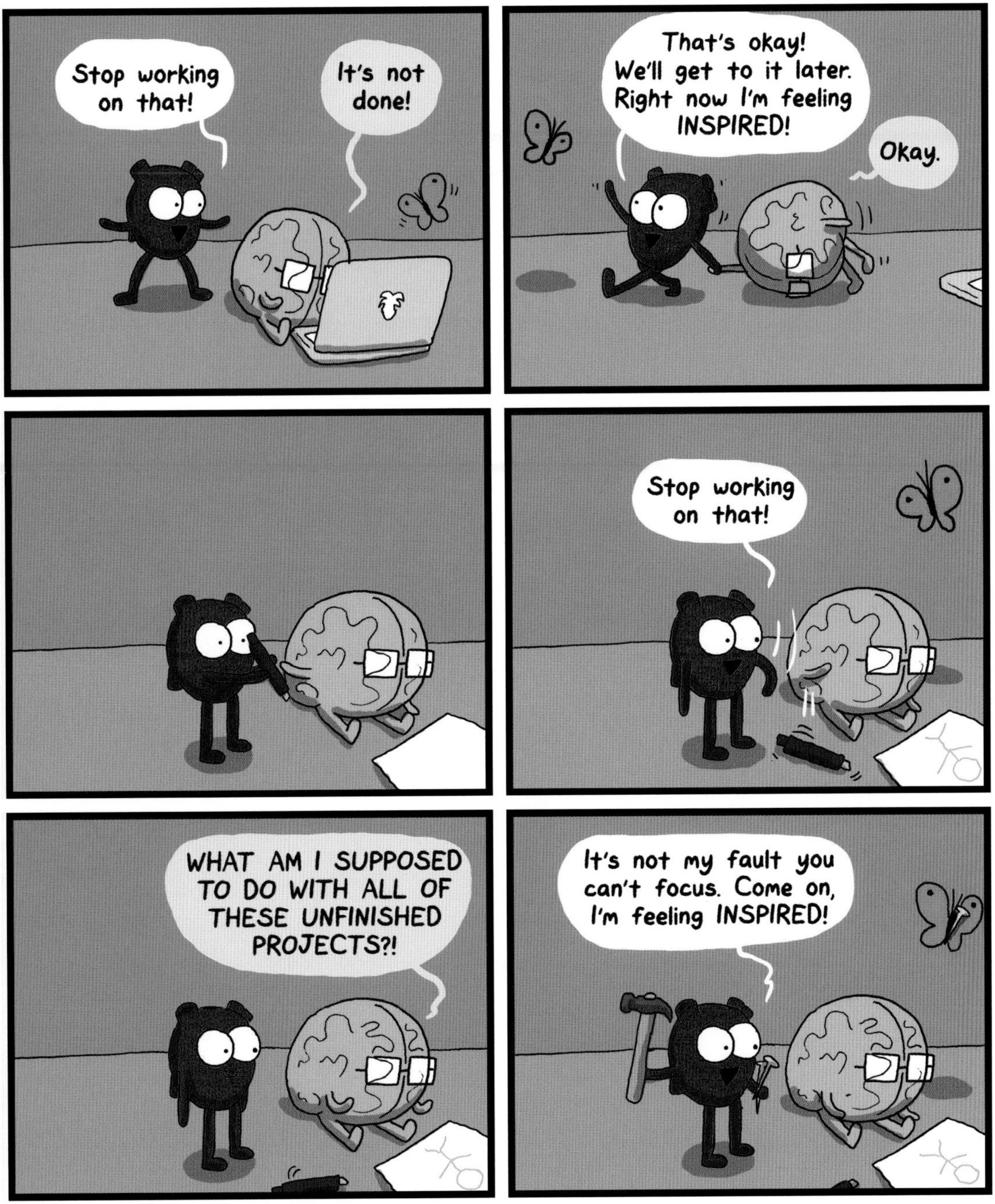
Stop working on that!
It's not done!
That's okay! We'll get to it later. Right now I'm feeling INSPIRED!
Okay.
Stop working on that!
WHAT AM I SUPPOSED TO DO WITH ALL OF THESE UNFINISHED PROJECTS?!
It's not my fault you can't focus. Come on, I'm feeling INSPIRED!

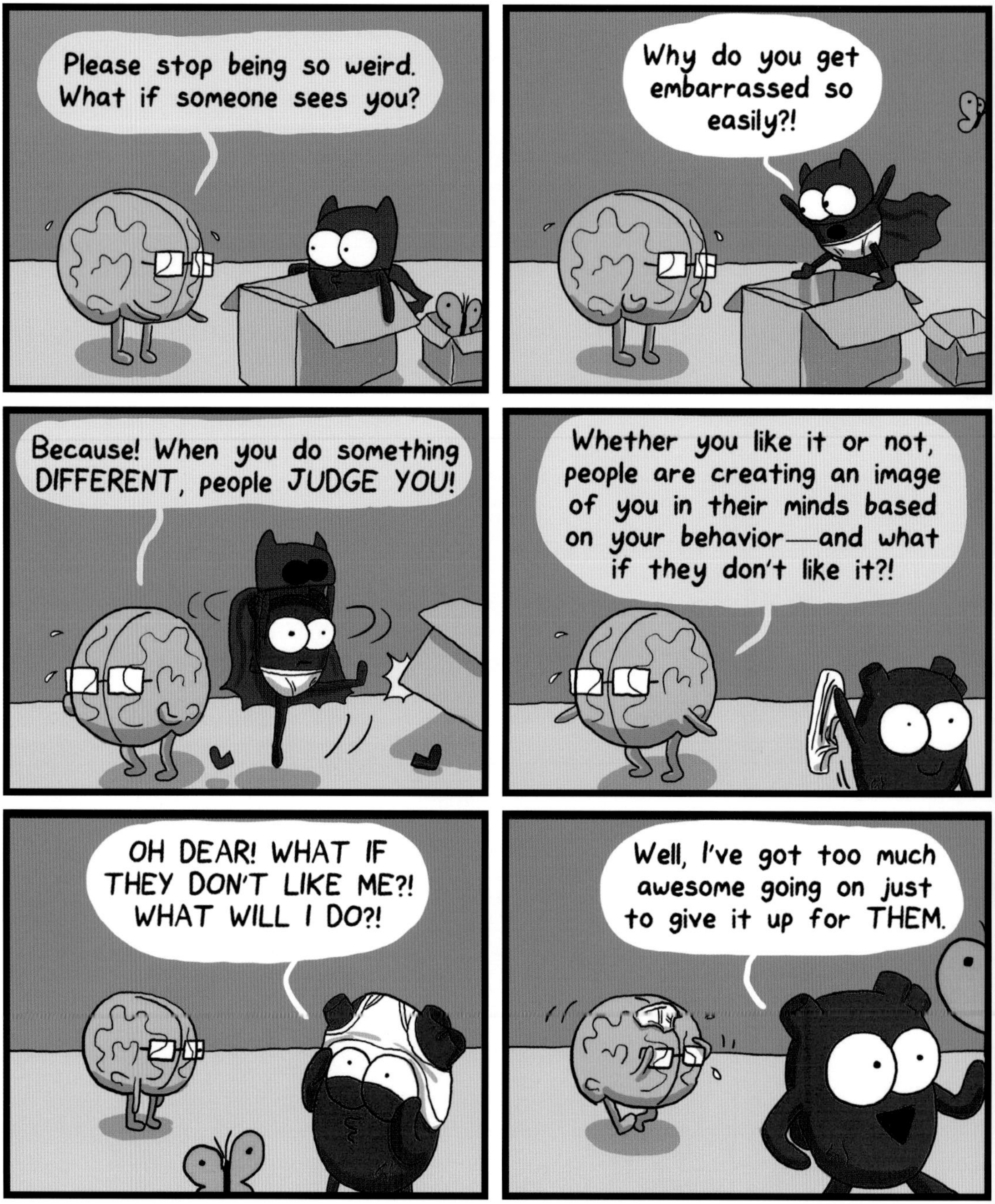
Please stop being so weird. What if someone sees you?
Why do you get embarrassed so easily?!
Because! When you do something DIFFERENT, people JUDGE YOU!
Whether you like it or not, people are creating an image of you in their minds based on your behavior—and what if they don't like it?!
OH DEAR! WHAT IF THEY DON'T LIKE ME?! WHAT WILL I DO?!
Well, I've got too much awesome going on just to give it up for THEM.

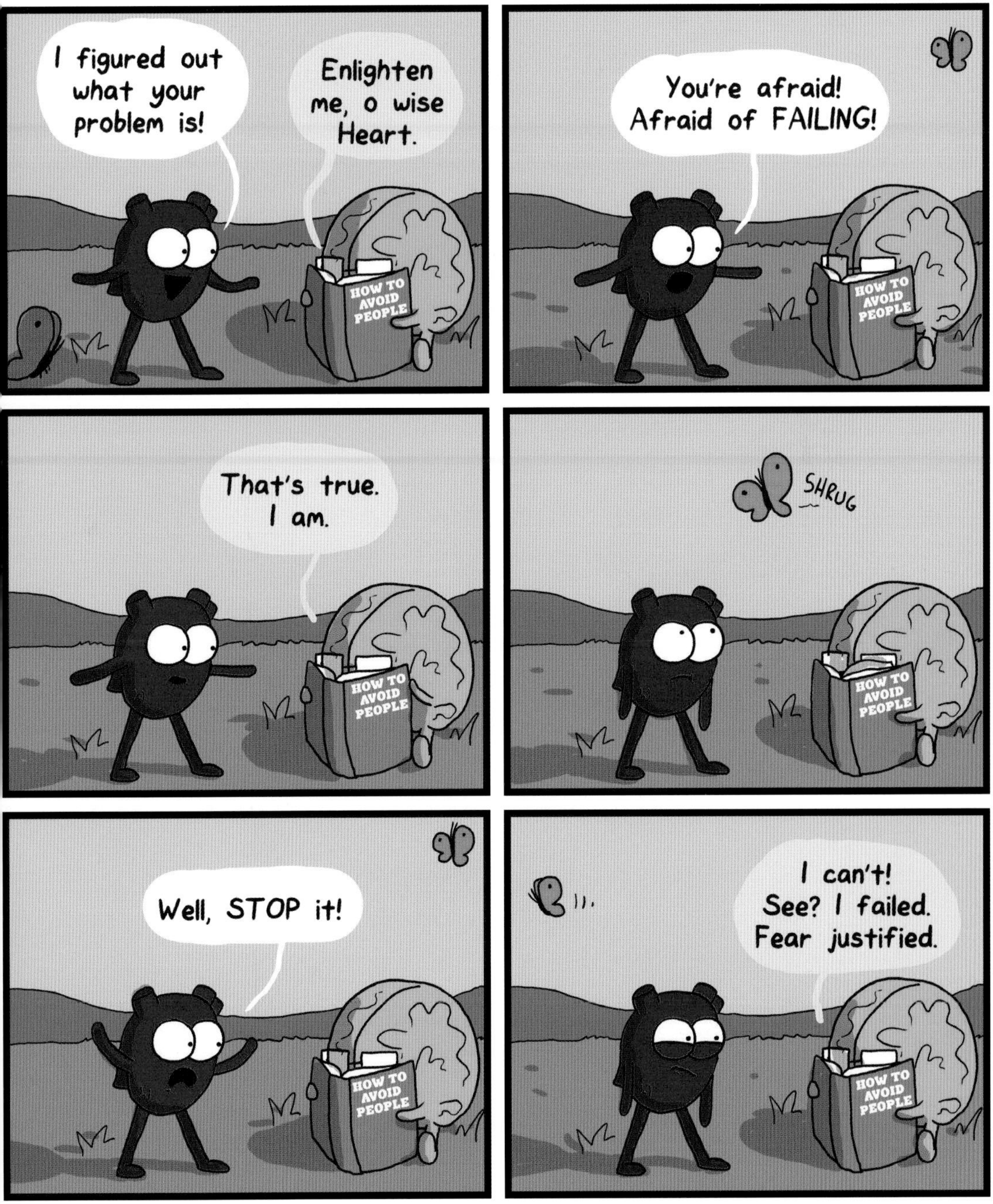
I figured out what your problem is!
Enlighten me, o wise Heart.
HOW TO AVOID PEOPLE
You're afraid! Afraid of FAILING!
HOW TO AVOID PEOPLE
That's true. I am.
HOW TO AVOID PEOPLE
SHRUG
HOW TO AVOID PEOPLE
Well, STOP it!
HOW TO AVOID PEOPLE
I can't! See? I failed. Fear justified.
HOW TO AVOID PEOPLE

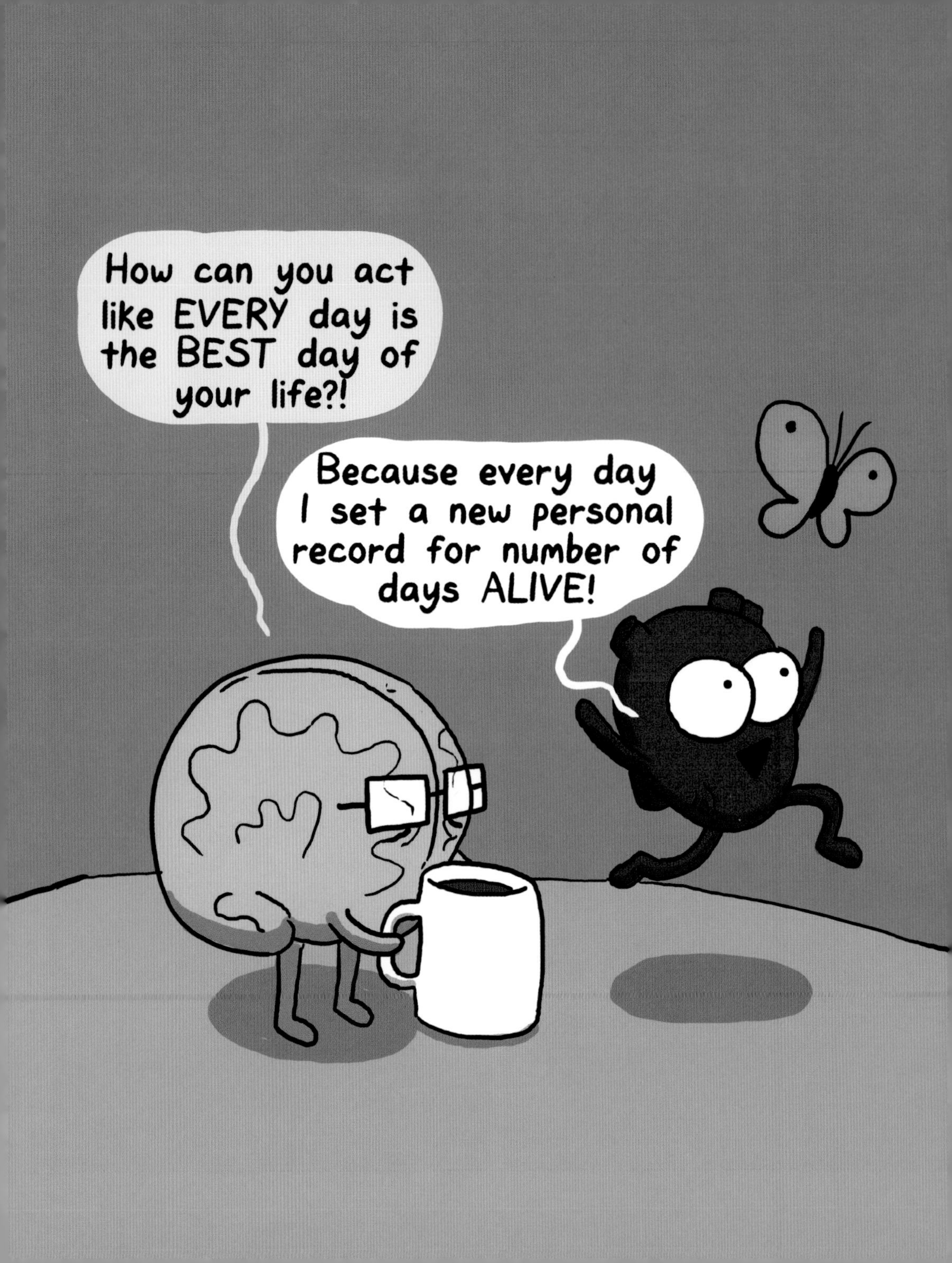
How can you act like EVERY day is the BEST day of your life?!
Because every day I set a new personal record for number of days ALIVE!

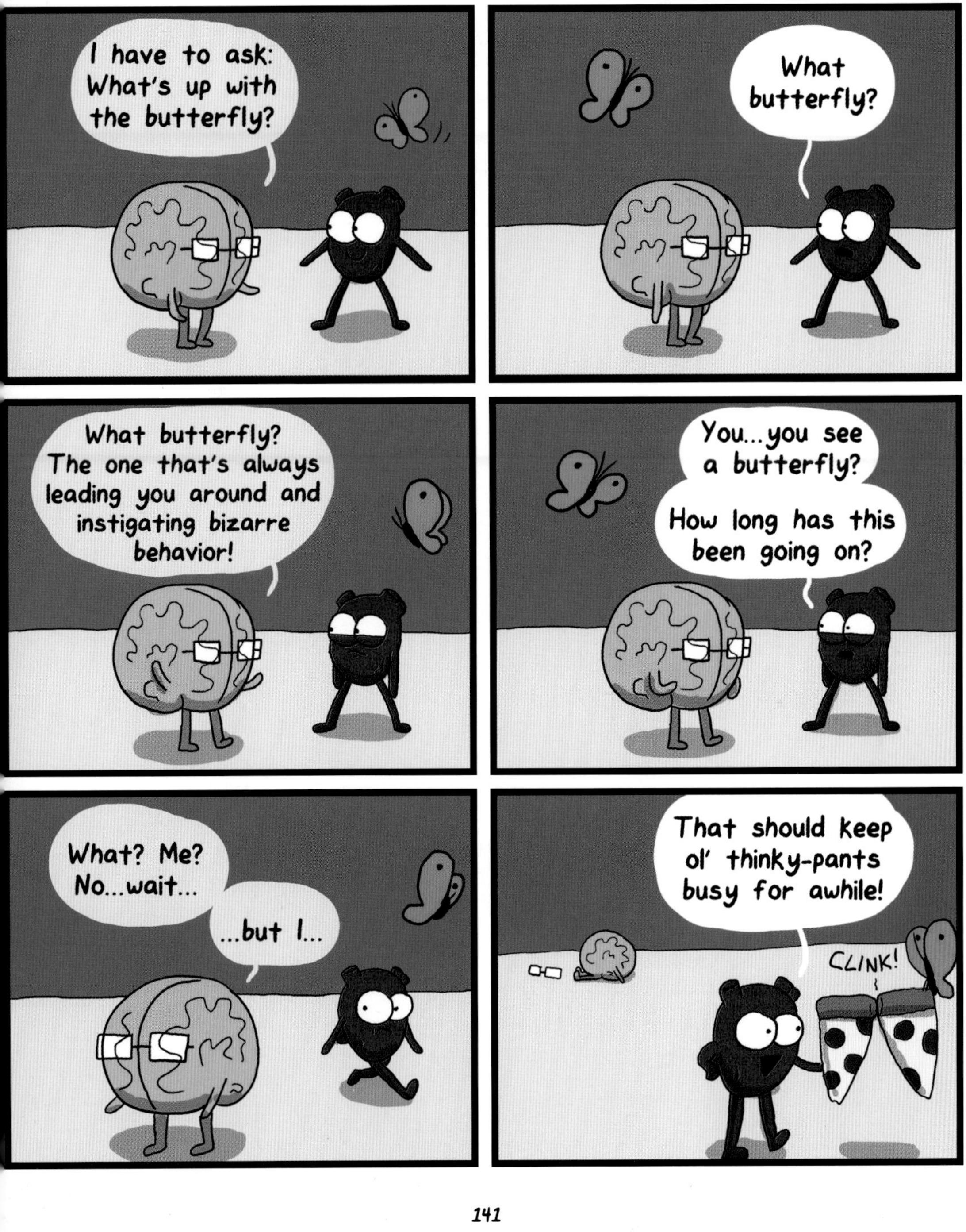
I have to ask: What's up with the butterfly?
What butterfly?
What butterfly? The one that's always leading you around and instigating bizarre behavior!
You...you see a butterfly?
How long has this been going on?
What? Me? No...wait...
...but I...
That should keep ol' thinky-pants busy for awhile!
CLINK!

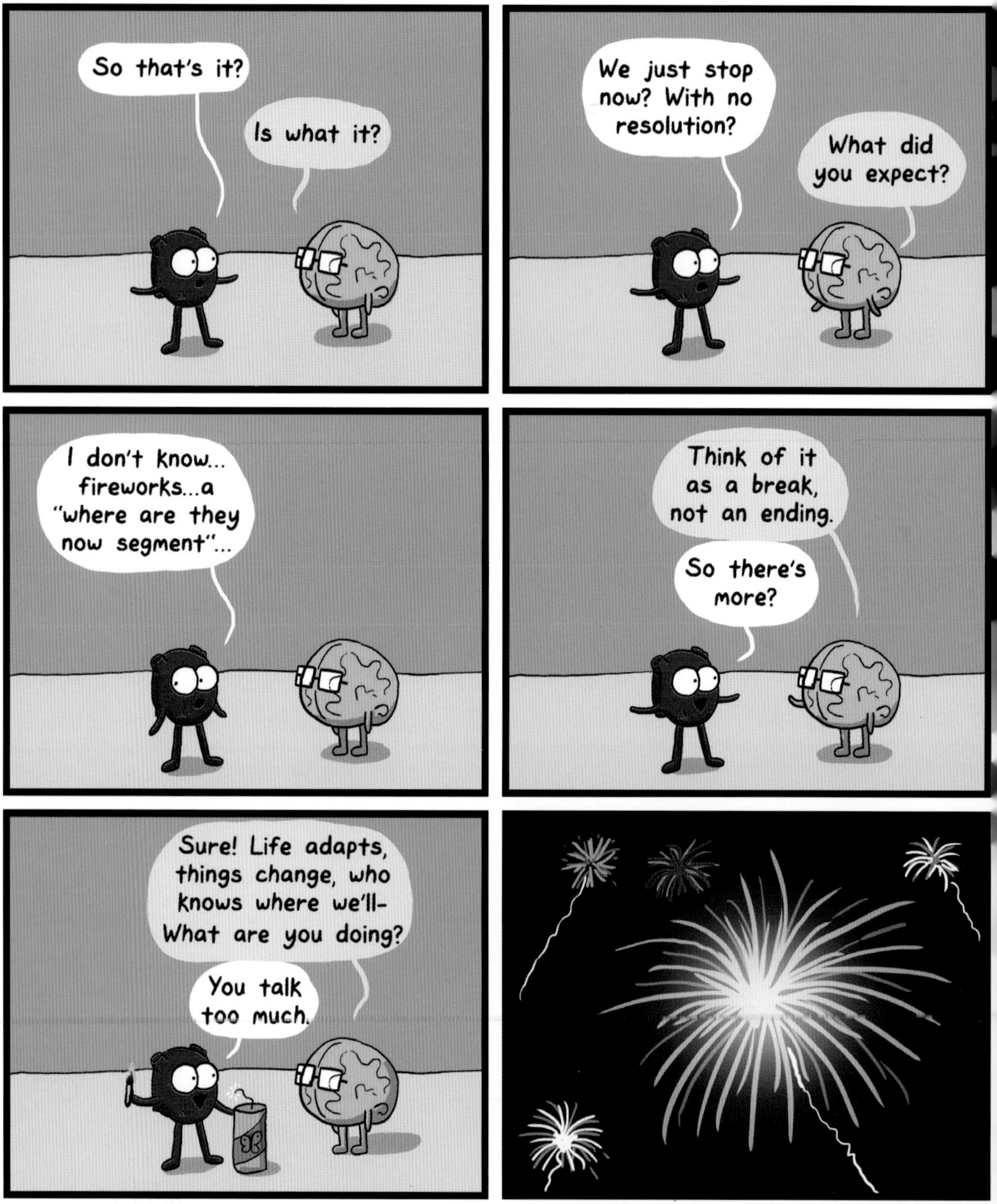
So that's it?
Is what it?
We just stop now? With no resolution?
What did you expect?
I don't know... fireworks...a "where are they now segment"...
Think of it as a break, not an ending.
So there's more?
Sure! Life adapts, things change, who knows where we'll- What are you doing?
You talk too much.